THE

LOYAL MOUNTAINEERS

OF

TENNESSEE

BY

THOMAS WILLIAM HUMES, S. T. D.

"The noblest word in the catalogue of social virtues is Loyalty"—JOHN RUSKIN.

The Reprint Company, *Publishers*
Spartanburg, S.C.
1974

This volume was reproduced from an 1888 edition in the Special Collections, University of Tennessee Library, Knoxville.

Reprinted: 1974
The Reprint Company
Spartanburg, South Carolina

ISBN 0-87152-159-8
Library of Congress Catalog Card Number: 73-23071
Manufactured in the United States of America on long-life paper.

73091

Library of Congress Cataloging in Publication Data

Humes, Thomas William, 1815-1892.
  The loyal mountaineers of Tennessee.

  1. Tennessee, East—History—Civil War.　I. Title.
E531.H92　1974　　　976.8′6′04　　　73-23071
ISBN 0-87152-159-8

BELMONT COLLEGE LIBRARY

E
531
H92
1974

ASSAULT ON FORT SANDERS.

THE

LOYAL MOUNTAINEERS

OF

TENNESSEE

BY

THOMAS WILLIAM HUMES, S. T. D.

"The noblest word in the catalogue of social virtues is Loyalty"—JOHN RUSKIN.

KNOXVILLE, TENN.
OGDEN BROTHERS & COMPANY
1888.

Copyright, 1888,
By THOMAS WILLIAM HUMES.

Ogden Bros. & Co.
Printers and Stationers,
Knoxville, Tenn.

DEDICATED

IN

LOVE AND GRATITUDE

TO

The Memory

OF

LLOYD P. SMITH AND EDWARD EVERETT,

FRIENDS AND HELPERS

OF A

SUFFERING PEOPLE.

PREFACE.

THE attitude which a large majority of the people of East Tennessee deliberately assumed and persistently maintained in the Civil War of 1861–'65, was remarkable. It had no precise parallel within the limits of the ten seceded States, and there was no distinctive and numerous population in any one of the loyal States whose surroundings were so greatly unfavorable to a like attitude of devotion to the Union.

The majority of citizens in each of the border slave States of Maryland, Kentucky and Missouri adhered to the United States, and their respective governments were administered accordingly. But their territorial and other important relations were altogether different from those of East Tennessee. Maryland lay contiguous to the district and capital, where the Federal Government must and did especially defend itself. It is separated from Virginia not only by the District of Columbia but by the Potomac River and Chesapeake Bay, and it had no nearness to any other seceded State; while Pennsylvania stretched all along its northern border, and the other loyal States of New Jersey, New York and Ohio were not far distant. Kentucky was bordered by the States of Ohio, Indiana and Illinois. And Missouri was almost surrounded by Illinois, Iowa, Nebraska and Kansas. A majority of the people of West Virginia were steadfast in their friendship for the Union, notwithstanding the State, of which they were citizens, seceded. But West Virginia bordered chiefly upon Pennsylvania, Ohio and Kentucky. It was easy of access to influences favorable to the Union. At the same time the armies of the United States could without great difficulties enter and occupy its territory, and this fact helped to confirm the loyalty of its people.

East Tennessee was entirely removed from thoroughly loyal States. The only contiguous one that did not join in the work of secession was Kentucky, which was held to its place in the Union against the will of a considerable minority of its citizens. Otherwise, East Tennessee was bounded on the north and east by Virginia, on the east by North Carolina (lying between Virginia and South Carolina), and on the south by North Carolina and Georgia. High mountains surrounded it on every side, and on the west separated it from the other grand divisions of Tennessee, where prevailed a spirit of disunion that found sympathy and support in the adjoining Gulf States of Alabama and Mississippi.

The wonder is that the people of East Tennessee, situated as they were—far removed from States and populations where slavery did not exist; having railway connections and water communications only with those States that were hostile to the United States—should yet have set their faces as a flint against secession. The wonder is, not only that they sprung quickly with uplifted hands to the defense of the Union at the very beginning of the assaults upon its life, but were also its active or suffering friends to the close of the strife. Difficulties and dangers on that behalf, they encountered without flinching. Reproaches, and severities that in some instances were cruel persecutions, they endured with fortitude. Under the influence of an ardent patriotism, most of their able-bodied men, in order to save their personal liberty or life, or to escape being forced to fight against the Nation, left home and family and fled, as they then called it, to "God's Country"; crossing difficult rivers and mountains by day, and snatching at night short sleep in the dark forests through which they passed; suffering from hunger and fatigue, from drenching rains and alarms from foes, until at length, where the star-spangled banner was floating securely in the air, they enlisted by tens of thousands, to help with arms in saving the Nation's life.

During the War period, in more than two years of which the Southern Confederacy ruled over East Tennessee, the property of these refugees and that of Union people who remained at home, was seized and used or destroyed, until impoverishment and want prevailed to an alarming extent. In numerous instances, starvation, like a gaunt wolf, threatened the door, and the hearts of many were sickened by hope of succor long deferred; but the fire of devotion to the Union still lived and glowed within them strong and bright until the end came.

The scene in a momentous tragedy, thus presented in a region of country so isolated from the great world that its actors could have no stimulus to their constancy in the heard applause of admiring spectators, was phenomenal, even in that time of heroic deeds. In was the reproduction, upon the same stage, after nearly a vanished century, of the same broad patriotism—to some extent inherited—which sent a thousand riflemen from Sycamore Shoals on the Watauga River, to win for the American colonies a victory at King's Mountain; and which afterwards triumphed over a spirit of revolutionary separation, in retaining the allegiance of the people of Frankland to the mother State of North Carolina. Without doubt, the chief sentiment that animated the hearts of loyal East Tennesseeans in 1861-'65 was one of duty. "The duty of preserving the liberty which their ancestors, through God's blessing, won, established and handed down" to them—a duty which has been said to be "no less imperative than any commandment in the second table; if it be not the concentration of the whole." * To whatever causes their conduct may be attributed, it at least conveys the impression of their strong individuality as a people and invites the closer observation and study of the political philosopher.

It is certain, also, that the steadfast attachment of East Tennessee to the Union and the efficient aid it gave to its preservation, formed an important factor in the war and contributed in no small degree to its final result. Had its territory been friendly ground for the encampment, sustenance and transit of Southern armies, and had the ranks of those armies been recruited with the thirty thousand East Tennesseeans who volunteered in the service of the United States,

---

* Two Brothers Hare—in "*Guesses at Truth.*"

the course of events might have been seriously deflected and the war been prolonged, to the hurt of the whole country.

It is of occurrences during the conflict in that territory, shut in by rock-ribbed mountains, and chiefly in its central town, that these pages will tell. The purpose of the narrative is to instruct as well as to interest the general reader, and it may afford a help, however slight, to some gifted mind that shall in the future attempt the history of the War of 1861–'65 in the spirit of a sound Christian philosophy.

It is also the hope of the author that this volume will serve to confirm the reader's patriotism, or to quicken the sentiment into life, if it only slumber within him. The love of country has justly been extolled by the tongue of the eloquent orator and the pen of the gifted poet. Both the philosopher and the religious teacher commend it, and it is profoundly interesting to know that the Author of Christianity cherished that sentiment in its purity, and in full harmony with his wide-reaching love for other nations than His own of Israel. Some of His countrymen once interceded for His favor in behalf of a Roman centurion, with the reason, "he loveth our nation." The plea was not rebuked by Him, and as the petition which it aimed to strengthen was quickly granted, we may infer that it influenced Him.

Every one will probably admit that the spirit of patriotism is praiseworthy, but it is well to consider that it is sometimes liable to slip from the guidance of wisdom and to be narrowed down in its range of working to a section or a party. On the contrary, it should be as broad as it is ardent; its boundaries those of the Nation; and while it rises immeasurably above the base greed for office, it should equally rise above the bitterness and contentions of partisan zeal into the pure and serene atmosphere of fellow-citizenship. It may be blindly perverted, but a true love of country can never be intelligently applied to the uses of an inordinate ambition, or to supply the necessities of a huge wrong. "History," it is often repeated, "is Philosophy teaching by example." If so, then it would be wrong to let the splendid example of unadulterated patriotism given by the Union people of East Tennessee in the War of 1861-'65, go unchronicled. No popular leaders induced it. The courage and fortitude it presents sprang from deep and strong love for the Union of the States in one Nation—deep and strong love for their *whole country.*

Impressive also are the lessons of true and

far-reaching patriotism given by the heroic Rhode Islander and his fellow-soldiers, in rescuing East Tennessee, at great pains, danger and loss, from a usurped power; and by the generous people of Massachusetts, Pennsylvania, New York, Maine and other States, in relieving it from impending famine. These interpositions, not to destroy, but to save its people, should teach Americans, as long as the Republic lasts, that, in the words of Mr. Edward Everett: "If the Union means anything, it means not merely political connection and commercial intercourse, but to bear each other's burdens and to share each other's sacrifices; it means active sympathy and efficient aid."

CONTENTS.

INTRODUCTION.
PAGE.
FIRST SETTLEMENT IN EAST TENNESSEE—NATURAL FEATURES OF THE REGION—ITS PEOPLE—ITS CENTRAL TOWN. 19

CHAPTER I.
EARLY HISTORY—THE FRONTIER—PATRIOTIC SPIRIT—CALL TO ARMS—MARCH TO BATTLE................................ 37

CHAPTER II.
EARLY HISTORY—THE PURSUIT—THE BATTLE—THE VICTORY... 49

CHAPTER III.
EARLY HISTORY—MOUNTAINEERS DISSATISFIED—AN INDEPENDENT STATE—CONFLICT OF AUTHORITIES.................... 57

CHAPTER IV.
EARLY HISTORY—FRANKLAND'S CORRESPONDENCE—ITS STRIFES—ITS DEATH, UPON DEFEAT OF ITS CHIEF—HIS ESCAPE.... 67

CHAPTER V.
SHADOWS OF COMING EVENTS—POLITICAL HARANGUES—A SUSPECTED "INCENDIARY"—BIBLE SOCIETY COLPORTEUR IN SCOTT COUNTY.. 77

CHAPTER VI.
THE STATE FOR THE UNION—A STRANGER IN TOWN—SECESSION OF TENNESSEE PRE-ARRANGED—BIBLICAL CO-INCIDENCE—UNION ORATORS—AN ASSASSINATION...................... 90

CHAPTER VII.
THE UNION CONVENTION AT KNOXVILLE—THE UNION CONVENTION AT GREENEVILLE....................................... 103

CONTENTS.

CHAPTER VIII.

Growing Wrath—Joy over Victory—Gen. Zolicoffer—A Yankee Boy's Passport—Lights and Shadows—Escape of Congressmen—Forged Letters to Boston—A Military Zealot—Bridge Burning.......................... 120

CHAPTER IX.

Severe Treatment of Union Men—Oaths of Allegiance—Imprisonments—Executions........................... 138

CHAPTER X.

Reign of Terror—A Noted Patriot—His Painful Experiences and Final Deliverance—A Refugee's Perilous Journey—Conscription—Capture of Fleeing Men...... 152

CHAPTER XI.

Generals Kirby Smith, J. E. Johnson and Bragg—Refugees Invited Home by Proclamation—Mrs. Brownlow, Her Children and Mrs. Maynard Exiled—General Condition of Things Resulting from Secession............ 169

CHAPTER XII.

News and Literature in the Confederacy—A Mixed Dinner Party and Its Conversation—Carter's Raid and What Befell a Recruiting Officer—An Unterrified Yankee Citizen of Georgia—Sanders' Raid—Death of Pleasant McClung.................................... 188

CHAPTER XIII.

Gen. Buckner's Retreat—A Citizen's Adventure—General Burnside; His Welcome; His Expedition—Cumberland Gap; Its Surrender—An Eccentric Farmer—Military Movements in East Tennessee—Fight at Blue Springs—Affairs at and near Loudon—Burnside and the People....................................... 208

CHAPTER XIV.

Grant at Chattanooga—Peril of Burnside—Their Co-Operation—Longstreet at Loudon—Burnside Retreats and is Pursued—Battle of Campbell's Station—Military Conditions at Knoxville—Escape of Leading Unionists.. 234

CONTENTS.

CHAPTER XV.

Siege of Knoxville—Its Defenders and Defences—Colonel Sanders—His Death and Funeral—Progress of the Siege—Burning of North Knoxville. 250

CHAPTER XVI.

Hospital Needs—A Scene at Headquarters—Increased Destitution—Assault on Fort Sanders—Longstreet Retreats—Sherman's Approach—Burnside Gives Honor to His Army... 268

CHAPTER XVII.

Capt. Poe's Conclusions—President Lincoln's Proclamation—Generals Sherman and Grant—Intercessions with Gen. Foster—Battle of Resaca—Influx of Refugees to Knoxville... 285

CHAPTER XVIII.

Deplorable Condition of East Tennessee—Watauga Scenery—Landon C. Haynes at a Dinner Party—Nathaniel G. Taylor—His Wrongs—His Fears for the People—His Mission to the North and Work at Philadelphia—Edward Everett's Speech at Faneuil Hall.. 301

CHAPTER XIX.

Fund for Relief of East Tennessee at Boston, Portland and New York—Mr. Taylor and Family in Great Trouble—Their Timely Relief—Knoxville East Tennessee Relief Society—Pennsylvania Committee—Effective Work in Relieving Destitution—Summary of Results...

Appendices 337

ILLUSTRATIONS.

ASSAULT ON FORT SANDERS	*Frontispiece.*
PORTRAIT OF HON. EDWARD EVERETT	22
PORTRAIT OF MR. LLOYD P. SMITH	34
PORTRAIT OF REV. WM. G. BROWNLOW	77
PORTRAIT OF HON. THOMAS A. R. NELSON	90
PORTRAIT OF HON. JOHN BAXTER	108
PORTRAIT OF HON. ANDREW JOHNSON	129
PORTRAIT OF HON. CONNELLY F. TRIGG	153
PORTRAIT OF HON. HORACE MAYNARD	174
PORTRAIT OF GEN. A. E. BURNSIDE	208
PORTRAIT OF GEN. S. P. CARTER	245
PORTRAIT OF GEN. JOSEPH A. COOPER	294
PORTRAIT OF REV. NATHANIEL G. TAYLOR	313

INTRODUCTION.

FIRST SETTLEMENT IN EAST TENNESSEE—NATURAL FEATURES OF THE REGION—ITS PEOPLE—ITS CENTRAL TOWN.

"With gold and gems if Chilian mountains glow;
If bleak and barren Scotia's hills arise;
There plague and poison, lust and rapine grow;
Here peaceful are the vales, and pure the skies,
And freedom fires the soul, and sparkles in the eyes."
BEATTIE.

THE first English fort built in Eastern Tennessee was that of Loudon, in 1757, so called for the Earl of Loudon, at the time Governor of Virginia. It stood at the junction of the Tellico and Little Tennessee rivers, now in Monroe County, and 35 miles southwest of Knoxville. Its garrison of from two to three hundred men was, with three exceptions, massacred by the Indians in 1760, and with it a number of women and children.

The first permanent settlement of Anglo-Americans in the region was made on the Watauga River, not far from the present northwestern border of North Carolina. As early as 1748, explorers, traders and hunters from Virginia had visited that part of the land. Thirteen years afterwards, nineteen men were attracted to it from the same State by the abundance of its game and were employed as sportsmen on Clinch and Powell's rivers for eighteen months. Another company went towards it from North Carolina, but with the exception of the famous Indian hunter and fighter Daniel Boone, they halted at the spot where now is Abingdon, Virginia. Probably he had before been on the waters of the Watauga, for a beech tree, that stands on Boone's creek, a tributary of that river, not far from Jonesboro, still bears this inscription,

"*D. Boon cilled a Bar on tree in the year 1760.*"

These visits were followed by others from companies of hunting pioneers. In 1764 Boone returned to the same region from his home on the Yadkin River, North Carolina. Another pioneer gave him a glowing description of the country which is now Kentucky, and in 1771 he endeavored with a party of eighty persons—forty of whom were hunters—to pass into it through Cumberland Gap. They were waylaid and fiercely assailed by Indians and were forced to abandon the enterprise. Some four years later it was successfully renewed, and Boone, passing over the Clinch and Cumberland mountains from East Tennessee, led in the establishment beyond them of a great Commonwealth.

An eminent historian of the United States, after relating the wrongs to which the people of North Carolina were subjected in 1770–71, under the provincial Governor, Tryon, proceeds to tell how and where they fled from oppression.

"Without concert—instinctively impelled by discontent and the wearisomeness of life exposed to bondage—men crossed the Alleghanies and descending into the basin of the Tennessee, made their homes in the valley of the Watauga. There no lawyer followed them; there no King's Governor came to be their Lord; there the flag of England never waved. They rapidly extended their settlements. By degrees they took possession of the more romantic banks of the broader Nolachucky, whose sparkling waters spring out of the tallest mountains in the range. The climate was invigorating; the health-giving westerly wind blew at all seasons; in spring the wild crab-apple filled the air with the sweetest perfumes. A fertile soil gave to industry good crops of maize; the clear streams flowed pleasantly, without tearing floods; where the closest thickets of spruce and rhododendron flung the cooling shade furthest over the river, trout abounded. The elk and the red deer were not wanting in the natural parks of oak and hickory, of maple, elm, black oak and buckeye. Of quails and turkeys and pigeons there was no end. The golden eagle built its nest on the topmost ledge of the mountain, and might be seen wheeling in wide circles high above the pines, or dropping like a meteor upon its prey. The black bear, whose flesh was held to be the most delicate of meats, grew so fat upon the abundant acorns and chestnuts that he could be run down in a chase of a hundred yards; and sometimes the hunters gave chase to the coward panther, strong enough to beat off twenty dogs, yet flying from one." *

The entire valley of East Tennessee, extending from the southwestern border of Virginia to Northern Georgia, embedded in the mountains, offers peculiar attractions. Nearly fifty years ago an English gentleman, who had lived there several years, published a pamphlet in London,† in which he said:

"To one who has resided some years in the valley of East Tennessee, breathing the pure air from its mountains and drinking of its crystal springs, enjoying the sunny smile of its temperature and the cooling shade of its noble forests, delighting the eye and the heart with its fields of fruitfulness which at every turn present a new aspect, it is not 'England's laughing meads,' nor 'her flowering orchard trees,' nor yet Lomond and the Trosachs, with all their beauty and historical associations and the magic thrown around them by the exuberant imagination of the poet, that could tempt him again to quit the peaceful solitude, the clear blue sky, the song of the mocking-bird, the note of the dove, the hum of the humming-bird, and the silence of nature where all is echo."

The Hon. Edward Everett, in an address he delivered in Faneuil Hall, Boston, February, 1864,

---

* Bancroft. Ch. XLVI.: Ed. 1854.

† "A Brief Historical, Statistical and Descriptive Review of East Tennessee, Developing its Immense Agricultural, Mining and Manufacturing Advantages. By J. Gray Smith." * * * London, 1842.

HON. EDWARD EVERETT.

which was called forth by the then suffering condition of the people of East Tennessee in consequence of the war, said of it :

" A more interesting region, or one more entitled to our most active sympathy, is not to be found within the limits of the United States. Forming a part of the noble State of Tennessee, it is in many respects a State in itself, and not a small one either. It consists of the broad valley of the magnificent river, which traverses it from northeast to southwest, three hundred miles in length, and with a varying width of from fifty to seventy-five miles—and of the slopes of the mountains, which separate it on the north from Kentucky, on the southwest from Middle Tennessee, and on the southeast from North Carolina and Georgia : a beautiful valley, between beautiful enclosing hills, fertile many of them to their summits, sparkling with a hundred tributaries to the noble stream which forms its principal feature.

" That river is in some respects one of the most remarkable on the continent. Its northern affluents rise in the State of Virginia, but, as if to read a lesson of patriotism in the very face of the soil, as if to prop the fabric of the Union by the eternal buttresses of the hills, instead of flowing to the Atlantic like the other rivers of Virginia, it gathers up the waters of its tributary streams, Holston and Clinch and French Broad, and connecting Virginia and the Carolinas with East Tennessee, flows southward down to the northwestern corner of Georgia. There, after kissing the feet of the glorious hills of Chattanooga, instead of flowing to the Gulf, its seeming natural direction, it coquets with Northern Alabama, breaks into the Muscle Shoals, plants Decatur at their head and Florence at their feet, and then sweeping back to its native North, traverses the entire width of Tennessee a second time, apparently running up hill—for while it is flowing northward, the Mississippi, parallel to it, and at no great distance, is rolling its floods southward—enters the State of Kentucky, and empties into the Ohio, fifty miles above the junction of that river with the Mississippi, thus binding seven States in its silver circuit, and connecting them all with the great central basin of the continent.

"The soil of Eastern Tennessee is rich; the mountains are filled with coal and almost every variety of ore; their slopes bubble with mineral springs; the climate is temperate and healthful; the territory divided into farms of a moderate size, for the most part tilled by frugal, industrious men, who own the soil, which yields them its well-earned abundance. In no part of the State are there so few slaves; in none is there a more substantial population; in no part of the South is the slave interest so feeble. East Tennessee greatly resembles the lower ranges and fertile valleys of the Alps, and it has been often called the American Switzerland. It is divided into thirty counties, and its population does not, I think, fall short of 300,000 souls. *

* Its population was 301,056 in 1860, and 428,929 in 1880.

"But this grand valley, with the hills that enclose it, possesses an interest for us far beyond that which attaches to their geographical features, merely as such. It is one of the most important links in that chain of valley and mountain which traverses the entire North American continent, from northeast to southwest, separating the streams which flow into the Atlantic from those which seek the St. Lawrence, the Ohio and the Mississippi. Forcing its way down into the heart of the region whose alluvial plains are devoted to the culture of tobacco, cotton, rice and sugar by slave labor, this ridge of highlands, with the valleys embosomed in them, from the time you begin to leave the State of Pennsylvania, begins to assume the highest political importance in reference to the present stupendous struggle. Extending to the southwest as far as Northern Alabama, this noble mountain tract, and the valleys enclosed in its parallel and transverse ridges, is, by the character of its climate, soil, and natural productions, the natural ally of the North. Here, if nowhere else, we may truly say, with the German poet:

'Auf den Bergen ist Freiheit; der Hauch der Grüfte
Steigt nicht hinauf, in die reinen Lüfte.'

That means—

'On the mountain is Freedom; the breath of the vales
Rises not up to the pure mountain gales.'"

East Tennessee has been sometimes called the Switzerland of America, and certainly there are strong resemblances between the two countries. They are unlike in that the former is wanting in the lake feature that distinguishes Switzerland. East Tennessee, however, abounds wonderfully in natural springs of pure and limpid water, and has a multitude of creeks and rivers. Some of these last bear euphonious names, as Watauga, Nolachucky, Tellico, Hiwassee and Tennessee. The climatic advantages of the region result, partly, at least, from its having a Southern location and a Northern elevation—peculiarities which a Swiss gentleman who visited it thirty years ago, in fulfillment of his long cherished desire, was quick to observe.

Following the first immigrants to the region, who were from Virginia and North Carolina, and among whom were some of Scotch-Irish ancestry, others came, particularly to the county seats, directly from the north of Ireland; but the great majority of the settlers were of American birth—hardy and adventurous spirits, in great variety, such as are apt to seek a frontier life.

In the valleys and along the highways and rivers have always been much intelligence and moral worth, with admixtures, as elsewhere found, of ignorance and vice. Sufficient public schools have been sadly wanting in former years; yet education, by which comparatively few profited, has been esteemed and promoted in the Commonwealth from its beginning. Three colleges were established in East Tennessee before the Territory became a State: one each in Washington, Greene and Knox counties; and soon after this century began, county academies were chartered throughout the State.

At first the Presbyterian Church existed almost if not altogether alone, but before long it was succeeded by Methodist and Baptist churches. *

Accustomed as have been the people of the more mountainous counties to ruder modes of living and narrower means of education, their social condition is freer, even from healthy restraints. They are gifted with good natural qualities, but these have not been always cultivated to the repression of other traits and tendencies. They are brave, but many of them are liable to needless tests of personal valor; independent, but prone to notions of individual liberty inconsistent with right ideas of law and order; social, but inclined to promote good cheer by artificial means of excitement.

In 1848 a recent diplomatic agent of the United States in India† found his way to this very secluded region, seeking, under the pressure of severe domestic bereavement, to "get rid of himself." He succeeded in doing so by dwelling for the winter at the southern base of the Cumberland Mountains. Afterwards he ascribed to the highlanders among whom he hibernated, three favorite sources of excitement, namely, political stump-speakings, religious camp-meetings, and home-made liquors. An unlearned population, far removed from the world and its thoroughfares, they highly prize their

---

* See Appendix: Note A. † Mr. Balestier.

right of suffrage to make legislatures and judges, members of congress, governors and presidents. Their religious instinct, once awakened, is quick to respond to fervent preaching that is sustained by stirring devotional songs. Their animal spirits are apt to be depressed by the monotony of their daily life, and the juice of Indian corn gives relief.* That corn is the grain that is chiefly grown in the highlands. Its meal and the salted flesh of hogs are principally their food. Eager candidates for office supply them with mental aliment at heated discussions pending the elections, and the result is that although many of them are without the knowledge acquired at school, all of them are informed concerning questions of public policy. Probably no people of equal numbers can be found in the land who excel those of East Tennessee in acquaintance with current politics. It is to be confessed that more than a few of the mountaineers are deficient in historical lore. Certain great events of the Nation's earlier life, whose results they have exaggerated, have a firm lodgment in their minds, but lie there unqualified by knowledge of later occurrences. An anecdote related by John Mitchell will illustrate.

Scarcely had the United States diplomatic agent just now spoken of, departed upon an Oriental mission, when the weary Irish patriot arrived from Australia, in this isolated region. He, too, sought retirement, and in Tuckaleechee Cove, near the

---

* In 1887 East Tennessee voted in favor of a State prohibition law by a majority of nearly 13,000.

Smoky Mountains, he found it, with his family. One day some of the neighbors met together, after the not unfrequent idling custom of men in the mountains—perhaps for friendly gossip, or to shoot at a mark in rivalry of skill for a prize. One said:

"Who is this stranger, anyhow? He don't do nuthin' only him and his son go fishin' and shootin'."

"O," another replied, "don't you know who that is? That's John Mitchell, the exile of the British Government."

"British Government indeed!" said the first speaker. "I thought we had whipp'd that consarn out long ago." *

One virtue obtains almost universally among the people of East Tennessee—that of hospitality. It has to some extent diminished in the valleys, where the inhabitants live as did their ancestors from plentiful tables and various dishes, but where, since the war ended, the increase of travel and of commercial intercourse with other parts of the country have checked generosity and enlarged prudence. Yet it has lost none of its olden-time proportions in the mountains, where the table lacks nothing in abundance but a good deal in variety; where the narrow range of habitual diet affords small opportunity for skill in cookery, and even that opportunity has not been improved. There the signs of an advanced civilization—the steam-engine, the telegraph and the telephone—have never invaded the air with whistle or wires; but the stranger will

* The mountaineers are innocent of the dialect given them in recent novels.

be kindly entertained for the night at little or no charge, and probably when he departs in the morning, will be cheered on his way by the expressed hope of his host that he will come again. Not that the landlord thinks money is worthless. For he and his countrymen are sharp traders. Without adventuring at the start upon fixed sums, they "beat about the bush" to find out how much can be had or how little be paid by them, and both buyer and seller are wide awake to "get the best of the bargain." They also know points of law, and are unduly given to litigation in defense of their real or supposed rights.

Slavery, even in the modified, domestic garb it wore among them, had a depressing, degrading influence upon the white common laborers. This was more obviously so with the several thousands of inert, improvident people, such as are to be found more or less in all regions, but who are apt to be more numerous where the climate is genial and a few acres of land with a poor tenement can be cheaply rented. These led an Arab sort of life, living in a log cabin and growing a crop of corn, then, not "folding their tents," but packing up their "plunder"—the synonym for household goods—and flitting away with their children and dogs to a cabin of another proprietor. For this class, who lived "from hand to mouth," and whose contentment was partly due to the fact that their covetousness had no incitements to indulgence, the negroes of substantial families had an unconcealed contempt. Another and better class consisted more numerously of diligent and thrifty farming people. In them slavery induced, by some subtle, indefinable influence, an industrial languor. It approximated them to the slaves, despite their difference in color and personal relation to the masters; and it barred their way to improvement of condition, by pushing them as tenants from the more fertile acres which the slaves tilled, to the thin soil of the hillsides. Now, under the reign of freedom, these small but industrious farmers have access by lease to the richer lands.

The mountaineers, strictly speaking, felt no concern about the institution of slavery itself, and knew but little. Here and there among them were men of competent means, some of whom owned a few negroes. Generally they looked upon slavery as something foreign to their social life, but they had no imperative, philanthropic impulses to contend against it. They would have been displeased at its coming near their homes in the imperious majesty it wore in the cotton States. At the same time they were satisfied to let men of the South keep serfs at pleasure, but they counted it no business of theirs to help in the work. If the perpetuity of the Union or that of slavery were the question at issue, they would have no hesitation in deciding. Let slavery perish and the Union live. Yes! the Union—the Government handed down to them from Washington and his compatriots! *It* must survive. For it they would fight, and, if necessary, die.

While the men high up on the hills had no philosophic reflections nor any humanitarian hate towards slavery, a strong aversion to it had been manifested from an early period by some men of the valleys. "A powerful appeal for the abolition of slavery" was published as a communication in the *Knoxville Gazette*, 1797. It called a meeting of the citizens of East Tennessee at a town in Washington County, March, 1797, to form a Manumission Society. The communication bears internal evidence of having been written by a member of the Society of Friends. Not then, but in 1815 the proposed society was organized.* The Rev. John Rankin, born February 4, 1793, Jefferson County, East Tennessee, graduated at Washington College, was ordained a Presbyterian minister, but having imbibed anti-slavery sentiments from his mother in Rockbridge County, Virginia, he removed his residence from Tennessee to a free State and became a leading abolitionist. Before his recent death at the advanced age of nearly ninety years, at Ironton, Ohio, he gave authority to the statement that "the sentiment of abolitionism originated in Tennessee about 1814, there being then an anti-slavery society in Jefferson County, East Tennessee.† The Manumission Society first mentioned, prosecuted its work diligently for years. In March, 1819, "*The Manumission Intelligencer*," a weekly newspaper, was issued at Jonesboro, and its publication gave place, the year following, to

---

* Moses White, Esq., in an address to the Tennessee Press Association, has made these historical statements.

† See letter of "Gath" (George Francis Townsend)—Cincinnati Enquirer, September, 1885.

"*The Emancipator*," monthly, by Elijah Embree, one of two brothers, Friends, from Pennsylvania, who manufactured iron near Elizabethton. On his death, it was succeeded by "*The Genius of Universal Emancipation*," at Greeneville, published by Benjamin Lundy, a Friend, from New Jersey. It lived until 1824.

After that date, the sentiment of aversion to slavery survived and in various ways was manifested, and although it was eventually counteracted by the political strife which grew out of the subject, it never ceased to exist firmly in many minds. A home in the great valley of East Tennessee was not formerly adapted to the cultivation of pro-slavery sympathies in persons of humane disposition and healthy sensibilities. For along the highway through that valley, slave-dealers transported negroes whom they had bought in Virginia and intended to sell in Southwestern States. The sales of these unfortunates, often because of their masters' necessities, had in some instances separated families: and lest the men, moved by sorrow over the disruption, by aversion to their destined market, or by desire for freedom, should escape on the way, the dealers fettered them two and two to a strong chain running lengthwise between. It was pathetic to see them march, thus bound, through the towns, and to hear their melodious voices in plaintive singing as they went. By-standers then saw slavery without the disguise, with which Laurence Sterne pronounced it "still a bitter draught," and the spectacle was apt to create or strengthen antipathy to the institution in unbiased minds.

Knoxville, the central town of this entire region, stands on the northern bank of the Tennessee River, four miles below the junction of the Holston and French Broad rivers, which rise, the first in Virginia and the second in North Carolina. From 1792 to 1796 it was the capital of the "Territory south of the river Ohio," and from 1796 to 1816, that of the State of Tennessee. Its society had at that time a relative distinction for character and influence which it has never lost. In 1865 the town received a strong impulse to growth, from which its population in 1870 was 8,682, in 1880 it was 9,693, and in 1886 it was about 30,000. The great, and of late, rapid increase is largely owing to immigration from Northern States. Thrifty and enterprising new-comers have added in a marked degree to the trade and prosperity of the place. Like results have followed more or less throughout East Tennessee, especially at Chattanooga, since the war disclosed the natural advantages of the whole region to the knowledge of the world outside of it. So obvious are the benefits that will accrue to it from worthy immigrants, that even the most zealous sectionalists have yielded their prejudices so far as to give even "Yankees" not only a welcome, but an invitation to dwell in the land.

Lloyd P. Smith and Frederick Collins, of Philadelphia, visited the region in March, 1864, upon a benevolent errand. In their published report of the visit they said: "The existing war is clearly

LLOYD P. SMITH.

destined to introduce Northern men, Northern ideas and Northern enterprise into the border States, and, as our military lines advance, throughout the whole South. * * * East Tennessee, with its fertile lands, its rich mines and valuable water-power, presents a fine field for the application of Northern labor and capital; and when this calamity is overpast, and a direct railroad communication with the North is secured, it will prosper as never before. Especially will this be the case when the incubus of slavery is thrown off." These words are now in a measure fulfilled prophecy.

Topographically, East Tennessee is at the very heart of the Atlantic States. It has been observed that "Knoxville is the exact geographical center of the eastern half of the United States: the corners of the eastern half being Eastport in Maine, Key West in Florida, the mouth of the Rio Grande in Texas, and a point in Lake Superior on the northwest boundary (water or lake) line of Michigan. The point is north of Isle Royal in the lake. The opposite sides of the figure formed by lines drawn from and to these corners are respectively parallel and equal, and its diagonals intersect at Knoxville. The more exact the map, the more exactly is Knoxville found to be at the point of intersection." *

* Hon. Henry R. Gibson.

The Loyal Mountaineers of Tennessee.

CHAPTER I.

Early History—The Frontier—Patriotic Spirit—Call to Arms—March to Battle.

> "Men who their duties know,
>   But know their rights, and knowing, dare maintain;
>   * * * * * * *
> These constitute a State."
>
> Sir William Jones.

THE hardy and brave settlers on the Watauga, Holston and Nolachucky rivers, among lofty mountains, dwelt in such peace as their savage neighbors permitted, and in contentment with their great distance from the busy world. Having leased the territory from the Indians, they proceeded to organize the

FIRST REPUBLIC EVER FORMED IN AMERICA.

There was no established government of any kind within their reach, whose protection they could enjoy while they owned its authority. Therefore, under the pressure of a civil necessity, they met in convention, entered into a written association, prescribed laws and elected commissioners for the administration of justice and the conduct of public affairs. Their commonwealth existed for several years.

In 1774 the Shawnees and other Indian tribes assailed the western frontier of Virginia. Lord Dunmore, Governor of that State, called for volunteers to resist the invasion, and of those enlisted from southwestern counties of the colony, a regiment under Col. Christian assembled at New River. To it a company of more than fifty men from Sullivan and Carter counties (East Tennessee), commanded by Capt. Evan Shelby, joined themselves, and with it went to Greenbrier, where Gen. Lewis, commander in chief, assembled his forces. From there the army marched with difficulty for twenty-five days through the wilderness, along the rugged banks of the Kanawha River, to Point Pleasant on the Ohio. Two of Capt. Shelby's men were instrumental in preventing the Indians, before day on the 10th of October, from surprising and probably overthrowing the army of Gen. Lewis. In the hotly contested battle which immediately followed, some of the same company dislodged a body of the savages from an important vantage ground, and thus ensured victory to the Americans. The defeat of the Indians was so complete that they were subdued into a peace which lasted for two years. Judge Haywood, in commenting upon the unexpected discovery of the enemy by men from East Tennessee, to the salvation of the whole army of the provincials, remarks: "Thus it has happened that East Tennessee, in the earliest stages of her infancy, has been called on to contribute all in her power to the common defense, and seems to have been made much less for herself than for the protection of her neighbors."

In the resistance made by the American Colonies to the Government of Great Britain, these settlers early expressed their sympathy. Important events touching the welfare of a people may be remotely separated in space while they are closely related in time. On the fifth day of September, 1774, when the army of Gen. Lewis at Greenbrier was about starting on its hard march down the Kanawha River, to win a victory that would compel the Indians into peace, the first Continental Congress met in Philadelphia, to deliberate for the liberty and welfare of the American people. The King of Great Britain rejected the offers of that Congress. The British Parliament met in November, and again after the holidays. The twentieth day of January was the first day of the session in the House of Lords. On the very same day the men of the settlements beyond the Alleghanies, where the Watauga and the Holston flow to the Tennessee, united with the men of the southwestern corner of Virginia in council near Abingdon. On hearing what Congress had done, they unanimously declared their adhesion to it. To the Virginia delegates in Congress they wrote:

"We explored our uncultivated wilderness, bordering on many nations of savages, and surrounded by mountains almost inaccessible to any but these savages. But even to these remote regions the hand of power hath pursued us, to strip us of that liberty and property with which God, nature and the rights of humanity have vested us. We are willing to contribute all in our power, if applied to constitutionally, but cannot think of submitting our liberty or property to a venal British Parliament or a corrupt ministry. We are deliberately and resolutely determined never to surrender any of our inestimable privileges to any power upon earth, but at the expense of our lives. These are our real though unpolished sentiments of liberty and loyalty, and in them we are resolved to live and die."

The War of the American Revolution began at Lexington and Concord April 19, 1775 (on the anniversary of which day, eighty-six years afterwards, was the fight at Baltimore). In describing the swift travel of the war message from Massachusetts throughout the Colonies, the historian Bancroft represents it as overleaping bays and rivers and the Dismal Swamp, passing through pines and palmettoes, and transcending hills and mountains. "The Blue Ridge took up the voice and made it heard from one end to the other of the valley of Virginia." And westward still: "The Alleghanies, as they listened, opened their barriers that the 'loud call' might pass through to the hardy riflemen on the Holston, the Watauga and the French

Broad," who, for some years after the beginning of the war, knew that it was going on, but the scenes of its battles were far removed from their secluded homes. The echoes of their wooded hills were now and then awakened by the notes of the "spirit-stirring drum and ear-piercing fife," but never by any martial sounds from conflicts with arms in the American Revolution. Georgia, in 1779, was brought into subjection to the King. About a hundred patriots, led by Col. Clarke, had fled to the mountaineers for refuge, and obtained helpers in their conflict with the British, in order to renew which, they returned home. Refugee Whigs had also come from east of the Alleghanies to the Washington District, into which North Carolina in 1777 organized the Watauga and adjacent settlements. The accounts given by all these of the persecutions and cruelties inflicted by the British and Tories, had moved the frontier men to friendly sympathy with the sufferers, and to slumbering wrath against the oppressors, and they only needed opportunity to actively join their brethren in the struggle of the Colonies for independence. The summer of 1780 had opened, and that opportunity was soon offered.

On the 11th of May, Charleston was surrendered by General Lincoln to Sir Henry Clinton. Shortly afterwards the British power was so triumphantly extended over South Carolina as to rally to its support all timid, wavering and disaffected people. North Carolina was in danger of being conquered. Col. Ferguson, of the British army, was marching towards it and threatening it with invasion. Col. Charles McDowell, temporarily chief commander of the Whig forces in North Carolina, called on Colonels John Sevier and Isaac Shelby, of Washington District, for help, "as soon as possible," against the invader. They promptly responded, and in July, Sevier, with two hundred mounted riflemen from Washington County, and Shelby, with an equal number from Sullivan County, joined McDowell's camp on Broad River, South Carolina. They did good service in several conflicts with the enemy, in capturing the fort held by Col. Moore on the Pacolet River and its garrison, and in winning the battle at Musgrove's Mill, where more than two hundred British prisoners were taken. Upon the heels of this victory came news to McDowell of Gen. Gates' defeat at Camden and Sumpter's disaster. This disheartened the army; it was in a position of danger and could only withdraw. So great indeed were its apprehensions and sense of inability to hold its own in the field, that it fairly dissolved. Shelby and Sevier, with their regiments, returned at once to their distant homes, yet ready of mind soon to renew the warfare. Not long after, McDowell, with a company of several hundred men, sought refuge in the same hospitable region.

Meanwhile, Cornwallis, flushed with his victory over Gates (August 16) at Camden, was eager for other triumphs, and by his direction Ferguson and his troops pressed their way up to the present Rutherfordton, North Carolina. The result was to encourage the Tory inhabitants and rally them to his support. Already, to his displeasure, the mountaineers had given him lessons of their prowess in battle. In September he sent a message to the officers on the western rivers that "if they did not quit their opposition to the British Government, he would march over the mountains, hang their leaders, and lay their country waste with fire and sword." This fierce missive did not frighten or deter those to whom it went. It rather incited them to hostile action. The presence in their country of refugee Whigs, some of whom had but recently arrived, was a constant reminder of the bitter and relentless hate of their enemies, that provoked them to sturdy resistance. Their patriotic spirits only needed an incentive to go forth to war, and Ferguson's threat furnished it. Col. Shelby, on receiving it, immediately rode fifty miles to confer with Col. Sevier. They determined to anticipate Ferguson, to call their riflemen to arms and march unexpectedly upon his camp. Col. Wm. Campbell, of Washington County, Virginia, near by, was asked and consented to join the expedition. Sycamore Shoals, Carter County, Tennessee, was chosen as the place, and September 25, as the time, for assembling the forces. On the appointed day, one thousand and forty men met at the Watauga River, armed with Deckard rifles—many of them with their feet in moccasins. Officers and men wore hunting-shirts; every soldier had a shot-pouch, knife, tomahawk, knapsack and blanket. Four hundred men under Campbell were from Washington County, Virginia, two hundred and forty under Shelby were from Sullivan County, North Carolina, and the same number under Sevier, from Washington County, North Carolina. One hundred and more, under Col. McDowell, were exiles from east of the Alleghanies.

The scene was picturesque in its natural features. In the valley and on the surrounding hills the thick woods were no longer dressed in summer green. Their leaves, touched by the first frosts, had begun to put on their autumnal coats of yellow, orange and red, mingled with the perpetual verdure of cedars and pines. In the midst stood a thousand men in simple, homely attire. They were healthy, because of the pure, tonic air they breathed—strong, by physical exercise among the hills—alert, by living in dangers from savage foes—equipped with guns, which their sharp eyes and skillful fingers made sure of aim and deadly in effect. Altogether, there were plentiful materials present for the pencil of an artist. The patriotic enthusiasm that filled the hearts of the gathered mountaineers, in harmony with the natural surroundings, gave a nobility to the scene that could not be portrayed on canvas or described but imperfectly in verse.

They who led in the enterprise had reverence of mind. It was a bold undertaking for a body of raw militia to encounter trained and tried soldiers in deadly fray, but their trust was not chiefly in themselves. There were Scotch-Irish Presbyterians among them who had strong faith in God, and the influence of their teaching and life had been felt by other settlers. Before the march began, prayer was offered by the Rev. Samuel Doak to Him who is supreme in heaven and earth. The minister associated the occasion and its purpose with the wars of Israel, under a departed dispensation of religion. One historian relates that the petitions were " accompanied with a few stirring remarks befitting the occasion, closing with the Bible quotation, 'the sword of the Lord and of Gideon,' when the sturdy Scotch-Irish Presbyterians around him, clothed in their tidy hunting-shirts and leaning upon their rifles in an attitude of respectful attention, shouted in patriotic acclaim: 'The sword of the Lord and of our Gideons!'" *

Buoyant with hope of triumph they went forward: on over the Little Doe and Big Doe rivers, —then through a gap between the Yellow and the Roan mountains,—then down along Roaring Creek and Big Toe River, following ravines, over stony ground. All around them from the start, the mountains stood, sublime in grandeur,—one, not far distant, higher than any other in the Atlantic States,—and mountains were ahead of them. On they went,—through the Blue Ridge at Gillespie's Gap,—then over Silver and Linville mountains to the Catawba River,—along its bank and across Linville River to Quaker Meadows. There Col. Cleveland and Maj. Winston, with three hundred and fifty North Carolinians, joined them.

When encamped in the gap at South Mountain,

---

* "History of the Battle of King's Mountain," by Dr. Lyman C. Draper: (the fruit of laborious historical research, and exhaustive of its subject.)

they supposed Ferguson to be at Gilbert-town, about eighteen miles distant, and for the impending conflict with him, it was needful they should have a commander. Who should it be? Their choice fell upon Col. Campbell, who had the largest regiment. Cleveland, McDowell and Shelby encouraged the men in brief and pithy words, and every one unwilling to go into battle was allowed to withdraw, but no one left. The march was resumed. They soon learned that the enemy had retreated.

On top of the Yellow Mountain, the second night after leaving Watauga River, two men had deserted from Sevier's regiment, and carried word to Ferguson that the mountaineers were advancing. He was alarmed, because, not only that he knew their mettle in fight, but that he had furloughed many Tory soldiers to visit their homes. Three days before, he had changed his camp a short distance (from Gilbert-town to Green River), in the hope of capturing Col. Clarke and his men, on their way from Georgia to Nolachucky. Quickly, upon learning that "the Back-water men," as he called them, were on the way to assail him, he sent word (September 30) to Lord Cornwallis, sixty miles distant, whom the message did not reach for a week. To the British commander at Ninety-Six he also wrote for reinforcements, which could not be given. In beginning to retreat, he went, not towards Charlotte, Cornwallis' headquarters, but southward, as if his destination were, as he said it was, Ninety-Six; and by this attempt to deceive, revealed his sense of danger.

Military prudence required that he should call the Tories to his help. Accordingly, on the second day of the retreat, there went out from his camp a circular to "the inhabitants of North Carolina," in which he described the on-coming descent of Whigs from the hills as "an inundation of barbarians." "If you wish," he said, "to be pinioned, robbed, and murdered * * * by the dregs of mankind; * * * if you wish or deserve to live and bear the name of men, grasp your arms in a moment and run to camp. The Backwater men have crossed the mountains. McDowell, Hampton, Shelby and Cleveland are at their head, so that you know what you have to depend upon. If you choose to be degraded forever and ever by a set of mongrels, say so at once, and let your women turn their backs upon you and look out for real men to protect them."

The next day, changing the direction of retreat, he went a few miles, watched all night for an attack, then marched twenty miles and halted forty-eight hours, with only thirty-five miles between him and Cornwallis. In a dispatch to that General, he spoke of his enemy as "of some consequence" by reinforcements, and of his hopefulness, yet doubt, of success. "Three or four hundred good soldiers—part dragoons," he said, "would finish the business. Something must be done soon." Sixteen miles more of travel brought him to King's Mountain, a ridge sixty feet high, six hundred yards long by two hundred and fifty wide at its base, and from sixty to one hundred yards wide on top. Upon it he encamped, October the sixth. Without fortifying the position, he expressed entire confidence in maintaining it. Several Whig leaders in their narratives attribute sayings to him on the subject that are boastful and blasphemous.

CHAPTER II.

Early History—The Pursuit—The Battle —The Victory.

> "Hark to the trump and the drum,
> And the mournful sound of the barbarous horn,
> And the flap of the banners that flit as they're borne,
> And the neigh of the steed, and the multitude's hum,
> And the clash, and the shout, 'They come! they come!'"
>   Lord Byron.

FERGUSON'S foes heard, on October 4, of his retreat, but were doubtful of its direction. Following his footsteps, they made little progress that day, for men and horses were weary. Maj. Candler, with thirty of Clarke's refugees from Georgia, joined them; also, in the march on the 5th, Maj. Chronicle, with twenty men from the Catawba River. Col. Lacey arrived that night at their camp on Green River, from an encampment of four hundred and thirty Whigs, in Rutherford County, two hundred and seventy of whom were South Carolinians under Colonels Lacey and Hill, and one hundred and sixty were North Carolinians —one hundred commanded by Col. Williams, and sixty by Colonels Graham and Hambright. Lacey gave the mountaineers definite information concerning Ferguson, and it was agreed that they and the forces Lacey represented should meet at the

Cowpens and combine. The same night, about seven hundred of the troops commanded by Col. Campbell and his compatriots, whose horses were in condition for rapid movement were selected, and on the next day they marched to the Cowpens, leaving seven hundred men under command of Maj. Herndon to follow more slowly.

At the Cowpens, a junction of forces as prearranged was made. The four hundred and thirty soldiers commanded by Lacey and others, were reduced by selection to two hundred and ten. These made the whole body of chosen cavalry, nine hundred and ten. At 9 P. M. October 6, they started and rode all night in a drizzling rain to overtake Ferguson, whose army, as a spy informed them, numbered fifteen hundred men. With the return of daylight, they made better speed, but still the rain fell and they could scarcely keep their guns dry. They forded the deep waters of Broad River at sunrise, halted a few minutes to breakfast from the scanty food they carried, and would have halted at noon, because of the stormy weather and their fatigue. Campbell, Sevier and Cleveland proposed to do so, but Shelby, with profane words, refused. He would brook no delay until night fell or Ferguson was found. A scout who had visited a Tory family, disguised as "a true King's man," brought them word that the British army was posted on King's Mountain. When within a few miles of it, they captured from a courier a dispatch sent by Ferguson to Cornwallis, calling for help by reinforcement and declaring his purpose against the rebels in very uncourteous and profane language. It was told to the American troops, and only quickened their speed. With galloping horses they went forward in sight of the enemy's camp.

It was early in the afternoon of the seventh of October, 1780. The rain had ceased and the clouds were rolling away before the bright shining of the sun. This was auspicious. These plain men from west of the Alleghanies may not have understood how critical was that hour of the American Revolution, even as well as did the harried Whigs from the Carolinas who were their companions in arms; but they were wide awake to the value of the rights for which their countrymen contended, and of the opportunity at hand to help them. Not one of those who were about to go into battle for the Colonies saw, as the men of to-day can see, along with the greatness of the danger to the struggle for American independence, the important consequences of their own heroic conduct. Men engaged in war are intent upon present deeds rather than thoughtful of future results.

That day's conflict would roll away the clouds that filled the civil and political sky of the Colonies, or would make them darker and thicker. As that day went, would go the destiny, not only of the infant Republic, but with it, that of hundreds of millions of the human race. The battle might close the door or open it to "a Government of the people, by the people, and for the people," on a mighty continent, where families of every nation and language should dwell in the faith of Christ and brotherly love. O, men of the hills, where freedom always has a home, be brave of heart and firm of hand, in the presence of such a grand possibility! And those plain, hunting-shirted riflemen were not afraid. Therefore they shall be honored by all people of right mind and true heart until time ends.

Dismounted from their horses, they formed for battle in four columns around the mountain. Two columns were on the right—one, Campbell's regiment of Virginians, and the other, Sevier's regiment, with McDowell's and Winston's battalions. Two columns were on the left—one composed of Shelby's regiment and Williams' command; the other of North Carolinians, under Cleveland, Chronicle and Hambright, and of South Carolinians, under Lacey and others. The chief officers briefly exhorted their men to do valiantly. Campbell, addressing each corps in turn, told those who were afraid to stand back, but no one moved. Instead, men threw their hats into the air and wrapped their heads tightly in handkerchiefs, that their quick step through the woods might be easier. Up the mountain sides they went, in the face of an equal and boastful foe.

And now, the red-haired Campbell begins the attack, moving over the roughest ground. The shouts of his men swell on the air. Shelby's troops respond, and then others, until the whole mountain is enveloped in sound. Ferguson and his second, Capt. De Peyster,* hear the outcries.

* Dr. Ramsey writes, "Dupoister."

Ferguson's mind is touched with fear of defeat. De Peyster says, "These things are ominous." Soon, Campbell, nearly at the hill-top, opens a deadly fire, and quickly the shrill notes of Ferguson's whistle, inciting the British to battle, mingle with the roll of his drums. Campbell is forced to retreat down the mountain to its very foot, so fierce is the bayonet charge of regulars and Tories. But he rallies his men and again they ascend, driving back their enemy. Lacey and Hill, with their troops, join in the conflict. The left center, under Shelby, is almost to the summit, and pours hot volleys through the slight defences, putting Ferguson's person in danger. De Peyster confronts the assailants, charges them with bayonets, and Shelby also is compelled down the mountain. Back from successful repulse of his foes, De Peyster returns to repel the "brave and gentle Cleveland," Chronicle and Hambright. Chronicle is slain, and Williams dies, fighting bravely. Meanwhile, Campbell, McDowell and Shelby, on the other side of the mountain are again ascending, in conflict with Tory riflemen, shouting, "Huzza, boys!" as they advance. Sevier has gained the hill-top. He presses the British center, and is charged by the regulars but holds his ground. As the combat deepens about him, Campbell and Shelby have won to the summit. Then all the contending forces are face to face, and there is a general *melee*—firing with guns and charging with bayonets. Bailie Peyton says that at the first of the conflict " the mountain appeared volcanic; there flashed along its summit and around its base and up its sides one long sulphurous blaze." Judge Haywood says that at a later moment "the mountain was covered with flame and smoke, and seemed to thunder."

Soon the end of the battle is at hand, and all is a more violent storm of strife and tumult, freighted with wounds and death. Ferguson is in the midst of it, calmly courageous but restlessly active. He is here and there all over the field—wounded in his right hand, but heedless of personal danger—giving courage to others as he goes, and bearing the silver whistle, whose sharp sound quickens his men's pulses to the fray. He orders the cavalry into action and his regulars to charge, but at last, in vain. The Americans press him on all sides into ever narrowing limits. A white flag goes up from the Tories and he pulls it down. Another is raised at a distance, and quickly he is there to level it with the dust. A surrender is suggested to him by friends, repeatedly, but he will not listen to it. He *will not* give up his sword to men whom, with a curse, he calls "banditti": but he will escape by cutting his way through the hostile ranks with a sword in his left hand. Two officers join him in the attempt. Dashing at a weaker point in the Whig lines, he strikes with his sword until it is broken, and falls, pierced with bullets. Instantly De Peyster surrenders. The battle is finished. It was about an hour long.

In the confusion that followed, the Whigs ceased not at once from firing. The British called for quarter, but kept their weapons. The fearless

Shelby galloped up to their lines and commanded, if they wanted quarter, to lay down their arms. Perhaps animosity against the Tories would not die in some Whigs as soon as white flags were raised, for wars between neighbors are apt to be next in bitterness to religious wars. Some allowance also is to be made for the difficulty of self-restraint common to men in the heat of passion and strife. Their destructive zeal is slow to abate. Col. Campbell had to cry out to his men, "Don't shoot!" "Cease firing!" and actively to promote mercy; but when De Peyster profanely complained to him of the unfairness, he declined with dignity, to reply, except by ordering the prisoners into position. The victory was complete. Of the soldiers composing Ferguson's army, two-thirds were prisoners and the other third were killed and wounded in nearly equal numbers. Of the Americans, twenty-eight were killed and sixty-two wounded. Eight days after the battle the conquerors began their march westward. They had received information, which proved untrue, that Tarleton, a bold, skillful and ruthless British officer, was advancing upon them. On the contrary, Cornwallis and Tarleton were fleeing at the time from Charlotte to South Carolina, in fear that the mountaineers by thousands were about to assail them. The intention and hope of the British commander to bring North Carolina, and then Virginia, into like subjection with South Carolina and Georgia, were frustrated by the defeat of Ferguson. It disheartened Tories who had openly taken sides with the British, and deterred others from following their example. At the same time the victory of the Whigs inspired their friends everywhere. Their revived faith in the final success of the Colonies, moved them to more hopeful effort in its behalf.

The up-rising of the mountaineers—so spontaneous and yet so deliberate—their cheerful march over natural difficulties, their eager and persevering pursuit of a formidable enemy, their well-planned and swiftly executed attack on his chosen ground—all these combined, give their enterprise a high place in military annals. Add to them the great need at that time to the struggling Colonies of the victory they won and its important good results, and its title to the niche of fame it fills in the temple of American history, cannot be impeached. It turned the tide of battle. It led the way to the surrender of Cornwallis at Yorktown, and then to peace with Great Britain. The king and his counselors were already discouraged by military reverses and tired of their vain efforts for seven years to conquer. They were compelled to acknowledge the independence of the United States.

CHAPTER III.

Early History—Mountaineers Dissatisfied—an Independent State—Conflict of Authorities.

> "Hail sacred Polity, by Freedom rear'd!
> Hail sacred Freedom, when by Law restrain'd!
> Without you what were man? A grovelling herd,
> In darkness, wretchedness and want enchain'd."
>
> BEATTIE.

THE early history of East Tennessee, like that of all frontier regions of the United States in their westward march to wider empire, has its romantic and thrilling incidents of war with savages. Those may here be fitly omitted, but there is one episode in that history that should be briefly told. For it throws light upon the character of the first inhabitants, and so upon that, not only of their descendants, but also of the newer population, which it is reasonable to suppose has been more or less assimilated to the strong original type.

The State of Frankland or Franklin, as it is differently called by the two historians of Tennessee, Haywood and Ramsey, had a brief and troubled life. Several causes co-operated to bring it into being. One was the uncertain legislation of North Carolina concerning its western lands, and its insufficient regard, apparent or real, for the welfare of their inhabitants. A second cause lay in the triumphant spirit of freedom and independence cherished by the mountaineers when the war of the American Revolution was over, and their quickness to assert natural rights in the face of presumed governmental neglect.

The people of North Carolina west of the Alleghanies were in frequent conflicts with the Indians, but there was a difference in opinion as to the payment by the State of the expenses incurred. Mutual jealousies arose between the eastern and western counties, followed by contention.

At length in May, 1783, North Carolina ceded its western lands to the United States, *provided* that Congress should accept the cession within two years: until such acceptance the sovereignty of the State in the premises being reserved. The North Carolina Bill of Rights contained provision for the formation of a new State from that territory; and if its people, as they supposed, were to be left during two years to depend upon themselves for their protection and well-being, they considered it a propitious time to establish an independent State Government. The necessities of their civil society seemed to demand it, for the District of Washington was as yet without a Superior Court, and there was no existing law authorizing a call of the militia by its general to resist the Indians, whose hostilities continued. In this emergency a convention of delegates chosen by the people of Sullivan, Washington and Greene Counties, was held at Jonesboro, August 23, 1784, and formed an Association. It also declared the disadvantages to those counties from union with others more numerous and powerful east of the mountains, and the benefits they would derive from a separation. It provided for a delegate and memorial to Congress, and for the detention of all moneys collected by public officers "until some mode be adopted and prescribed to have accounts fairly and properly liquidated with the State of North Carolina." The convention finally adjourned to meet again at Jonesboro, which it did in December of the same year, but before then the Legislature of North Carolina met and repealed the Act ceding its western lands to the United States, organized the counties established on those lands into a new District, for which a Superior Court should be held in Washington County, and provided for it judicial officers, formed the militia of the District into a brigade and appointed Col. Sevier its general. These acts were thought by that officer sufficient to redress the grievances of the offended counties, and both by speech and letter he endeavored to influence the electors to desist from further measures looking to a separation from North Carolina, but shortly he was persuaded to a different mind. The election of new delegates to a convention was completed, and when assembled in December, it adopted a State Constitution, subject to the will of its successor, to assemble in November, 1785; and also ordered the election of a Legislature, which should hold its first session early in the same year. The

Legislature, upon convening, elected John Sevier Governor, and other State officials, and through the Speakers of its two Houses informed Governor Martin of North Carolina that the inhabitants of Sullivan, Washington and Greene Counties had declared themselves independent of the authority and government of the parent State.

To this communication Governor Martin replied courteously but firmly, and at length. He argued the fallacy or insufficiency of the reasons given by the western people for their conduct. He emphasized the facts, that the sovereignty of North Carolina over the ceded territory had been reserved until Congress should accept the gift, and that the Legislature had subsequently repealed the Act of cession. He affirmed that the good will of the State to the disaffected counties, had been shown by its recent ample provision for the regular administration of justice and the authoritative use of the militia. He denied that goods to compensate the Indians for their lands had been stopped by the State on the way and that in consequence murders had been committed by the savages. The goods, he averred, had only been delayed, that should the cession be accepted by Congress, they might go under its regulations. With some eloquence of words he exhorted all loyal citizens of the western counties to be firm in their adherence to the State he represented, and warned all persons concerned in the revolt who "had probably been seduced from their just allegiance by ambitious and designing men," to refuse obedience any longer to "the self-created power and authority unknown to the Constitution of the State and unsanctioned by the Legislature." The lessons which history teaches concerning needless revolutions were referred to by him, and the reflection advised that "there is a national pride in all kingdoms and states which inspires every citizen and subject with importance—the grand cement and support of government which must not be insulted." That insult he felt had been inflicted by the western counties; "the honor of the State had been especially wounded" in their "premature seizure by violence of that independence which in time no doubt would have been granted by consent." And he besought them "not to tarnish the laurels they had won at King's Mountain in supporting the independence of the United States, by supporting a black and traitorous revolt."

The circulation of this document strengthened the wills of the friends of North Carolina and increased their number among the western people, but the majority in the new State were unmoved from their previous purpose, and the work of governmental organization went forward. Courts and Magistrates were appointed and new counties formed. Salaries were allotted to State officials, to be paid in current money of Frankland, (six shillings to the dollar) or in specified articles received from the people in payment of taxes and at like rates of value. These miscellaneous articles included "flax and tow linen, woolen and cotton linsey, beaver, otter, raccoon, fox and deer skins, bacon, tallow and bees-wax, rye whisky, peach and apple brandy, home-made sugar and good tobacco."

The inchoate State gave due attention to its relations with the Indians, and conducted all its affairs without serious difficulty until near the close of the year 1785. Before that time an attempt was made in Washington County, Virginia, to use the privilege accorded to its citizens by the original Association of western counties, to join the new Commonwealth, but the movement was speedily prevented by Patrick Henry, then Governor of Virginia. The Convention of Frankland appointed to be held in November 1785, met at Greeneville in that month, adopted a Constitution like that of North Carolina, and sent a memorial to Congress by William Cocke, Esq., which was fruitless. Five days later the Legislature of North Carolina convened and passed an Act declarative of its desire "to extend the blessings of civil government to citizens of the western counties until such time as they might be separated with advantage and convenience to themselves," and "to hear and redress their grievances." It offered amnesty to all persons concerned in establishing the State of Frankland who should renew their allegiance to the State of North Carolina. It provided for an election of members of the General Assembly next succeeding, to be held in the revolted counties, and also appointed civil and military officers for those counties, who should supersede like officers of the State of Frankland. Ever since the repeal by North Carolina of the Act ceding its western lands to the United States, there had been opposition to the new State among its citizens. The two parties were now brought into closer antagonism. Under the authority of both rival governments, courts were held in the same counties, different laws were enforced, taxes levied and the militia called into service. Of course it followed that mutual animosities grew more intense, and practical collisions were frequent. On several occasions armed men of the respective parties visited rooms where courts were held by their adversaries; violent seizures were made of public records, and officers of the courts turned out of doors. In one instance the papers of a Frankland clerk having been forcibly abducted by partisan friends of the parent State, they were afterwards recaptured, and their official owner, to secure their future safety, hid them in a cave. These spoliations on both sides were more or less disastrous to litigants and owners of real estate. They also excited contentious followers of the two governments beyond self-control, and their exasperated feelings found vent at public meetings in pugilistic encounters. The combatants did not so far forget that they were neighbors, as do men at this period of more advanced civilization, and resort to the use of deadly weapons. They contented themselves with fisticuffs as means of drawing blood.

Gen. John Sevier, Governor of Frankland, and

Col. John Tipton, Judge, by appointment of North Carolina, were universally recognized as chief champions of the two State sovereignties that struggled for the supremacy. Even they were once betrayed into a trial of personal prowess after a primitive and comparatively harmless method. In colloquy they were led into discussion upon the exciting questions of the day and locality, then into an exchange of angry words, and finally to engage in pommeling each other with clenched and ungloved hands, without important results. The encounter, however, occurring as it did early in the history of social alienations, served hurtfully as an example that was abundantly imitated by members of the chieftains' families and by their adherents.

Col. Tipton, at the election in Washington County to the North Carolina General Assembly, was elected Senator. At the same time many of the people manifested the change wrought in their political sentiments by enrolling their names, in token that they accepted the amnesty offered by North Carolina in 1785, and returned to their allegiance. It was evident that hostility to the revolution in government had become strong enough within its own orbit of movement to endanger the ultimate success of the new State. In 1786 disorder prevailed in the disputed territory concerning ordinary revenues from the people. For, on the plea of uncertainty as to the validity of taxation by either government, no payment would be made to either; and both governments feared to enforce collections from delinquents, lest they might lose the taxpayers' allegiance.

In November of the same year, the three western counties of Sullivan, Washington and Greene had representatives in the North Carolina Legislature. Not of their number, but on a special mission from those counties, Wm. Cocke appeared before the North Carolina House of Commons, and made a long and able speech on their behalf. He told how the Act ceding them to the United States had led to their separation. Left, as they then were, without any certain authority over or vested in them, without means of defense against frequent attacks from Indians, and with no protection or aid from any human power, they were compelled by the necessities of the case to provide for their own welfare and safety. To be sure, in the winter following the Act of Cession, it was repealed by North Carolina, but the repeal found them penniless and defenseless, with even more urgent reasons than before to care for themselves. North Carolina sent them no help in money or supplies, nor a single soldier, while their savage foes were angered and threatening, because of the stoppage of goods for them by the way. He represented the condition of the western people to be one of distraction, suffering and poverty,—such as should move a magnanimous State to banish its animosity, to bury the past with its differences and errors, and to extend friendly sympathy and relief. "If," said he, "the mother should judge the expense of adhesion too heavy to be borne, let us remain as we are and support ourselves by our own exertions: if otherwise, let the means for the continuance of our connection be supplied with the degree of liberality which will demonstrate seriousness on the one hand and will secure affection on the other."

The address was well received by the House of Commons, and influenced the General Assembly to a spirit of moderation in dealing with the estranged counties. It proceeded to pardon all offenders who had returned to their allegiance and restore them to civic rights; being careful at the same time, by further legislation to maintain the authority of the State and provide for the due administration of justice under its laws. The effect of its temperate conduct was to increase the number of its friends in the west.

CHAPTER IV.

EARLY HISTORY—FRANKLAND'S CORRESPONDENCE—ITS STRIFES—ITS DEATH, UPON DEFEAT OF ITS CHIEF—HIS ESCAPE.

> "Contention, like a horse
> Full of high feeding, madly hath broke loose,
> And bears all down before him."
> SHAKS.; *Henry IV.*

> "How just soever
> Our reasons are to remedy our wrongs,
> We're yet to leave them to their will and pow'r,
> That to that purpose have authority."
> MASSINGER.

THE State of Frankland, although weakened by defections of its former friends at home, still stood with unbroken frame, but over it hung portentous signs of more deadly strife among its citizens and of disaster to itself that might be fatal. In view of them, all aid and support that could properly be had, were important to it. As early as 1784, at Gov. Sevier's suggestion, the General Assembly had, by a competent diplomatic agent, expressed to the Governor of Georgia, its willingness to unite with that State in a war which threatened to become necessary against the Creek Indians. The Legislature of Georgia gave respectful consideration to the letters, and friendly communications were interchanged in 1787; but the Governor of Georgia, while acknowledging gratefully the readiness of the Frankland government to co-operate as desired, was prudent to limit his assurances of reciprocal service to his power, and to consistency with the interests of the State of Georgia and its paramount duty to the United States. Less reserve of sentiment was shown by prominent citizens of Georgia. They spoke in warm praise of the zeal for liberty manifested by the Franks, and of the independent State they had organized. Sevier was addressed by letter as its Governor, and in social circles men drank "success to the State of Frankland, His Excellency, Governor Sevier and his virtuous citizens."

Dr. Benjamin Franklin had a wide reputation for great wisdom concerning public affairs, and Gov. Sevier wrote to him for advice as to the new State. He replied from Philadelphia, June 30, 1787, acknowledging the honor done him by "His Excellency and Council." "There are two things," he said, "which humanity induces me to wish you may succeed in: the accommodating your misunderstanding with the government of North Carolina, and the avoiding an Indian war by preventing encroachments on their lands. Such encroachments are the more unjustifiable, as these people in the fair way of purchase, usually give very good bargains, and in one year's war with them you may suffer a loss of property and be put to an expense vastly exceeding in value what would have contented them perfectly in fairly buying the lands they can spare. * * * I have no doubt of the good disposition of your government to prevent their receiving such injuries; but I know the strongest governments are hardly able to restrain the disorderly people who are generally on the frontiers, from excesses of various kinds, and possibly yours has not as yet acquired sufficient strength for that purpose. It may be well, however, to acquaint those encroachers that the Congress will not justify them in the breach of a solemn treaty; and that if they bring upon themselves an Indian war, they will not be supported in it. I will endeavor to inform myself more perfectly of your affairs by enquiry and searching the records of Congress; and if anything should occur to me that I think may be useful to you, you shall hear from me thereupon.

"I conclude with repeating my wish that you may amicably settle your difficulty with North Carolina. The inconvenience to your people of attending so remote a seat of government, and the difficulty to that government in ruling well so remote a people, would, I think, be powerful inducements to it to accede to any fair and reasonable propositions it may receive from you, if the Cession Act had now passed."

The course of events in the last months of 1787 moved rapidly towards their definite conclusion. John Sevier was still addressed in letters by Dr. Franklin and the Governor of Georgia as Governor of Frankland. While the eminent, philanthropic statesman persuaded to a policy of peace, —the fruit of fair dealing with the Indians; the

Legislature of Georgia passed an Act to levy three thousand of its own citizens for war with the Creeks as irreconcilable enemies, and Gov. Mathews sent a copy of that Act to Gov. Sevier with the request for fifteen hundred men from Frankland to assist in the campaign. Gov. Sevier yielded to this solicitation, and about the end of the year gave orders for arraying his militia.

Meanwhile the rival Governments proceeded with their respective affairs in the disputed territory. The Legislature of Frankland met at Greeneville in September, 1787. It appointed two prominent citizens to represent it before the North Carolina General Assembly, to which members were elected from all the western counties. That Assembly met in November, offered anew to all who had departed from their allegiance full pardon and restoration to citizenship, and passed other lenient measures relating to non-compliance with the State revenue laws and delay in reporting taxable property. A proof of the waning fortunes of Frankland was given in the acceptance of a Superior Court Judgeship for the West by David Campbell under an appointment from the North Carolina Legislature at that session. He had been a member of the Convention of 1784 that led to the formation of the new State, and of the Convention in 1785 to frame a Constitution, and had also been a Judge of its Superior Court by election of the Legislature in 1785: and his consent to serve its adversary at such a juncture, though it brought upon him severe reproach for desertion, in one instance directly from Gen. White, a fast friend of Frankland, nevertheless tended to convince some that he had left "a sinking ship."

At the same time the internal dissension drew near its crisis. Late in the year 1787, a writ of *fieri facias* had been issued, and early in 1788, the sheriff, under authority of North Carolina, executed it against the estate of Gov. Sevier; visited his farm on the Nolachucky River, carried off his negroes and lodged them securely at the house of his principal foe, Col. John Tipton. Sevier, at the time, was absent from home and near Greene County, providing for defence of the people against a threatened attack by Indians. Hearing of the sheriff's procedure, he at once rallied to him one hundred and fifty men from the Counties of Greene and Sevier and what is now Blount County, and went with them to the house of Tipton, against whom the fuel of his wrath had but a short time before been freshly kindled by his adversary's attempt, foiled by Sevier's absence, to seize his person. Tipton had but fifteen men in his dwelling when the Governor arrived with his militia and a small piece of artillery. It was in the afternoon. Sevier demanded an unconditional surrender, and was answered defiantly, with an expletive. The oral summons to yield was then followed by one in writing. To it Tipton made no reply, but sent it to Col. Maxwell of Sullivan County, with a call for help. Several days passed, but Sevier forbore to make an assault. Messengers successfully escaped from the house to gather recruits, some of whom afterwards made their way into it. The third night a reinforcement of one hundred and eighty men under Col. Maxwell arrived, awaited the break of day and then approached the beleagured dwelling simultaneously with an attack upon its defenders by the Governor. The recruits fired their guns and dashed forward with a ringing shout that was answered by another from the besieged, and followed by a sally. The united forces triumphed. Sevier's men were thrown into a panic and fled. Some of them and their one unused piece of artillery were captured. Among the prisoners were two of Sevier's sons, whom two brothers Webb would have killed in revenge for the death of their brother in the fight, but Tipton prevented them. According to a more dramatic account, Tipton himself was determined to hang the two youths, but was dissuaded by friends, who drew an imaginary picture of his own sons as captives and about to be slain in enmity to their father. He was melted to tears, and with strong self-reproach for his weakness, gave the young men their liberty. Indeed the two parties appear to have been animated throughout the affair by a spirit not altogether unneighborly. Sevier, from the beginning of the troubles, had been disposed to moderation. He sought on this occasion the recovery of his slaves, but delayed, although urged by others, to make an assault. Many of the men on both sides were unarmed, and some having weapons did not load them, or loading them, fired into the air. One of them said:

"We did not go there to fight. The men did not try to hit anybody. Most of us went to prevent mischief, and did not intend to let the neighbors kill one another."

Account is given of only two persons who were killed during the whole encounter, and but two or three were wounded. Right royal citizens were these in carrying on a civil war! Their example of mutual forbearance deserves at least historical transmission. A fatal blow had been received by the Government of Frankland. In May, 1788, the authority of North Carolina was established without dispute over the western counties. Sevier, after his defeat, devoted himself unreservedly to the service of the people against the Indians, and collecting troops led them victoriously into that enemy's country. While employed in military duties on the frontier, a bench warrant was issued from the Superior Court of North Carolina, at Jonesboro, against him for the crime of high treason. His seizure, arraignment for trial and perhaps his punishment were therefore from that date, reasonably certain; but the time of their occurrence was to be determined by circumstances. His eminence among the men of his day was partly owing to solid and brilliant qualities, which under proper culture would have given him distinction in much less rude society and more peaceful surroundings than those in which he lived. The facts that he served as first Governor of Tennessee three successive terms, and after an interval of a few years, three other terms by election of the people biennially and was then twice chosen a Representative in Congress, are weighty evidences of his ability, as well as his popularity. Judge Haywood, who was the Governor's contemporary during the latter part of his public life, says that John Sevier "had by nature a talent for acquiring popular favor, * * a friendly demeanor, a captivating address, * * * * * was generous, liberal and hospitable, * * and to crown all, was a soldier. To him it was no secret that in republican government, where the democratic principle is a main ingredient in its composition, the love of the people is substantial power. The frontier people adored him. They called him familiarly 'Nolachucky Jack.' Whenever at future elections that name was pronounced, it had the effect of electrical power in prostrating the pretensions of every opposing candidate." *

The State of Frankland was numbered among the things that were and are not. All that remains in this brief narrative is to tell what afterwards befell him who was its faithful head while it survived, in consequence of his official connection with it.

In October, 1788, Sevier returned home from the frontier and appeared openly among the people. At Jonesboro in company with some personal followers, he was charged by a returned soldier with failing to prevent, when he had the power, the murder of certain friendly Indians, and there was a quarrel, followed soon afterwards by another

* Haywood's History of Tennessee: Knoxville, Tenn., 1821. 8vo.

in the vicinity. A door was thus opened to the revival of animosities and to violent procedures against him for grave reasons of State. He was pursued during the night by armed men, was sought for at several houses, and found about sunrise, when he surrendered without resistance. After running the risk of injury from his enemies in the first flush of their wrath, he was led a prisoner to the county town and from there was sent under guard to Morganton, North Carolina. In the journey, his hands were unbound, and he attempted to escape. The earliest historian of Tennessee has been followed by the second in stating that Sevier failed in that attempt and in representing that he was rescued by a few of his friends from the custody of the sheriff, in the presence of the judge, at Morganton: but according to an oral tradition which has been recently published and appears to be authentic, Sevier succeeded in escaping while on the way to that town. The narrative heretofore accepted as accurate beyond doubt, is, in substance, appended, and also, the statement lately made, in contradiction of it.*

In November of the same year, the Legislature of North Carolina excluded Sevier from its amnesty to political offenders and from all State offices, but he was elected with great unanimity to the State Senate in August, 1789. Of that body he was admitted as a member

* See Appendix: Note B.

—not without a brief delay after his appearance at the capital; and subsequently he was appointed to his former office of Brigadier General of the western counties, now included in East Tennessee.

WILLIAM G. BROWNLOW.

CHAPTER V.

Shadows of Coming Events—Political Harangues—A Suspected "Incendiary"—Bible Society Colporteur in Scott County.

> "When clouds are seen, wise men put on their cloaks;
> When great leaves fall, then winter is at hand;
> When the sun sets, who doth not look for night?
> Untimely storms make men expect a dearth:
> All may be well; but if God sort it so,
> 'Tis more than we deserve, or I expect."
> — Shaks., *Richard III.*

THE Civil War begun in 1861 had for years its premonitions even in so retired a portion of the United States as East Tennessee then was; but they were not understood by the wisest of observers. The increased alarm among friends of the institution of slavery for its safety, would alone have been ominous; for strong fear of losing possessions tempts to rash and violent means of relief. There were other signs of coming evils:—the growing desire, especially of politicians in the South who were extremists, not only to preserve slavery within its existing limits but to fortify its perpetuity by extending its area; and also the widened direction of an intense and long-cherished animosity against abolitionists, so as to include in it all "Yankees" or "the North" in general. These sectional sentiments were not shared by the great body of East Tennesseeans. The large majority of them were not slave-holders. Cotton was not grown in the region, except that a very few farmers had small "patches" for domestic use. Even where slaves were owned, "the peculiar institution" most often wore a homely aspect. The negroes after a patriarchal fashion, were part of one household—the white and black children played together without fastidious reserve, and mutual kindly affections prevailed throughout the whole family. In 1860 the slaves were about one-tenth only of the population, and in over one-third of the counties less than one-seventeenth. The unlikeness of the mountainous region which is located centrally in the Atlantic States, to that of the planting States, is positive, and the dissimilarity in social and other conditions between their respective inhabitants could scarcely have escaped the observation of sagacious minds at the period named, when contemplating the political future. It may have been not without reference to possible coming emergencies, and to the promotion of sympathy with sectional sentiments among these mountaineers that one of the "Southern Commercial Conventions" which were feeders to disunion, was held in 1857 at the central town of East Tennessee. For its population then was only something over four thousand and its commercial vitality was small. Conspicuously apparent in the deliberations of that Convention was a spirit of sectional zeal, which once fairly excited and diffused, might easily upon opportunity or need be turned into a political dissolving temper. It would be interesting to know how many of those who were prominent in that and other "Southern Commercial Conventions" were also not long afterwards, active in the work of secession. Of the *lawyers* who figured in the Knoxville mercantile assembly was a Virginia "Hotspur." A few years later he told the South Carolinians who stood ready, if possible, to dissolve the Union; "strike a blow and Virginia will go out!" The blow was struck, Fort Sumpter fell, and Virginia went out.

As the *ante-bellum* decade drew nigh its close, a South Carolina gentleman of distinction visited the same very interior town. Currently told, he was father of the saying that "the Yankees know nothing of government; their only idea of it is that the majority shall rule." To this sentiment a ready-witted editor responded, that its author "differed from the Yankees in but one particular, his only idea of government being that the minority shall rule." This gentleman was of an aristocratic turn of mind. Evidently he considered the country men among whom he dwelt for the time fit subjects for a study, the precise nature and conclusions of which others could only conjecture. One day at his hotel he was wrapped in long and quiet but intent contemplation of the people on the street. A citizen friend who had looked on him as he mused, fancied in the light thrown back on memory by the flames of war shortly afterwards kindled, that the silent reflections of the stranger had reference to the impending conflict; not as an emissary from a dissaffected State, much less bent individually upon unfriendly espionage of the land, but as a political philosopher, forming an estimate of the capacity of the people before him for sharing in a life and death national struggle, and weighing in the scales of his judgment the relative probabilities of their inclining to favor one or the other of the antagonists in that struggle.

In 1860, late in the canvass for the Presidency of the United States, a political discussion took place at Knoxville between three of the candidates for Elector from the State at large: Mr. W. C. Whitthorne on the Breckenridge ticket, Mr. Nathaniel G. Taylor on the ticket for Bell, and Mr. Hopkins on that for Douglass. Mr. Whitthorne spoke respectably well. Mr. Taylor was truly eloquent. His description of the civil war, which he declared the friends of Mr. Breckenridge were contriving to bring upon the country in the event of their party being defeated and the Republican candidate's election to the Presidency, was vivid and powerful. Few, if any, of his hearers, however, had a real expectation that the calamity he so graphically depicted would shortly befall the land. He said that the people of East Tennessee were "determined to maintain the Union by force of arms against any movement from the South throughout their region of country to assail the Government at Washington with violence, and that the secessionists of the cotton States in attempting to carry out their nefarious design to destroy the Republic, would have to march over his dead body and the dead bodies of thousands of East Tennessee mountaineers slain in battle."

The speech of Mr. Hopkins was lucid and logical, and reflected much credit upon his skill and power in debate. His antagonism was especially to the followers of Mr. Breckenridge as the authors of a ruinous breach in the unity of the Democratic party that had so long ruled the nation and dispensed its offices and emoluments.

Shortly before the Presidential election in the autumn of 1860, William L. Yancey of Alabama, came to Knoxville by pre-arrangement with resident extremists on the subject of "Southern rights," and spoke to a popular assembly in the open air. He labored to show that the South did not receive justice at the hands of the North, that the negro was never intended by the Federal Constitution and its authors as anything more than property, that it was the interest of the white man of the South to perpetuate slavery, because it gave the South a political power in Congress it would not otherwise have, and also for other reasons which he stated.

Among those who then heard him for the first time some were disappointed that they did not find in him the able orator whom Fame had heralded. His voice, without being disagreeable, had no special good qualities, and was too monotonous of tone. He showed, however, great earnestness, and now and then rose to eloquence. Evidently he had a quick, high and imperious temper, a bold and determined will, superior readiness and skill in debate, and the disposition to domineer over opponents. His determination seemed to be not to heal existing dissensions but to maintain by strife the South's rival power in the nation.

His speech was not well received by many of those who heard it. At one time being rudely interrupted by a man in the crowd, he peremptorily silenced the intruder. Before concluding his discourse, a note was handed to him. Having read it, he asked the writer to come upon the platform. The note conveyed a desire to know, if, in the event of Mr. Lincoln's election to the Presidency, Mr. Yancey would favor the secession of the Southern States from the Union and forcible resistance to the Federal Government? The person so unexpectedly elevated to the side of the orator was Mr. Maney, from Pennsylvania, but for some years a citizen of Tennessee; endowed with much good sense, large acquaintance with public affairs and considerable readiness of speech. A brief colloquy ensued, in which Mr. Yancey endeavored without success to bring Mr. Maney into ridicule. At length it came to light that the latter was the representative of others in the assembly whose names were signed to the note, and which were then called aloud by Mr. Yancey, with a request that the persons bearing them should ascend to the platform. They complied accordingly: Rev. William G. Brownlow, Judge Samuel R. Rodgers, O. P. Temple, John M. Fleming, and Wm. R. Rodgers, M. D.

The orator proceeded to read an extract from a

published speech or letter of the Hon. John Bell of Tennessee, declaring his mind as to the course of conduct the slave States ought to adopt, should Mr. Lincoln be elected. He then desired to know severally from the gentlemen before him, whether they endorsed Mr. Bell's sentiments? Mr. Temple answered that he approved them, if the words in which they were expressed were taken with their context and rightly interpreted: at the same time adding, that in his own opinion, any forcible resistance to the Federal Government would be improper. Of like purport in general, was the reply made by each of his companions, except that of Mr. Brownlow. When called on to answer he said "that not only would he refuse to join in any secession or armed opposition to the authority of the National Government because of Mr. Lincoln's election, but that any body of men attempting to march on Washington City with hostile purpose through East Tennessee, would find there thousands of men ready to prevent them by force of arms. Among those defenders of the Union, he," Mr. Brownlow, "would take his stand, and that over their dead bodies they who sought to overthrow the Government would have to make their way."

Mr. Yancey replied. He gave it as his opinion that the statement from Mr. Bell that had been read, favored the idea of resistance under certain circumstances. Declining to answer at once and in few words the inquiry first propounded, he went into a historical statement of the question of secession as it had been agitated in Alabama, and of his connection with it. Finally he said, that as a loyal son of that State, he would abide by its decision in the case and go as it might go. "As for this man," he said; turning to Mr. Brownlow, "who talks of confronting the sons of the South in a contest for their rights, with the armed opposition of East Tennesseeans,—if his (Mr. Yancey's) State determined upon resistance, he would meet Mr. Brownlow in the bloody strife, and" making a violent gesture towards Mr. B.'s person, "would give him the bayonet up to the muzzle." At this utterance and action, a strong sensation passed through the assembly. The orator went on to reproach his opponent, that being by profession a minister of the Gospel, he should be a fomenter of strife, and counseled him to amend his conduct. Mr. Brownlow replied in his peculiar style with pungent words, and soon the people dispersed.

The Alabamian's friends seemed to be jubilant over the victory they claimed to have won in the wordy encounter. The other party were less demonstrative but more determined than before, and were moved to various degrees of wrath by the disunion sentiments to which they had listened. Some, while stirred to indignation by the sentiments, which they considered atrocious, and at the speaker's audacity in uttering them, had yet a feeling of regret that their own champions were put on the platform at disadvantage; had been subjected in turn to questioning by their adversary, as witnesses might be in court by an adroit attorney; and were compelled to relative silence, while he, on the point at issue, fully delivered his mind with an air of triumph to the exhilaration of his friends.

When the result of the Presidential election was known, the political excitement greatly increased. There had been no electoral ticket in Tennessee for the Republican candidates: and had any citizen of the State openly advocated Mr. Lincoln's election, he would have had to suffer indignity and injury, or to flee from his home. The general public sentiment was hostile to the Republican party and at the same time friendly to the continuance of slavery where it existed, without interference from abroad. As between secession and the preservation of the Union, opinions differed both in kind and degree of strength. A single incident will illustrate the situation:

A citizen of Ohio, selling fruit-tree scions arrived at Knoxville from Asheville, North Carolina. He was closely followed by the newspaper of that village, fixing strong suspicion upon him from slight evidence, as a peregrinating Abolitionist with a sinister purpose. Meanwhile he with his chattels personal, had found temporary lodgment on the Deaf and Dumb Asylum grounds. Some medical students at Philadelphia from Mississippi and Alabama, influenced by political fervor, when the work of secession began, incontinently abandoned their professional studies, and departed homewards. Arriving at Knoxville on their way, and hearing of the alleged anti-slavery Ohioan, they went without delay and demanded his expulsion from the community. But because of the Asylum's Principal, they failed in their errand, and as rumor told, were humorously rebuked by him for their impertinent wrath and intolerance.

Their visit was soon succeeded by one of more formidable proportions from indignant citizens, with a local office-holder of the United States at their head. The suspected political "incendiary" was arrested and led a prisoner to the court-house. There excited people gathered, until the room was filled to its utmost capacity. Nor could this fact justly occasion surprise. Slaves bore the fatal stigma in public estimation, generally, of being not *persons*, but *things*. Their classification therefore, in common with houses, goods and whatever else could, like them, be bought and sold, was under the head of property. And any alarm raised that peaceful possession of them was endangered, naturally enough assembled a crowd. A citizen, attracted to the meeting by its understood object, entered the court-room, as Parson Brownlow in concluding a speech, gave no opinion *pro* or *con* about the stranger, but advised the people to watch, for that fomenters of trouble with the negroes were abroad in the country.

Afterwards, the committee of citizens appointed to consider and determine the extent of grievance inflicted upon the community and what should be its redress, reported through its chairman,—who had led in making the arrest,—that the stranger was guilty of Abolitionism and should be ordered to leave the town which his presence put in danger. But further proceedings in the direct line of a vote upon the proposition, were halted by the courageous interposition of the Deaf Mutes' Asylum Principal in behalf of the prisoner, with whom he had conversed, and who, he averred, was not an extreme and dangerous anti-slavery man. This reduction of the guilt of the accused, was promptly and hotly resented by the committee's chairman as a denial of his personal veracity, not to be borne. The Principal, without disputing the logical sequence of that deduction, stoutly maintained the truth of his statement, and an altercation ensued that threatened to end in a general row. The assembly became tumultuous. Men ready for fight with sticks and pistols sprang upon the platform, where stood the disputants, between whom a third person, urged on by others, had interposed himself and essayed to speak. But he could not be heard because of the great clamor, accompanied by violent gesticulations, of the assembly. At length a few words from the *tertium quid*, minimizing the difficulty into a mere difference of opinion between two gentlemen, were listened to, and the excitement subsided.

As for the troubled Ohioan, he "stood not upon the order of his going" from a locality inhospitable and dangerous to strangers who felt free to say that they did not find their Bibles and human slavery altogether harmonious. It is to this day, however, an unsolved question, whether as he went, righteous indignation at the treatment he had received or sincere joy at his escape from worse ills, prevailed in his soul.

The mental agitations of people living in towns and in less remote parts of the country, caused by the work of secession as it progressed, were painfully shared by many older and conservative persons. They could not bear the thought of a dissolution of the Union, and in some instances were moved by it to tears, alternating with anger. As the possibility of so dire an event grew in their apprehensions, they shrank back from witnessing its occurrence, as one might do from looking on at the death of a beloved kinsman.* But the dwellers in the more mountainous parts of East Tennessee, "far from the madding crowd," were comparatively free from all such agitations and griefs.

In the autumn of 1860 a Colporteur of the Knoxville Bible Society† distributed the Book among the people of Scott County, Tennessee, a very elevated region near the Kentucky border line. On returning home, he made a report of his labors to Mr. C.,—Depositary of the society,—who greatly deplored the possible destruction of the Union. The Colporteur soon afterwards met another Unionist, and said:

"Do you know that Mr. C. is going to Scott County to live?" The other, knowing Mr. C. to be a person of wealth, who would by such an exchange lose comfortable surroundings, answered:

"No! how is that?"

"O," said the Colporteur, "I told him that I

---

* See Appendix, Note C. † Note D.

asked the people over in Scott County 'how were times with them,' and they said, 'not very good.' I inquired if that was because of the troubles in the country? They asked, 'what troubles?' I said: 'Troubles to the Union. Haven't you heard that South Carolina has seceded?' They answered, 'no!' "

"Now," the Colporteur added, "I told this to Mr. C. and he says he is going to Scott County to live: for if the Union should be dissolved, *he will never hear of it over there.*"

CHAPTER VI.

THE STATE FOR THE UNION—A STRANGER IN TOWN—SECESSION OF TENNESSEE PRE-ARRANGED—BIBLICAL COINCIDENCE—UNION ORATORS—AN ASSASSINATION.

> "Between the acting of a dreadful thing
> And the first motion, all the interim is
> Like a phantasma, or a hideous dream;
> The genius and the mortal instruments
> Are then in council; and the state of a man,
> Like to a little kingdom, suffers then
> The nature of an insurrection."
> SHAKS.; *Julius Cæsar.*

TENNESSEE was unwilling to depart from her wise sisters in the Union and join the others in committing what one of her adopted sons,—a General of the Confederate army,—said to his friend after the war had ended, "was one of the greatest blunders in history." The Legislature of the State proposed a convention to decide what the State should do concerning its national relations. Governor Isham G. Harris and his sympathizers, no doubt considered the secession of Tennessee could be most conveniently accomplished through that instrumentality: and it was ordered that the question of holding such a convention should be determined by the people at the ballot-box, February 9, 1861.

HON. T, A. R. NELSON.

Love for the Union had not yet weakened in many persons throughout the State, who at later points of time could not withstand the accumulated force of motives to give it up,—some of whom in finally surrendering it, hushed their lingering objections with the plea of necessity. The majority of people were used to think of the Union as a precious heritage from their ancestors, and they were unable to see that they ought to throw that inheritance away, because the Republican candidate for Chief Magistrate of the Nation had been elected. Even at the city of Memphis an enlightened public sentiment in favor of maintaining the Union widely existed in the fall of 1860, and found expression at a large public meeting, called and participated in by more than a few of the best citizens. Before the February election the question of secession was often discussed, not only by politicians before assemblies, but by citizens in conversation. While enthusiastic disputants threw arguments thick and fast without convincing one another, they still parted in friendship, that was sometimes abated by the controversy. The time had not then come for the wrathfulness of the political atmosphere and excitement of men's passions, to prevent colloquial and peaceful interchange of opinions. As a general rule, secessionists and the disaffected towards the newly chosen Government at Washington, were more numerous in East Tennessee among the rich and persons of best social position, and were greatly out-numbered among the middle and poorer classes.

The election in February resulted in a majority of more than sixty thousand voters for Tennessee continuing in the United States, and also in a decided majority against holding the proposed convention. It was clearly to be seen that the people were content to continue in old and tried paths, and did not think it wise or expedient even to send delegates of their own choosing to discuss the vital questions that agitated and threatened the country. Many of them looked upon the convention with apprehension as a contrivance for mischief. What if the enemies of the United States intended and should use it as a hot-bed to mature an ordinance of secession, which, like the gourd over the head of the displeased and murmuring Hebrew prophet at Nineveh, quickly grown, would quickly perish? Has not experience any lesson to teach on the subject of unusual gatherings of inflammable materials, which a spark may kindle into a great fire, when the air is very dry from intense heats?

With the advent of spring, in 1861, the muttering of the storm gathering in the national heavens became louder and longer. The inauguration of Mr. Lincoln on the fourth of March, was affirmed by men in Tennessee with others in the South, who were bent upon separation, to be an ample reason in itself for a dissolution of the Union. His words when he took the oath of office,—so full of friendship and good will to the South, fell idly on their ears, and his abstinence from any act to disturb its peace, did not abate their hostility a fraction.

During the month of March a young New Yorker arrived at Knoxville, returning home from Havana, where he had dwelt in the winter for the sake of health. He found New Orleans, through which his journey lay, all in a ferment over the cauldron of political troubles in the land. Not being versed in State-craft nor fully impressed by the gravity of the national situation, he was disposed to look with a lenient eye upon the insubordination to the Federal Government prevailing in the Queen City of the South. Louisiana desired to have a government of its own, and with great generosity, he said it might be well to let its people make the experiment. He, at least, was not inclined to coerce them into obedience. Now and then in his leisure at Knoxville, as the times were ominous, he kept on the alert for news. One day, being told of the fall of Fort Sumter, he inquired of an ardent secessionist standing near:

"Was the attack upon the Fort without provocation?"

The citizen addressed, took the question, not as it was intended, merely to learn how the fight began, but as a provocation. At once he spoke with stern manner and strong words of Southern rights and as his sectional zeal grew more fervid with its venting, he asserted that "one Southern man could whip five or six Yankees." He himself "could whip three or four."

"My friend," was the reply, "you are mistaken. We are all of one Anglo-Saxon blood and Northern men can fight, as well as Southern."

A few hot-bloods not far off, overheard the conversation. One of them told his companions he knew the stranger by his peculiar speech to be a Yankee, whom the party at once talked of subjecting to the indignity of "a ride on a rail." He caught enough of their words to learn the hostile meaning, and obeying the instinct of his courage, to which his strength looked unequal, he calmly walked up to the company and stood, waiting their pleasure. They kept silence, being discomfited by his composed bearing and shortly went their way.

This boastful estimate of the greatly superior fighting capacity of Southern men, compared with Northern, was widely entertained and expressed in terms not much less exaggerated. It had its root in the idea that Northern people were not "chivalric," and were so devoted to money-making that they would not go to war for the sake of any principles involved in the attempt to dissolve the Union. The two notions helped no little to embolden the secessionists in their purpose of disintegration.

The experience of the young stranger with the effervescence of warlike feelings on the street, did not end with the above incident. Not many days afterwards, the town postmaster was seen emerging from his office with an unnatural paleness of face, that indicated intense mental excitement. The cause was soon explained by his mounting a goods'-box on the principal business street, for want of a better rostrum, and reading aloud to the crowd which immediately gathered, President Lincoln's Proclamation calling for seventy-five thousand men. A copy of it had just arrived by mail. The reading was followed by enthusiastic and martial oratory that stimulated to greater heat the temper of hearers whom the Proclamation offended. At that moment the New Yorker appeared on the scene and desired to see the document. Having no opportunity, he passed along the street with a friend to a distant point where the postmaster was about to read it from a doorstep to another audience, which they joined.

Profound attention was given by all listeners, until the words "loyal citizens" were read, when a strong voice cried out:

"If there is a loyal citizen present, let him now speak!"

No one made reply. The call came from one of a company of young men who were exceedingly zealous, and had it moved the inoffensive Yankee to speak indiscreetly in the surroundings, it may easily be inferred that he would have been handled with severity. When the reading was concluded, he and his friend joined in a subdued laugh over escaped mischief and joyfully departed.*

Governor Isham G. Harris, fired with increased zeal by the beginnings of actual hostilities, called an extra session of the Legislature for May, 1861. The certainty of war determined some minds to favor resistance to the Federal Government by force, which had before adhered to the Union without reference to such an ordeal. A conserv-

* See Appendix: Note E.

ative regard for institutions derived from the past, had influenced them at first to cherish Union sentiments, but their intimate personal and social relations were more with men who were already enlisted in sympathy with the intended revolution. They had resisted the influence of these associates while the peace was unbroken, yet they had combative temperaments and the President's Proclamation roused their slumbering pugnacity. Their own passions being loosed from bit and bridle, as they must have a share in the contention, on whose side should it be but on that of nearest kith and kin. The cause they had deemed unrighteous and against which they had argued and voted, became righteous in their eyes, when seen through the red and lurid atmosphere of Mars.

Others there were who had little strength of character, and had been opposed to secession chiefly because it threatened to disturb the even tenor of their lives. The noise of war in the air did not stir their blood or change their minds: but the same easy-going disposition—the same aversion to be disquieted which had made them Unionists at first, led them to fall into the current of popular feeling in their vicinity, which the entrance upon bloody strife made stronger and swifter for secession. Some for the first time, then heartily responded to the pleas they heard for sympathy and co-operation from Tennessee with the Southern States, as more nearly its sisters, and needing its help. Others yielded to those pleas, because they feared the reproach of their communities for want of right affection and just conduct, or worse still, to be called "scalawags" and "Lincolnites."

The material interests which were affirmed, and by many believed to be at stake in the conflict for "Southern rights," had their influence to increase the number of secessionists in parts of Tennessee after the appeal to arms. The growth of disunion sentiments, like their germination, depended more or less upon the climate and soil. In West Tennessee, where cotton is the chief product and slaves were very numerous, the friends of the Union eventually, were few and far between. At the city of Memphis, a large cotton port, where a strong Union sentiment existed in the autumn of 1860, the voters against secession four months later, could be counted on the fingers of one hand. In Middle Tennessee the secessionists increased in numbers, less in proportion to population, than in West Tennessee: but in East Tennessee, there was no important change in the relative strength of parties produced by the commencement of hostilities. During April, the political excitement in the chief town of the latter region, rapidly waxed strong as it did elsewhere in the land: but it differed then and afterwards in the bitterness mixed with it growing out of the close and sharp divisions among neighbors. The near prospect of a general civil war increased the disposition of the revolutionary party to vigorous proceedings and added something to its confidence. The friends of the United States were put more on the defensive against the charge of disloyalty to their own section of country, and found it necessary to use discretion as well as firmness. Sometimes the adverse parties came near to collisions on the streets.

Tidings of "the fight at Baltimore" vibrated on men's nerves like a shock of electricity. It was on Friday, April 19. On Sunday, people went to church with the exciting news yet ringing in their ears. Singularly enough, as a coincidence, widely observed, and thought by some to be prophetic, the first lesson for the day (third Sunday after Easter) read in the worship of God in many churches of the land, began with the ninth verse of the third chapter of the prophet Joel, in these words:

"Proclaim ye this among the Gentiles; prepare war, wake up the mighty men, let all the men of war draw near; let them come up; beat your plough-shares into swords, and your pruning-hooks into spears: let the weak say, I am strong."

Universally the worshippers were unprepared to hear a portion of God's Word, long before prescribed, but so well suited to the particular time that it might have been selected that morning, and they were impressed or startled. Another portion of Holy Scripture read on the same occasion by like prescription, and which had special fitness to existing circumstances, breathed no martial strains, and therefore received less attention as a coincidence. It was in the Epistle for the Sunday, from St. Peter's first Epistle:

"Submit yourselves to every ordinance of man for the Lord's sake: whether it be to the king as supreme; or unto governors, as unto them that are sent by him for the punishment of evil doers, and for the praise of them that do well. For so is the will of God."

Aiming to promote a spirit of order and peace, the minister who conducted these religious services at Knoxville preached that morning upon the importance of right government and obedience to it—of using freedom, not in the service of evil passions, but of neighborly, kind affections, from the apposite words;

"For, brethren, ye have been called unto liberty; only use not liberty for an occasion to the flesh, but by love serve one another."

As if, however, the hour for discord had come, and its footsteps would not tarry, the result of the day was the loss to the church of several leading families whose sympathies were strongly with "the South," including that of a church warden. He was a worthy citizen and sincere christian, but he "could no longer attend as a worshipper and listen to the 'prayer for the President of the United States and all in authority,'" as set forth in the Book of Common Prayer. The prayer dates back to the year 1789.

The agitations and mutual wrath of parties at the locality, each of them being strong, were sensibly increased by the secession of Virginia and the forcible seizures of Harper's Ferry and the Portsmouth Navy Yard, which followed not long after the Baltimore fight. Notwithstanding the people of Tennessee had voted against secession in February, 1861, by a majority of 60,000, now, in the absence of any later expression of their will on the subject through an authorized channel, the State Government entered into a military league with the Southern Confederacy and passed an ordinance of secession subject to the ratification of the people at the polls on the eighth of June. Under that league troops were enlisted throughout the State, and so without having seceded or become a member of the Confederacy, Tennessee was placed independently in actual rebellion against the United States. Some eight hundred of these soldiers were stationed in camp near Knoxville. One day Andrew Johnson and Thomas A. R. Nelson addressed the people on the principal business street of the town, the court-room being too small to receive them. The meeting was disturbed by the loud music of a Confederate band from a neighboring hotel, and by the threatening demeanor of armed men who had just been addressed by secession orators and were parading the streets. A bloody collision was only prevented by the friendly interposition of peaceably disposed men from both parties. The same two Union leaders were soon afterwards stopped in addressing the people at Blountville in the strong Democratic county of Sullivan, and compelled to desist.

On the twelfth of May the United States flag was raised by some Unionists to the top of a liberty pole fixed near a spot of public resort in the town, and a stirring speech in keeping with the occasion was made by Connelly F. Trigg, Esq. Among his sympathizing hearers was Charles Douglass, a citizen of violent disposition and addicted to the use of strong drink, which without detaining him at home, tended to increase his contentiousness. Being a democrat and an ardent admirer of Andrew Johnson, he followed that distinguished politician into the Union party. Between him and a Major of the Military League State troops—Wash. Morgan—a few angry words were spoken after the flag raising, and Douglass was subsequently fired upon by his adversary and a military companion, when not expecting an assault.

He escaped with slight hurt, but the shots aimed at him mortally wounded a harmless countryman entering a store door. The soldiers in camp were excited upon being informed at once of the affair by Major Morgan, and some hundreds of them under his leading, intent upon Douglass's death were intercepted on their way to town by a discreet Colonel of their army—with help from influential citizens, and persuaded to return to their tents.*

The offending Unionist was not however to escape from his enemies. While seated before a front window of the second story of his house he was shot from a hotel upper window, a hundred yards distant. After a few days of suffering he expired. His murderer was unknown, but was thought to be either the Major or some one of that antago-

*See Appendix Note F.

nist's fellow-soldiers procured for the purpose. The circumstances of his death excited wide regret in the community, except among a few extremists whose over-heated passions had so beclouded their moral sense, that they could hear of the assassination with the same indifference they would hear of a man being slain in battle. By many of the Union men he was looked upon as a martyr in their cause.

The eighth of June, on which day the people were to vote upon the ordinance of secession adopted by the General Assembly, was drawing nigh, and as East Tennesseeans in a majority of cases were averse to it, special efforts seemed advisable at Nashville to influence them in its favor. Certain persons therefore, Hon. John Bell among them, visited Knoxville and other places in the eastern division of the State, but their addresses and labors were of little or no avail. Mr. Bell would not advocate secession, being still hostile to it as a political doctrine, but he was understood to declare himself "a rebel." Other visitors from Middle and West Tennessee were less reserved in advocating the doctrine, and in commending the ordinance to the people for their suffrages. Meanwhile Andrew Johnson, Horace Maynard and Thomas A. R. Nelson were active in making public speeches for the Union. This they did at imminent risk of injury or death from soldiers of the Confederacy (who were transported at that time from the Southwest through East Tennessee to the defence of Virginia), or from the State allied troops.

CHAPTER VII.

The East Tennessee Union Convention at Knoxville. The East Tennessee Union Convention at Greeneville.

> "You must not think
> That we are made of stuff so flat and dull
> That we can let our beard be shook with danger,
> And think it pastime."
> — HAMLET.

> "True fortitude is seen in great exploits
> That justice warrants and that wisdom guides;
> All else is tow'ring, frenzy and distraction."
> — ADDISON'S *Cato*.

TO a thoughtful observer at that time, Tennessee's condition was novel—unlike that of any other State. For while its people had not called for or ratified any Act declaring it no longer a member of the Union, its Governor and Legislature had formed a military league with the enemies of the Union, and in doing this appeared to have done several wrongs. They had exercised a right of sovereignty expressly denied to the several States by the Constitution of the United States, to which the State was certainly subject while in the Union, as it must be allowed to have then been, even upon the admission that an Act of secession when ratified by the people would be valid. And in forming an alliance between Tennessee and the

Southern Confederacy and levying troops from the citizens of the State to promote the objects of the Confederacy, they had assumed authority and power not delegated to them by the people, and had also anticipated in effect the very action of the people upon the question of secession, which they professed to admit depended on the will of the people as it might be expressed on the following eighth of June. For by placing the State in military league with the Southern Confederacy and by levying Tennessee troops to carry out the purposes of that league, they had not only put the State into an attitude of *de-facto* hostility to the United States, but also placed the voters in surroundings which would secure a majority of them at the polls for secession; so that the popular will in the matter was practically pushed as far into the back-ground, as if the Governor and Legislature in passing an ordinance of secession, had altogether ignored the existence of the people. The popular vote in the ensuing June—considering all the appliances procured and brought to bear upon it—would not be an election between alternatives, but could only be decided in conformity with the already known will of the Governor and Legislature. In a word, the people were made a mere figure-head in the whole transaction.

Such were the views of many intelligent and patriotic East Tennesseeans. They thought that a bold attempt had been made to override the free will and real mind of the people through the usurpation of power and in defiance of State and

National constitutions; and by contrivance and force to array Tennessee in line with the States armed against the United States. Should they tamely submit to the usurpation without protest, while yet its purpose was not fully accomplished? The revolutionary scheme that had prevailed in other Commonwealths had now come by means of new devices to darken their very doors with its baleful presence and premature forces—ere long to be followed by many and dire ills. What should be done? In time of trouble and danger it is wise for men to counsel with one another. Let the people be invited to meet together by newly-chosen representatives, well informed of the serious political situation, who shall calmly deliberate and determine. This conclusion was expressed by the publication of the following notice:

"EAST TENNESSEE CONVENTION."

"The undersigned, a portion of the people of East Tennessee, disapproving the hasty and inconsiderate action of our General Assembly, and sincerely desirous to do in the midst of the troubles which surround us what will be best for our country and for all classes of our citizens, respectfully appoint a convention to be held in Knoxville on Thursday, the thirtieth of May, and we urge every county in East Tennessee to send delegates to this convention, that the conservative element of our whole section may be represented, and that wise, prudent and judicious counsels may prevail, looking to peace and harmony among ourselves.

"(Signed by), F. S. Heiskell, C. H. Baker, S. R. Rodgers, W. Rodgers, M. D., John Baxter, C. F. Trigg, David Burnett, John Williams, John J. Craig, W. H. Rogers, O. P. Temple, John Tunnell, W. G. Brownlow and others."

These were citizens whose names commended the appointment they made to general attention and to the co-operation of all who sympathised in its object: and at the time proposed, being Thursday, the Convention assembled at Temperance Hall, Knoxville. The delegates present numbered four hundred and sixty-nine, representing twenty-six counties, which with two other counties represented by two resident proxies, constituted nearly the whole of East Tennessee. As the meeting was held in Knox County, and therefore was more easy of access to its delegates, they were much more numerously appointed and in attendance than were those from any other county. Still there were three hundred and twenty-seven present from other counties. Contiguity to the place of assembling, would of course affect more or less the relative attendance from all parts of the region included in the convention, but so too would the degrees of Union sentiment existing in them. Accordingly, of counties immediately adjacent to Knoxville and strongly devoted to the Union, there were delegates from Anderson, Blount, Jefferson, Union, Roane and Sevier, aggregating one hundred and fifty-eight; Roane sending the largest number and Jefferson the smallest. Among delegates from other counties lying in the great valley, there were twenty-eight from Greene and twenty-four from McMinn: Hamilton, at the extreme southwest, equalled McMinn in numbers, and Sullivan, at the extreme northeast, had a sufficient Union element to send six representatives. Distance lessened attendance from the mountain counties: but Johnson sent thirteen delegates from the far east, and Carter five; and although travel on horseback was difficult at a time so troubled, ten were present from Campbell County on the north, and six from Morgan on the west. In Scott County, east of Morgan, the mountains pierce the clouds, the scenery is grand and the slaves were only one in forty-five of the population. It was its people in their high and peaceful homes who did not hear that South Carolina had seceded until the event lost all its freshness as news: and possibly tidings of the convention at Knoxville had not gone to them with enough fleetness of wing to give timely information. Yet they were alive and awake to the worth of "Liberty and Union,—one and inseparable,—now and forever!" and the time would come to them for action. The tidal wave of battle would ere long toss its foam and spray upon the foundations of the everlasting hills among which they dwelt; and they would do their part in saving the ship of state from being wrecked in the storm. Rhea County and Sequatchie, a little county embedded in the mountains north of Chattanooga, were the only ones in East Tennessee unrepresented in the convention; but why, does not appear.*

* See Appendix: Note G.

The deliberative body assembled on the 30th of May, was composed of intelligent, patriotic citizens, who were deeply impressed with the gravity of the political and civil condition and of the questions at issue: and they were mindful to turn, in that hour of perplexity and peril, to God, "the Governor among the nations," and to supplicate Him in faith for guidance and help. Prayer to Him was offered, upon request, by a Christian minister, and then the meeting was organized. The Hon. John Baxter was appointed President temporarily, and upon nomination of a committee of his selection, permanent officers were chosen by acclamation, as follows:

President, Hon. Thos. A. R. Nelson, of Washington County; Vice President, Col. J. G. Spears, of Bledsoe; Assistant Vice Presidents, R. D. Wheeler, of Campbell, J. C. Murphy, of Sevier, M. R. May, M. D., of McMinn, John Williams, of Knox, and William Heiskell, of Monroe. Secretary, John M. Fleming, of Knox; Assistant Secretaries, A. L. Greene, of Roane, S. P. Doss, of Bledsoe, and J. M. Meek, of Jefferson.

Before taking his seat, the President elect addressed the convention for above an hour, with more than his usual powers of argument and oratory. As described at the time, "he forcibly reviewed the history of the revolutionary movement that was convulsing the country,—exposed with masterly ability the usurpations of the Governor of Tennessee and the unconstitutional acts of the Legislature at its recent extra session, and closed

HON. JOHN BAXTER.

with an earnest, eloquent appeal to the members of the convention to discharge their responsible duties with calmness and firmness;—to submit to no wanton tyranny, and to acquiesce in the will of the people, if constitutionally and legally expressed."

On motion, the President then appointed a general committee to prepare and report business for the convention. It consisted as follows:

Connelly F. Trigg, of Knox; Alexander E. Smith, of Johnson; J. T. P. Carter, of Carter; S. T. Logan, of Washington; James P. McDowell, of Greene; William Mullenix, of Sullivan; Wm. C. Kyle, of Hawkins; William McFarland, of Jefferson; Samuel Pickens, of Sevier; Rev. W. T. Dowell, of Blount; Daniel Heiskell, of Monroe; John W. Wester, of Roane; Daniel C. Trewhitt, of Hamilton; R. M. Edwards, of Bradley; B. F. Staples, of Morgan; David K. Young, of Anderson; David Hart, of Campbell; George W. Bridges, of McMinn; T. J. Matthews, of Meigs; A. C. Yates, of Cumberland; J. M. McCleary, of Polk; S. P. Doss, of Bledsoe; E. E. Jones, of Claiborne; Isaac Bayless, of Union; Harmon G. Lea, of Grainger, and P. H. Easterly of Cocke. Marion County was represented on the committee by Wm. G. Brownlow, proxy; and he, with Wm. C. Kyle, as proxies, represented Hancock County of the distinctive mountain region.

While this committee was absent for deliberation, Gen. Thomas D. Arnold, of Greene County, a veteran in politics as well as the law, was introduced to the convention. He spoke at considerable length in opposition to "the schemes of the Governor and Legislature of Tennessee to plunge the people against their own will into a ruinous and unwarranted revolution." His speech was "bold, pointed, earnest and eloquent."

On the morning of the second day of the convention, the general committee submitted their report, which after discussion by various members and amendment, was unanimously adopted. It was as follows:

"In the enumeration of rights of citizens which have been declared under the solemn sanction of the people of Tennessee, there are none which should be more warmly cherished or more highly estimated than that which declares that 'the citizens have a right in a peaceable manner to assemble together for their common good.' And at no time since the organization of our Government has there been an occasion which called so loudly for the exercise of that inestimable right, as that upon which we are now assembled.

"Our country is at this moment in a most deplorable condition. The Constitution of the United States has been openly contemned and set at defiance, while that of our own State has shared no better fate and by the sworn representatives of the people has been utterly disregarded.

"Constitutions, which in other days were wont to control, and give direction to our public councils and to those in authority by the fiat of the people, have been wholly supplanted; and fanaticism, passion and prejudice have assumed an arbitrary sway. Law and Order seem to have yielded their beneficent offices for the safety of the country and the welfare of the people: and in their stead, Revolution, despite its attendant horrors, has raised its hideous head. The condition of the country is most perilous,—the present crisis most fearful.

"In this calamitous state of affairs,—when the liberties of the people are so imperilled and their most valued rights endangered, it behooves them in their primary meeting and in all their other accustomed modes, to assemble, consult calmly as to their safety, and with firmness to give expression to their opinions and convictions of right.

"We, therefore, the delegates here assembled, representing and reflecting, as we verily believe, the opinions and wishes of a very large majority of the people of East Tennessee, do resolve and declare:

"That the evils which now afflict our beloved country, in our opinion, are the legitimate offspring of the ruinous and heretical doctrine of secession; and that the people of East Tennessee have ever been and we believe still are opposed to it by a very large majority.

"That while the country is now upon the very threshold of a most ruinous and desolating civil war, it may with truth be said, and we protest before God, that the people so far as we can see, have done nothing to produce it.

"That the people of Tennessee, when the question was submitted to them in February last, decided by an overwhelming majority that the relations of the State towards the Federal Government should not be changed;—thereby expressing their preference for the Union and Constitution under which they had lived prosperously and happily, and ignoring in the most emphatic manner the idea that they had been oppressed by the General Government in any of its Acts,—legislative, executive or judicial.

"That in view of so decided an expression of the will of the people, in whom 'all power is inherent and on whose authority all free governments are founded;' and in the honest conviction that nothing has transpired since that time which should change that deliberate judgment of the people; we have contemplated with peculiar emotions the pertinacity with which those in authority have labored to over-ride the judgment of the people and to bring about the very result which the people themselves had so overwhelmingly condemned.

"That the Legislative Assembly is but the creature of the Constitution of the State, and has no power to pass any law or to perform any act of sovereignty, except such as may be authorized by that instrument: and believing as we do, that in their recent legislation the General Assembly have disregarded the rights of the people and transcended their own legitimate powers; we feel constrained,—and we invoke the people throughout the State as they value their liberties,—to visit that hasty, inconsiderate and unconstitutional legislation with a decided rebuke, by voting on the eighth day of next month against both the Act of Secession and that of Union with the 'Confederate States.'

"That the Legislature of the State, without having first obtained the consent of the people, had no authority to enter into a 'Military League' with the 'Confederate States' against the General Government, and by so doing to put the State of Tennessee in hostile array against the Government of which it then was and still is a member. Such legislation in advance of the expressed will of the people to change their governmental relations, was an act of usurpation, and should be visited with the severest condemnation of the people.

"That the forming of such Military League, and thus practically assuming the attitude of an enemy towards the General Government,—this too in the absence of any hostile demonstration against this State,—has afforded the pretext of raising, arming and equipping a large military force, the expense of which is enormous and will have to be paid by the people. And to do this, the taxes, already onerous enough, will necessarily have to be very greatly increased, and probably to an extent beyond the ability of the people to pay.

"That the General Assembly, by passing a Law authorizing the volunteers to vote wherever they may be on the day of election,—whether in or out of the State;—in offering to the 'Confederate States' the Capitol of Tennessee, together with other acts, have exercised powers and stretched their authority to an extent not within their constitutional limits and not justified by the usages of the country.

"That Government 'being instituted for the common benefit, the doctrine of non-resistance to arbitrary power and oppression is absurd, slavish and destructive of the good and happiness of mankind.'

"That the position which the people of our sister State of Kentucky have assumed in this momentous crisis, commands our highest admiration:—their interests are our interests:—their policy is the true policy, as we believe, of Tennessee and all the border States. And in the spirit of freemen, with an anxious desire to avoid the waste of the blood and treasure of our State, we appeal to the people of Tennessee, while it is yet in their power, to come up in the majesty of their strength and restore Tennessee to her true position."

The declaration concluded:—"We shall await with the utmost anxiety the decision of the people of Tennessee on the eighth day of next month, and sincerely trust that wiser counsels will pervade the great fountain of freedom,—the People,—than seem to have actuated their constituted agents."

Hon. Andrew Johnson, who had begun an address to the convention before the committee made their report, afterwards proceeded with it. According to the official record of the convention, "he spoke three hours and commanded earnest attention throughout his entire speech," which "was masterly in argument" and carried "conviction to every honest mind that heard it." During the two days' session, there was much friendly debate upon the report, &c. The set addresses of Messrs. Nelson, Arnold and Johnson were the conspicuous oratorical features of the occasion and made strong impressions; but whatever others said touching the subjects that had brought the delegates together, was listened to with the ready minds of men who felt profoundly.

It should be remembered that these things were spoken and done, not in a corner, but in the broad light and open air, and under the intimidating influence of hostile soldiers close at hand. They rode along the highway in sight of the convention and shouted at it their defiance and scoffs; but without otherwise molesting it.

THE CONVENTION IN GREENEVILLE

Was held nine days after the election, which was declared to be in favor of secession. It met on the 17th of June, according to adjournment from Knoxville on the 31st of May. The delegates present numbered two hundred and ninety-two, from twenty-six counties: four other counties being represented by proxies. The change of place greatly diminished the attendance from some counties and increased it from others.* The general committee appointed at Knoxville was continued with some changes, chiefly to supply absences; its new members being W. B. Carter, of Carter; Jas. W. Deaderick, of Washington; R. L. Stanford, of Sullivan; John Netherland, of Haw-

* See Appendix Note H.

kins; Jas. P. Swann, of Jefferson; Charles F. Barton, of Hancock; W. B. Staley, of Roane; J. Stonecipher, of Morgan; L. C. Houk, of Anderson; J. A. Cooper, of Campbell; R. K. Byrd, proxy for Cumberland; Wm. M. Biggs, of Polk; J. G. Spears, of Bledsoe; S. C. Honeycutt, proxy for Scott; and E. S. Langley, for Fentress.

On the second day the committee recommended to the convention, a Declaration of Grievances with Resolutions, which were discussed and finally adopted. In these were set forth at greater length their sentiments and the reasons for them, than were in the similar document at Knoxville.

The Declaration affirmed that so far as the convention could learn, the election held in Tennessee on the eighth of June "was free with but few exceptions, in no part of the State other than East Tennessee. In the larger parts of Middle and West Tennessee, no speeches or discussions in favor of the Union were permitted. Union papers were not allowed to circulate. Measures were taken in some parts of West Tennessee, in defiance of the Constitution and laws which allow folded tickets, to have the ballots numbered in such manner as to mark and expose the Union votes. * * * * "Disunionists in many places had charge of the polls, and Union men when voting were denounced as Lincolnites and Abolitionists. The unanimity of the votes in many large counties, where but a few weeks ago the Union sentiment was so strong, proves beyond doubt that Union men were overawed by the tyranny of the military power and the still greater tyranny of a corrupt and subsidized press. * * * For these and other causes we do not regard the result of the election as expressive of the will of a majority of the freemen of Tennessee. Had the election been conducted as it was in East Tennessee, we would entertain a different opinion."

The convention, in its "Declaration of Grievances," testified with emphasis to its love for the Union, whose virtues and benefits it extolled; and its hate of secession, whose "treacheries, falsehoods, violences and evil results," it arraigned in detail and condemned. Yet manifestly, it was averse to angry strife with fellow-citizens of the State who differed from it in opinion, and it was inclined to cultivate forbearance and peace with them. At first it had even contemplated standing aloof from any conflict with arms that might take place without and beyond the State. But it complained that its political opponents had shown a self-willed, intolerant and severe temper towards Union men. The Declaration said, in speaking of secession:

"Its bigoted, overbearing and intolerant spirit has already subjected the people of East Tennessee to many petty grievances."—They "have been insulted; our flags have been fired at and torn down; our houses have been rudely entered; our families treated with insult; our peaceable meetings interrupted; our women and children shot at by a merciless soldiery; our towns pillaged; our citizens robbed and some of them assassinated or murdered."

"No attempt has been spared to deter the Union men of East Tennessee from the expression of their free thoughts. The penalties of treason have been threatened against them, and murder and assassination have been openly encouraged by leading secession journals. As secession has been thus overbearing and intolerant while in the minority in East Tennessee, nothing better can be expected of the pretended majority, than wild, unconstitutional and oppressive legislation; an utter contempt and disregard of Law;—a determination to force every Union man in the State to swear to the support of a Constitution he abhors, to yield his money and property to aid a cause he detests, and to become an object of scorn and derision, as well as a victim of intolerable and relentless oppression."

"In view of these considerations and of the fact that the people of East Tennessee have declared their fidelity to the Union by a majority of about twenty thousand votes," the convention appointed three of its members to prepare and present a memorial to the State Legislature, asking its consent to the formation of a new State to be composed of East Tennessee and such counties in Middle Tennessee as desired to co-operate to that end. Other resolutions were adopted, which provided for a convention of delegates, duly elected at the polls by the constituency of the new State, to be held at Kingston. Unanimity prevailed, except that two of the Hawkins county delegates protested against the action of the convention.

It was in session four days, during which time

the "Louisiana Tigers" of the Confederate army halted at Greeneville on their way to Richmond. Their commander embraced the occasion to make a speech, and his soldiers expressed their ill-will to the convention by derisions and small indignities, but there was no blood shed. Unterrified and unmoved to acts of resentment, the delegates persevered in their work, fully persuaded of the honesty of their purpose and the righteousness of their cause. Because they felt the need of superior counsel and help, and trusted in Him who only is wise and powerful to bestow these, the daily proceedings of the convention were opened with prayer by various Christian ministers.

Enthusiastic delegates were in favor of forming at once a Provisional Government and organizing an army, with John Baxter for its General. But he, assisted by James W. Deaderick, A. H. Maxwell and others, advocated less hasty action, and moderate counsels prevailed. He advised that instead of hopeless war on the spot, all who chose should join the United States army in Kentucky. Spears, Byrd, Cooper, Houk, Clift and others did so speedily.

If the request to the Legislature for a new State should not be granted, it was expected by some delegates that an independent government would still be formed at the Kingston convention, but the adverse military occupation of the region, and the progress of events prevented further action.

CHAPTER VIII.

GROWING WRATH—JOY OVER VICTORY—GEN. ZOLICOFFER—A YANKEE BOY'S PASS-PORT—LIGHTS AND SHADOWS—ESCAPE OF CONGRESSMEN—FORGED LETTERS TO BOSTON—A MILITARY ZEALOT—BRIDGE-BURNING.

> "The days of the nations bear no trace
> Of all the sunshine so far foretold;
> The cannon speaks in the teacher's place—
> The age is weary with work and gold,
> And high hopes wither, and memories wane;
> On hearths and altars the fires are dead;
> But that brave faith hath not lived in vain—
> And this is all that our watcher said."
> FRANCES BROWN.

THE indignation of the Union men and the intolerance of the Secessionists were obviously increased by the election of the 8th of June and its announced result. The first declared the vote was fraudulent; the second exulted, that by it the State became a member of the Southern Confederacy. The railroads were busy much of the time, as they had been for a short time before, in the transportation of troops from the Southwest through East Tennessee to Virginia. This transit of soldiers was witnessed by people loyal to the Union with feelings of strong dissatisfaction, which sometimes grew into great animosity and wrath.

Once a mass-meeting of Unionists was in progress at Strawberry Plains, Jefferson County, during the excitement over the election, when a regiment from the South passed by on the railway. A conflict with fire-arms between members of the two hostile parties took place, but no life was lost. The incident tended to exasperate the public temper. It was exceptional, however. Generally the people repressed their grief and pain at such scenes—enough, at least, to avoid all violent demonstrations towards their adversaries. They vented them to one another, sometimes with bated breath.

The United States flag had been lifted up and displayed from liberty poles without a rival, at the beginning of the dissensions. Then it had for months contested supremacy in the air with the flag of the Southern Confederacy. At length the United States flags were taken down under compulsion, except in a few instances, where, being private property, their removal was prevented for a time by the boldness and firmness of the owners.

News of the first battle of Manasses in July, 1861, was hailed with gushing delight by the friends of the Confederacy. In the town they were not so strong numerically as in actual ascendency, and tidings of that victory encouraged the manifestation of their special sympathies in the war more freely and defiantly. In the overflow of their elation of spirits, various means of noisily celebrating the recent triumph were adopted. Even the bells of churches, innocent as they were of all connection with bloody fields of conflict between brethren, were joyfully rung. Zealous citizens, who never before had shown any particular interest in the musical instruments whose business it is to call Christian people to the house of prayer, were active in making them contribute their voices to the general Jubilee.* Words of bitterness and wrath against "the Yankees," and against Union men under several opprobrious names, were more freely used. Alienations of close kinsmen and ruptures of friendly relations, were widened and deepened. Other swords there are besides those of steel, wielded in civil wars. Quite as sharp and effective are they in wounding feelings and cutting through social ties, as are metallic blades in severing limbs and piercing bodies.

About this time Gen. Felix K. Zolicoffer, of Nashville, was appointed to the supreme command in East Tennessee, and with his military staff, he went into camp at Knoxville. Years before, he had been a journeyman printer in the town, and his friendships then formed among its citizens, had subsequently been increased in number. He seemed disposed to exercise authority over the people with a lenient hand, and to abstain from needless severities. At the beginning of the Southern Confederacy, complaint was made at some localities, that in filling offices under the new Government, Democrats were chiefly appointed to the rejection

---

* A Union man, who was also an elder of a Presbyterian Church, was grieved to hear its bell joining with merriest notes in the chorus of song. He sought with speed to know the reason, and found a citizen of good social position, whose intimate relations were more with this present world than with that which is to come, had got into the Church by a window, and was vigorously applying his gentlemanly muscle on the rope that led to the steeple.

of Whigs, who were equally or more competent. This may have been done, because Democrats were known as a party, to have had stronger sympathy with the secession movement at its initiation, and were believed to be worthy of fuller confidence in its interests. Zolicoffer, while the Whig party survived, was prominent in its ranks, and some of those who affiliated with him at that time, were in 1861 devoted to the Union. With them, after entering upon his military duties, he chose to continue friendly intercourse. This caused jealousy and ill-feeling towards him among intolerant observers, and the *Register*, a small daily newspaper of the town, blamed him in its editorial columns, for too mild use of his power. These censures did not seriously affect his mind. He still permitted the *Whig* newspaper edited by William G. Brownlow to continue its weekly issues, although its sentiments were in obvious sympathy with the United States, and its submission to the Southern Confederacy was clearly the result of necessity. At the same time he had the editor's son, John Bell Brownlow, arraigned before him upon accusation by Gen. Lane, of McMinn County, of circulating a copy of Helper's book, entitled "Impending Crisis of the South." The youth accidentally found a copy of the book which had been sent to the editor by mail, and loaned it upon urgent request to a friend. He was speedily acquitted of the alleged offence: but, under an order before issued concerning arrested civilians, he was, after three days' detention as a prisoner in camp, handed over to the Confederate Court. Judge Humphreys repeated the acquittal, but suggested the administration to the youth of the specific for doubtful loyalty, *i. e.* an oath of allegiance, which he refused to take, and was released. Altogether, Gen. Zolicoffer manifested sufficient official zeal, and a few months later he was severe in sending his cavalry abroad to disarm peaceable Union men in Anderson, Campbell, Scott and Fentress Counties.

People are apt to suppose that in time of war the authority of a General, like that of a Judge or Governor in time of peace, will be respected by his civilian allies, and that a wrong done by them in despite of it, is easily remedied. On the contrary, the excessive ardor of the allies sometimes blinds their respect for the authority, which then fails to redress the wrong. The sign manual of Gen. Zolicoffer proved of no avail to a young man from Connecticut, who had been a student of the University at Knoxville for two years. In 1861 a few of his fellow-students, catching the spirit of intolerance from their elders, annoyed and angered him with reproachful words because of his nativity. He decided to return home, and Gen. Zolicoffer gave an official letter that should permit him to travel without interruption into Kentucky by way of Nashville. But when about to leave that city by railroad, he was arrested without cause and taken before a committee of citizens, the chairman of which was also from Connecticut, and illustrated the opinion that "Northern men with

Southern principles" not unfrequently during the war exceeded Southerners in their sectional zeal. The student's letter of safe conduct through the State was adjudged insufficient, and the committee required him to take an oath of their dictation in order to prosecute his journey. Gen. Zolicoffer, when informed of the facts, promised an inquiry. The student, on reaching Connecticut, joined a company of United States volunteers, was repeatedly promoted for gallant conduct, left the army at the end of the war a Major, and is now a worthy, prosperous citizen of Los Angeles, California.

Gen. Zolicoffer had a pleasant military family at his encampment, where visitors were kindly received. Every circle of personal associates, composed of men who are in the front of the strife at such stormy periods, is liable to quick and fatal disruption. In this instance the speedy mortality was impressive.

On the bright, delightful morning of the second of September, 1861, a civilian from the town was conducted to the tent of Gen. Zolicoffer, with whom were Gen. William R. Caswell, Commander of Tennessee Provisional soldiers, and Major F. B. Fogg, only son of the eminent lawyer and excellent man, Francis B. Fogg, Esq., of Nashville, who was a steadfast friend of the Union. Major Fogg and other young men—members of the Chief's staff—talked with lively interest of the news they found in the mail just then brought to camp, that General Albert Sidney Johnston had arrived in the Atlantic States from California. The visiting citizen, having but a small stock of knowledge on hand concerning military men, asked: "And who is Albert Sidney Johnston?" The prompt reply was: "O, he is the greatest of all the Confederate Generals."

The annals of events in the succeeding twelve months, cast sombre shadows upon the remembrance of that scene:—the cheerful company, holding pleasant converse,—the fresh and sunny autumnal air, and the mingled light and shade of the forest playing among the tents. For during that short period, the principal persons in the scene were no more! General Zolicoffer was killed at the battle of Mill Springs, Kentucky, in January, 1862. Major Fogg was there mortally wounded. In August, General Caswell was murdered in the woods near Knoxville, as was believed by a fugitive slave whom he was endeavoring to arrest. And General Albert Sidney Johnston, the object of their special admiration, and around whom clustered thickly the confidence and hopes of friends of the Southern Confederacy, fell heroically contending for it on the battle field of Shiloh.

Early in August the usual bi-ennial elections in Tennessee for Governor, the Legislature and members of Congress took place. The Union candidates for Congress were elected by overwhelming majorities. They held that they were properly members elect of the *United* States Congress, and accordingly they were quickly furnished by the sheriffs of the counties with authenticated returns of the voting, that they might proceed at once to Washington, leaving vacant the seats in the Confederate Congress at Richmond which East Tennessee was entitled to fill. Had their purpose fully succeeded, a humorist might have found in the result a grim joke, to which considerations of even-handed justice would have lent a flavor. For the electors were friends of the United States, and if represented in any Congress, should have been so in that of the United States.

The result was not wholly successful with the three gentlemen chosen. The only route any one of them could take to Washington without certain arrest, led through the Cumberland Mountains which divide East Tennessee from Kentucky, and over the rough, hilly country that lies on both sides of those mountains. Ridge after ridge and river after river would have to be crossed and the journey be made on horse-back.

The Hon. Horace Maynard, Representative from the second or Knoxville District, in order to avoid armed arrest, was already on the way from his home to the Kentucky border when the election occurred, and soon after was safely beyond it. A sort of consternation among friends of the South in the town followed upon tidings of his adventurous exodus. And although he was an esteemed ruling elder in one of the Presbyterian Churches, some of the public petitions provoked by the unwelcome news were scarcely in harmony with the Spirit of the Lord, for they savored more of anathema than of benediction. Fortunately for the intended victim, as one may fairly conclude from subsequent events, the petitions did not ascend as high as the ceiling of the house.

The Hon. Thos. A. R. Nelson was less fortunate than Mr. Maynard. He attempted to pass from his home at Jonesboro through the southwestern corner of Virginia into Kentucky. At Cumberland Gap the lines of Virginia, Kentucky and Tennessee converge to a point. It was already occupied by Confederate troops, and a small body of them intercepted him on the road at night. He was taken by way of Abingdon, Va., to Richmond a prisoner, and had to run the gauntlet of infuriated and threatening people at the various railway stations. After a short detention in custody, he was released upon giving a written promise to the President of the Confederacy to abstain from overt acts of hostility against it, and returned to dwell peaceably in Tennessee.

The Hon. George W. Bridges, of the Third or Athens District, contrived to effect his escape into Kentucky through the Cumberland Mountains in Fentress County, Tennessee. It was pre-arranged that his wife and children should immediately follow him, but they were made the means of ensnaring his feet. The Confederate commander of a post on the border detained his family, decoyed him to return by a message of his wife's illness, and then placed him in arrest. Another instance was thus added to the many furnished by history, teaching that in all important and dangerous enterprises it is wise to "look not back," even for the

HON. ANDREW JOHNSON.

sake of cherished objects of natural affection, lest through the adroit use of them by enemies, they become fatal impediments. Mr. Bridges was carried to Knoxville, where he signed a pledge or took an oath of submission to the Confederacy. In a short time he obtained permission to pass into Kentucky to transact a matter of business, and improved that opportunity to extend his journey to Washington, where he served a term in Congress.

Hon. Andrew Johnson had preceded Mr. Maynard to that city. In June the *Richmond* (Va.) *Enquirer* had made publication concerning a recent transaction at Knoxville which, if Mr. Johnson were indeed a party to it, seriously involved him; but the facts went to show that an attempt had been made to obtain money for political uses by the forgery of his name. On the 30th of that month he published from Washington a statement, "in order," to use his own words, "to expose the dishonorable and wicked means resorted to by 'Secession' to carry out its nefarious and corrupt designs in attempting to overthrow and break up the best Government the world ever saw."

Mr. Amos A. Lawrence, of Boston, received a forged letter, marked PRIVATE, and dated "Knoxville, Tenn., May 15, 1861"—on which day Andrew Johnson, whose signature it bore, was addressing a Union Convention at Elizabethton, one hundred and eighteen miles from Knoxville. It read:

DEAR SIR: I received your kind favor on yesterday and hasten

H

to reply. Thank you for the high regard you seem to have for my patriotism and my devotion to my country.

What assurances can I have from you and your people of *material aid* in the way of money, men and arms, if I can succeed in arousing my people to resistance to this damnable treason in the South? This is very important. We have a formidable Union element in East Tennessee, which can be judiciously managed, if we can obtain the aid alluded to. Harris, Governor of the State, will not let us have arms nor money: therefore we *must appeal* to you. Let me hear from you forthwith.

Very respectfully, your obedient servant,
(Signed)   ANDREW JOHNSON.

To the above, this answer was sent:

BOSTON, May 18, 1861.

DEAR SIR: If your note to me were printed in our newspapers, it would be good for ten thousand dollars in three days' time. But of course I must only use it as a private letter. In order that you may be sure of something at once, I write below this a draft, which some of your Union bankers or merchants may be willing to cash at the usual premium for East exchange. Probably Gardner & Co., Evans & Co., Douglass & Co., of Nashville, will know it. The Government will soon exhibit a power which will astonish even you. The Nullifiers have been playing into Scott's hand for three weeks, and now they have lost the game.

Yours with regard,
AMOS A. LAWRENCE.

If you cannot use the draft, return it and tell me what to send.

The draft was as follows:

BOSTON, May 18, 1861.

At sight, without grace, pay to Andrew Johnson or order, One Thousand Dollars, for value received, and charge to my account.

AMOS A. LAWRENCE.

To MASON, LAWRENCE & Co., Boston.

The acceptance of Mason, Lawrence & Co., was on the face of the draft.

Mr. Lawrence received the following in reply:

KNOXVILLE, TENN., June 6, 1861.

Amos A. Lawrence, Esq., near Boston, Mass.:

MY DEAR SIR: I have received your two letters to-day. Thank

you most sincerely for your proffered aid. We need it,—need it badly. As yet I have not been able to use your draft; I am afraid to do so. Send me, if you can, $5,000 or $10,000 in New England currency, in large bills, by mail, *via* Cincinnati. Be sure to do it promptly. Don't delay. I can now purchase a lot of arms if I had the means.

How do you propose to introduce aid or arms into East Tennessee? By what route and by what method? Answer soon.

Respectfully, your obedient servant,

(Signed)   ANDREW JOHNSON.

To this communication no response was made. Mr. Lawrence, by some means or other, had his eyes opened to the game which the conspirators were attempting, and gave them no further attention.

Later in the autumn Gen. Zolicoffer moved his forces towards the Kentucky border. He even passed beyond Cumberland Gap and established his camp north of Cumberland (river) Ford, near Barbourville, Kentucky. After his departure there was a succession of officers in command at Knoxville. First, Col. Wm. B. Wood, of Alabama, whose zeal was intense and did not leave room enough in his mind for the exercise of that discretion, which is said to be the better part of valor. On the 28th of October, his want of self-control, and therefore, unfitness to command others, was signally shown. An affray occurred in the town between a few citizens and some of his men, growing out of an attempt by the police to subject the disorderly soldiers to the civil authority, and their resistance. He represented that the joy of Union men over the news that Gen. Zolicoffer with his army had fallen back on Cumberland Ford, became so irrepressible that "some eight or ten of the bullies or leaders made an attack on some of (his) men near the Lamar House and seriously wounded several." He immediately marched a company of cavalry and one hundred infantry into the town. In an overflow of wrath he slighted the proposal of the Mayor to unite with him in restoring and preserving order, and proceeded to search actively for the frightened guardians of the municipality. They, meanwhile, had made their escape. Entering the store-house of a leading mercantile firm, he demanded in a lordly style that the building should be thoroughly examined, and sternly threatened that if he found one of the alleged culprits secreted in the house, he would burn it down. The quiet and brave head of the firm assented to the demand, but as it resulted in no discovery there was no conflagration! The general bearing on the occasion of the wrathful officer may be inferred from this incident. It is manifest from the correspondence between Gen. Zolicoffer, Col. Wood and others, that the angry disaffection of friends of the Union in East Tennessee under Confederate domination made them restless. Col. Wood, writing from Knoxville on the first day of the month, to Hon. J. P. Benjamin, Secretary of War, at Richmond, said: "There can be no doubt of the fact that large parties, numbering from twenty to a hundred, are every day passing through the narrow and unfrequented gaps of the mountain into Kentucky to join the army. My courier, just in from Jamestown, informs me that a few nights since, one hundred and seventy men passed from Roane County into Kentucky. I do not believe that the Unionists are in the least reconciled to the (C. S.) Government, but on the contrary are as hostile to it as the people of Ohio, and will be ready to take up arms as soon as they believe the Lincoln forces are near enough to sustain them."

On November 8th, an organized plan was partially carried out, by parties of Union men, to burn the bridges of the two railways from Knoxville, one eastward to the Virginia line and the other westward to Chattanooga, and Dalton, Georgia. The bridges over the Hiwassee River, Lick Creek, Greene County, and three other streams, were destroyed. That over the Holston River at Strawberry Plains, Jefferson County, was saved by the bravery of its watchman. These violences created great excitement and alarm. They were the first overt acts of resistance from among the people to the power by which they were subjected; and were committed, no doubt, not in a spirit of mere wanton mischief, but of war upon an enemy and for the purpose of seriously interrupting the military communications of the Southern Confederacy. Some political friends of the destructive workers justified the burnings as acts of war. Others, while not dissenting from that opinion, yet thought them inexpedient,—hurtful to public convenience, and as a military movement, conducive to no important practical results, because unsupported by a sufficient armed force from outside the region.

The Confederate States authorities had apprehended an outbreak of the slumbering discontent of the people; but they could not at first measure the import of this particular aggression. They were therefore liable to suppose it was the forerunner of a general uprising against them, which would be sustained by United States soldiers from Kentucky. The circulation of the news concerning it was quick and general and bred universal agitation, especially among friends of the Confederacy. Citizens gathered in towns and soldiers in camps, to hear declamations. Everywhere, these assaults and the danger of others, were their topics of conversation. Telegrams flew on the wires and letters went by mail to Knoxville, increasing the alarm. A dispatch from Charleston, Tenn., said, "Seventy-five Union soldiers were to-day near Harrison. They had knapsacks." And again, "Jeff Mathes is within twelve miles of this place: has one hundred men." From Chattanooga: "About nine hundred men, part of them from Bradley County, leave Clift's in this county to-day in squads, either to organize for operations against this place and Loudon bridge, or to meet Union forces from Kentucky. The regiment is formidable." A later message said, "They have formed a camp at Bower's, near Smith's Cross Roads. They may return to this place or to Loudon. They calculate to organize one thousand men." From Athens it was written that "some fifteen hundred Lincoln men are under arms in Hamilton County, ostensibly for Jamestown. Their destination is more probably Loudon bridge." The

Major in command at Loudon, on the Tennessee River, thirty miles west of Knoxville, wrote: "The Union feeling in this county is exceedingly bitter, and all they want, in my opinion, to induce a general uprising, is encouragement from the Lincoln armies. They have a great many arms, and are actually manufacturing Union flags to receive the refugee Tennesseeans when they return. They are getting bold enough." Col. Wood wrote: "The whole country is now in a state of rebellion. A thousand men are within six miles of Strawberry Plains and an attack is contemplated to-morrow" (November 12). "They (the Unionists) are gathering in large force and may secure (Washington bridge) in a day or two." "About two miles from here in Sevier County, already three hundred in camp, are being re-inforced."

Knoxville was at once put under martial law. The people's houses were arbitrarily entered day and night by military direction and their guns and pistols demanded. Even weapons intended only for sporting uses or for rivalry in marksmanship were included in the exaction. In but few instances was the requisition evaded by timely secretion of the implements. In others, they were indignantly surrendered, carried off to the armory, and some of them never restored. No one was allowed to depart from the town without a pass-port signed by a committee of three leading secessionists from among the select few citizens, whom Editor Sperry, of the town newspaper, compared, not facetiously but seriously, to the few righteous men who might have saved Sodom and Gomorrah if they could have been found. At first no one was permitted to enter the town without a paper of that kind, which could only be procured from the committee centrally located. Church-going people from the vicinity were surprised on Sunday morning to find armed men in the way who refused them ingress until a messenger, sent by some friend known to be loyal to "the South," went and returned with the requisite passes. An old citizen of the county who had a mind of his own and stoutly adhered in sentiment to the Union, went to town without interruption, probably through oversight of the guard, but on returning homeward, his passport was demanded. He had none to show, for to procure such a document, it was necessary by order of the Committee of Three to take an oath of allegiance to the Southern Confederacy, and *that* he had predetermined he would not do. He was arrested, led back, arraigned before the committee, and refusing to take the prescribed oath, he was placed on confinement to the limits of the town until his case should be tried before the Confederate States Commissioner. Whether he was sent to jail, into which many were then being cast for what was called "Union talk," does not appear. Col. Wood, writing from Knoxville to Adjutant General Cooper at Richmond, said: "I feel it to be my duty to place this city under martial law, as there was a large majority of the people sympathizing and communicating with them by the unfrequented mountain paths, and to prevent surprises and the destruction of public property. I need not say that great alarm is felt by the few Southern men here. They are finding places of safety for their families and would gladly enlist if we had arms for them."

CHAPTER IX.

SEVERE TREATMENT OF UNION MEN—OATHS OF ALLEGIANCE — IMPRISONMENTS — EXECUTIONS.

> "Patience, my lord; why 'tis the soul of peace:
> Of all the virtues 'tis the nearest kin to heaven;
> It makes men look like gods: the best of men
> That e'er wore earth about him, was a sufferer,
> A soft, meek, patient, humble, tranquil spirit,
> The first true gentleman that ever breathed."
> DECKER.

THE attacks from armed Unionists upon different points that were expected and feared by the Confederate authorities just after the bridge burnings, did not occur. Previously, disaffected people in some instances and at various localities had been violently treated by over-zealous neighbors or by lawless soldiers in small squads—whipped with hickories or arrested for their Union sentiments and forced to pay money for their release. It was not considered the business of officials to redress such wrongs, even when brought to their attention; for to be a Union man was regarded in their minds as itself a crime, and injustices suffered on that account outside the operation of the law, could not rightfully be appealed into court. Besides, to interpose for their repression would tend to cool the ardor and check the activity of

Southern partisans, and that would be bad policy.

Now that the Union people had grown restive under a power which they felt to be alien and hostile to their Government and Country, and a few adventurous spirits among them had assailed that power, it was concluded that the whole population was blameable, and should be dealt with more severely by the Confederate Government. General Zolicoffer wrote from his headquarters at Jacksboro, Nov. 12th, to Col. Wood, at Knoxville:

> I will to-morrow send dispatches to the forces near Jamestown, the cavalry near Huntsville, that near Oliver's, and start out the cavalry here, to commence simultaneously disarming the Union population. You will please simultaneously send orders to all detachments under your command to inaugurate the same movement at the same time in their various localities. Their leaders should be seized and held as prisoners. The leniency shown them has been unavailing. They have acted with duplicity and should no longer be trusted.*

On the 20th of November Col. Wood wrote from Knoxville to Hon. J. P. Benjamin, Sceretary of War, Confederate States, at Richmond:

> SIR: The rebellion in East Tennessee has been put down in some of the counties, and will be effectually suppressed in less than two weeks in all the counties. Their camps in Sevier and Hamilton counties have been broken up and a large number of them made prisoners. Some are confined in this place and others sent to Nashville. In a former communication I inquired of the Department what I should do. It is a mere farce to arrest them and turn them over to the Courts. Instead of having the desired effect to intimidate them, it really gives encouragement and emboldens them in their traitorous conduct. Patterson, the son-in-law of Andrew Johnson, State Senator Pickens and several other members of the Legislature, besides others of influence and distinction in their counties,—these men have encouraged the rebellion, but have so managed as not to be found in arms. Nevertheless all their actions and words have been unfriendly to the Government of the Confed-

---

* See Appendix: Note I.

erate States. Their wealth and influence have been exerted in favor of the Lincoln Government and they are the parties most to blame.

They really deserve the gallows, and if consistent with the laws, ought speedily to receive their deserts. But there is such a gentle spirit of conciliation in the South, and especially here, that I have no idea that one of them will receive such a sentence at the hands of any jury. I have been here at this station for three months, half the time in command of this Post; and I (have) had a good opportunity of learning the feeling pervading this country. It is hostile to the Confederate Government. They will take the oath of allegiance with no intention to observe it. They are the slaves of Johnson and Maynard and never intend to be otherwise. When arrested, they suddenly become very submissive and declare they are for peace and not supporters of the Lincoln Government, but yet claim to be Union men. At one time, while our forces were at Knoxville, they gave it out that a great change had taken place in East Tennessee and that the people were becoming loyal.

At the withdrawal of the army from here to the (Cumberland) Gap and the first intimation of the approach of the Lincoln army, they were in arms and scarcely a man but was ready to join it and make war upon us. The prisoners we have, all tell us that they had every assurance that the enemy was already in the State and would join them in a few days. I have requested at least that the prisoners I have taken be held, if not as traitors, as prisoners of war. To convict them before a Court is next to an impossibility. But if they are kept in prison for six months it will have a good effect. The bridge-burners and spies ought to be tried at once."

To this communication was replied:

WAR DEPARTMENT, RICHMOND, November 25, 1861.
Col. W. B. Wood:

SIR—Your report of the 20th instant is received, and I now proceed to give you the desired instruction in relation to the prisoners of war taken by you among the traitors of East Tennessee.

First. All such as can be identified in having been engaged in bridge-burning are to be tried summarily by drum-head court-martial, and, if found guilty, executed on the spot by hanging. It would be well to leave their bodies hanging in the vicinity of the burned bridges.

Second. All such as have not been so engaged are to be treated as prisoners of war, and sent with an armed guard to Tuscaloosa, Alabama, there to be kept imprisoned at the depot selected by the Government for prisoners of war.

Whenever you can discover that arms are concentrated by these traitors, you will send out detachments, search for and seize the arms. In no case is one of the men, known to have been up in arms against the Government to be released on any pledge or oath of allegiance. The time for such measures is past. They are all to be held as prisoners of war, and held in jail to the end of the war. Such as come in voluntarily, take the oath of allegiance and surrender their arms, are alone to be treated with leniency.

Your vigilant execution of these orders is earnestly urged by the Government.

Your obedient servant,
(Signed)   J. P. BENJAMIN,
Secretary of War.

COL. W. B. WOOD, Knoxville, Tenn.

P. S.—Judge Patterson Andy Johnson's son-in-law, (Rem. Corresp.), Col. Pickens and other ring-leaders of the same class, must be sent at once to Tuscaloosa to jail as prisoners of war.

The Hon. W. H. Humphreys had been on the Bench of the United States District Court before Tennessee seceded. He had warmly espoused the cause of the Southern Confederacy and was appointed by it to a similar office under its Government. As preliminary to his new duties, he announced from the Bench his determination to punish all treason and rebellion against the authority he represented. Union men were arraigned before him upon various charges. The only crime of a majority of them was love of the Union. For their political purgation, an oath of allegiance was thought to be sufficient, and upon taking it they were summarily released.

The compulsory swearing of fealty during the progress of the war had in many instances a demoralizing effect. It made familiar to men the idea of an oath as having in itself no binding force, and therefore tended to increase the lenient regard which was before too prevalent for the crime of perjury. No doubt an oath of allegiance was administered to many men on both sides of the conflict, under compulsion of their wills, who in their hearts considered it null and void. They felt as Hudibras puts it:

> "He that imposes an oath, makes it,
> Not he that for convenience takes it:
> Then how can any man be said
> To break an oath he never made."

Said a Union man, when rumor was current that everybody would soon be made to swear loyalty to the Confederacy, he would take such an enforced oath "from the teeth out." And so too, an ex-Confederate soldier, made to swear loyalty to the United States, muttered to his friend the words of Galileo when compelled to abjure the Copernican system: "It still moves!" Yet both the Unionist and the Confederate were conscientious, worthy citizens, who alike in times of peace, would esteem the oath before a court of justice as "a recognizance to heaven," and again, to quote pithy lines from Hudibras, as—

> Being "not purposed more than Law
> To keep the good and just in awe,
> But to confine the bad and sinful,
> Like moral cattle in a pinfold."

However, despite all ethical objections to the miscellaneous administration of the oath of allegiance, and the numerous instances of its futility in the war, its reputation still held good as a specific for curing disloyalty; or at least, as a certain preventive of ill consequences from that political sickness through men afflicted with it. Therefore the extensive use of it by Judge Humphreys in his court-room with Union citizens indicated no lower degree of intelligence in him, although in the opinion of some it might show his lack of judicial wisdom. Instances were not wholly wanting in which the use of that requirement was denied him, because the patient thought the prescribed dose too astringent for health of conscience, as may be seen by the following from the *Knoxville Whig* of that period:

"On Saturday evening, Mr. Perez Dickinson, for the last thirty years a successful merchant of Knoxville, returned from the North whither he had gone with a written permit from Governor Harris, to attend to business connected with the two firms of which he is a member. On Monday morning he was arrested upon a warrant based upon an affidavit by Attorney Ramsey, setting forth that said Dickinson was born in the State of Massachusetts, and that he had been to the North and held intercourse with the Northern people. This was the charge, and this affidavit was all the proof offered against him. His Honor Judge Humphreys, bore testimony to the good character and high standing of Mr. Dickinson, and proposed to him that he should at once and without any investigation (by the court), take an oath of allegiance and fidelity to the Confederate States. Mr. Dickinson rose and responded in a brief address—spoke of his coming here when a boy some thirty years ago—of his being an orderly and law-abiding citizen—of his all being here, and of the bones of his mother, sisters and brother being here—denied that he had held any intercourse with the people of the North in violation of his parole to Governor Harris, and declined, under the circumstances of compulsion surrounding him, to take the oath. His Honor then instructed him that he would have to give a bond of ten thousand dollars for his good behavior during the few days allotted him to remain in the State."

The reputable merchant refused to give the bond, and was prepared to depart. Notwithstanding that refusal, the Judge, upon advice of political friends, permitted him to remain.

Arraignment of prisoners before the Judge sometimes rested on no foundation whatever. Rev. W. H. Duggan, a Methodist minister, of McMinn County, was charged in the indictment with having prayed for the United States Government: but the evidence showed that the praying had been done before Tennessee seceded from the Union. The manner in which he was treated was described at the time in the *Whig* newspaper, under the eyes of the authorities. It illustrated the condition of things in the region:

"Some twenty-five persons, citizens of McMinn County, were brought before Judge Humphreys on Monday, about twenty of whom were released on the ground that there was nothing against them. The truth is, they had voted the Union ticket and they had voted for years against certain men: and this explained their arrest. They were taxed with small fees to pay costs and required to take the oath, although they had committed no offense. The other five were retained for further hearing and sent into camps under a military escort for the night. Among these was Rev. W. Duggan, a member of the Holston Annual Conference, and the preacher in charge of the Athens Circuit, * * * a man of truth and integrity.

"He was arrested at a quarterly meeting on Friday night, and marched on foot on Saturday nine miles, being refused the privilege of riding his own horse: and on Sabbath he was landed at Knoxville. He is a large, fleshy man, weighs two hundred and eighty-one pounds, and was recovering from a long spell of fever. He gave out at a spring some seven miles from where he started. The day was warm, and his feet were sorely blistered. He begged permission to ride; he was refused, cursed, denounced and threatened with bayonets! His horse was led after him as if to aggravate him. They even refused him water to drink or anything to eat until Sunday."

He is represented in the same editorial to have had "the confidence of men of other denominations."

That he was "a very poor man, with a wife and

six helpless children" could have availed him nothing had he been guilty, but the absence of all evidence that he had done anything for which he should be punished, induced his discharge after three days custody in camp, "without entering into bonds or taking any oath."

Some of the Union men arraigned before Judge Humphreys were temporarily imprisoned. It was not, however, until his departure from the scene and after the bridge-burnings, that more severe measures were adopted against that class of citizens.

Commissioner Robert B. Reynolds presided over these stringent proceedings at first and for some time. He was a native Tennesseean, had "the courage of his opinions" and had been conspicuous as one of the few and faithful, who at the home of Hugh Lawson White, adhered to Martin Van Buren as Andrew Jackson's lineal successor. Afterwards he was a Paymaster in the United States Army. Probably his appointment to the office of Confederate States Commissioner was more due to two of his qualifications than to anything else. These were, his great zeal for "the South," according to a current phrase, "in its contest for its rights," and his understood inflexibility of will. There were members of the Bar who thought his knowledge of the Law to be deficient, and his adversaries attributed brusqeness and austerity to his judicial manner. On the other hand, his political friends commended his performance of duty to the Government he served with such full and ardent sympathy. No one could complain of him for want of diligence and energy as a worker.

A large number of political offenders were arrested. "Union talk" became a more serious misdemeanor. The common jail was filled up rapidly. Some prisoners were sent to Alabama for confinement. One of these was the Hon. Mr. Pickens, State Senator from the counties of Blount and Sevier. He had been already designated by name as a victim, in a postscript from Secretary of War, J. P. Benjamin, to Col. Wood. His son had been of the party that unsuccessfully assailed Strawberry Plains bridge, and was there wounded, but not mortally, evaded the soldiers who pursued him until his injury was healed, then escaped into Kentucky and joined the Federal army. Senator Pickens was a person of superior character and greatly esteemed by the people. He did not long survive, a captive and exile at Tuscaloosa, Alabama; and when death had released him at one and the same moment from "this prison of the body" and from a Confederate jail, his wife, too, sickened and went to the higher freedom into which his spirit passed.

A number of persons had been arrested at different places, who were accused of having shared in the assaults upon bridges or their destruction. Col. Ledbetter, in command of the Post at Greeneville (reputed to be a native of the State of Maine), "stuck in the letter" of Secretary Benjamin's instructions that "all such (prisoners) as can be

EXECUTIONS.

identified in having been engaged in bridge-burning are to be tried summarily by drum-head court-martial, and if found guilty, executed on the spot by hanging," and also " to leave their bodies hanging in the vicinity of the burned bridges." In consequence, two men—Hensie and Fry—were hung at Greeneville by Col. Ledbetter's immediate authority and without delay. Their bodies, instead of being quartered and distributed abroad after an old English custom, were left suspended for four days near the railroad track. In that exposure, they seem to have been less of a terror to Union men of the vicinity, than objects of merry observation to railway passengers. Had not the executions been so hasty, it might have been discovered, in time to save Fry's life, that not he, but another person of the same surname, was the real offender in the case.

Among the many prisoners at Knoxville, were some under like accusation with the two hung at Greeneville: but proceedings against them were more deliberate. They were tried by a court-martial, organized under Gen. Carroll, of Middle Tennessee, successor of Col. Wood at the Post, and by common repute of dissipated habits. For nearly one month, Wm. G. Brownlow was an inmate of the jail. He states that at the time he was cast into it, the prisoners numbered about one hundred and fifty; that on the lower floor where he was kept, there was not room for all to lie down at one time, and therefore they stood on their feet and rested alternately; that the only article of furniture in the building was a dirty wooden bucket, from which the prisoners drank water with a tin cup; and that their food consisted of meat and bread, scantily supplied, sometimes half raw, sometimes burned. To the truth of his description, in the main, there is extant, corroborative testimony. Some prisoners shook his hand silently with tears; some faces lighted with joy to see him; some manifested a sense of humiliation wrought by their condition, and many were depressed in spirits. A few notes taken from his diary in jail will show the nature and extent of the work carried on by the military towards suspected and convicted Union people:

SATURDAY, Dec. 7.—This morning forty of our number, under a heavy military escort, were sent off to Tuscaloosa. Thirty-one others arrived to take their places from Cocke, Greene and Jefferson Counties. They bring us tales of woe from their respective counties as to the treatment of Union men and Union families, by the * * * * cavalry in the rebellion. They are taking all the fine horses they can find and appropriating them to their own use; they are entering houses, breaking open drawers and chests, seizing money, blankets and whatever they can use.

MONDAY, Dec. 9.—More prisoners arrived this evening. Twenty-eight are in from Jefferson and Cocke counties.

WEDNESDAY, Dec. 11.—Fifteen more prisoners came in to-day from Greene and Hancock counties, charged with having been armed as Union men and accustomed to drill.

THURSDAY, Dec. 12.—Fifteen of our prisoners were started to Tuscaloosa this morning to remain there as prisoners of war. They had no trial, but were sent upon their admission that they had been found in arms as Union men, preparing to defend themselves against the assaults and robberies of the so-called Confederate cavalry. Poor fellows! They hated to go.

FRIDAY, DEC. 13.—Three more prisoners in to-day from Hancock and Hawkins Counties. Charge as usual—Union men, attached to a company of Home Guards.

IMPRISONMENTS.

Saturday, Dec. 14.—Three more prisoners from the upper counties were brought in to-day. They speak of the outrages perpetrated by these rebel troops, and of their murderous spirit.

Sunday, Dec. 15.—Started thirty-five of our lot to Tuscaloosa to be held during the war. Levi Trewhitt, an able lawyer, but an old man, will never get back.* His sons came up to see him, but were denied the privilege. Dr. Hunt, from the same county of Bradley, has also gone. His wife came sixty miles to see him, and came to the jail door, but was refused admittance.

Monday, Dec. 16.—Brought in Dr. Wells and Col. Morris, of Knox County, two clever men and good citizens. Their offence is that they are Union men, first, and next they voted and electioneered as old Whigs, * * * * years ago.

Tuesday, Dec. 17.—Brought in a Union man from Campbell County to-day, leaving behind six small children, and their mother dead. This man's offence is holding out for the Union. To-night two brothers named Walker, came in from Hawkins County, charged with having "talked Union talk."

Wednesday, Dec. 18.—Discharged sixty prisoners to-day who had been in prison from three to five weeks—taken through mistake, as was said, there being nothing against them. Business suffering at home—unlawfully seized upon and thrust into this uncomfortable jail—they are now turned out.

Thursday, Dec. 19.—To-night twelve more Union prisoners were brought in from lower East Tennessee, charged with belonging to Col. Clift's regiment of Union men, arming and drilling to go over to Kentucky and join the Federal army.

Saturday, Dec. 21.—Took out five of the prisoners brought here from the Clift expedition—liberated them by their agreeing to go into the rebel army. Their dread of Tuscaloosa induced them to go into service. They (the Confederate authorities) have offered this chance to all, and only sent off those who stubbornly refused.

Sunday, Dec. 22.—Brought in old man Wampler, a Dutchman seventy years of age, from Greene County, charged with being an "Andrew Johnson man and talking Union talk."

Friday, Dec. 27.—Harrison Self, an industrious, honest and heretofore peaceable man, a citizen of Greene County, was notified this morning that he was to be hanged at four o'clock, p. m. His daughter, a noble girl, modest and neatly attired, came in this morning to see him. Heart-broken and bowed down under a fearful weight

*He died in prison.

of sorrow, she entered his iron cage and they embraced each other most affectionately. My God, what a sight! What an affecting scene! (The prisoners looking on were moved to tears.) But her short limit to remain with her father expired, and she came out weeping bitterly—shedding burning tears. Requesting me to write a dispatch for her and sign her name to it, I took out my pencil and a slip of paper and wrote the following:

KNOXVILLE, Dec. 27, 1861.

Hon. Jefferson Davis:

My father, Harrison Self, is sentenced to hang at four o'clock this evening, on a charge of bridge-burning. As he remains my earthly all and all my hopes of happiness centre in him, I implore you to pardon him.

ELIZABETH SELF.

With this dispatch the poor girl hurried off to the office two or three hundred yards from the jail; and about two o'clock in the afternoon the answer came to General Carroll telling him not to allow Self to be hung. Self was turned out of the cage into the jail with the rest of us, and looks as if he had gone through a long spell of sickness. But what a thrill of joy ran through the heart of that noble girl! Self is to be confined, as I understand, during the war. This is hard upon an innocent man; but it is preferable to hanging."

There follows in the diary an account of an interview—at first refused, and finally granted for twenty minutes—between a small farmer from Sevier County, bearing the name of Madison Cate, and his wife—she with a babe in her arms, and the prisoner too ill with a fever to stand on his feet, but lying on the floor in one corner of the jail with "a bit of old carpeting" for a bed and "some sort of bundle as a pillow."

During the month of December three of the prisoners, having been convicted by court-martial of bridge-burning, were executed by hanging. One of these, C. A. Haun, was a young man, but the head of a small family. He was hanged alone on the eleventh day, and maintained a courageous spirit on the scaffold. The other two, whose name was Harmon, were father and son. They died after the same method six days later, and protested their innocence to the end. Whether for the sake of economy or for some other unknown reason, the military authorities had not provided for the solemn occasion suitable means for ushering more than one of the two souls into eternity at a time. The omission is to be deplored, as it left room for imputing to the managers of the pitiful spectacle a singular want of humanity in compelling the father to witness his son's ignominious death, while awaiting his own.*

* See Appendix Note J.

CHAPTER X.

REIGN OF TERROR—A NOTED PATRIOT—HIS PAINFUL EXPERIENCES AND FINAL DELIVERANCE—A REFUGEE'S PERILOUS JOURNEY—CONSCRIPTION—CAPTURE OF FLEEING MEN.

> "Go, say, I sent thee forth to purchase honor;
> And not the king exiled thee. Or suppose
> Devouring pestilence hangs in our air,
> And thou art flying to a fresher clime.
> Look, what thy soul holds dear, imagine it
> To lie that way thou goest, not whence thou comest."
> SHAKSPEARE, *Richard II.*

FOR a considerable time, including that in which these trials, imprisonments and executions occurred, there was a reign of terror over Union people. The vigilance of the party in power subjected even citizens of better social position to arraignment for slight or insufficient reasons. To have been born in a Northern State was *prima facie* a ground of suspicion, unless the person were a pronounced friend of the rebellion. Equally so was the fact that one had been a conspicuous Unionist before the secession of Tennessee, more especially if his position in reference to public affairs generally, was prominent. Dr. R. H. Hodsden, of Sevier, and Representative of that county and Knox, was hunted for, but evaded the search until he was induced to believe that he would not

HON. C. F. TRIGG.

be harshly treated. He then surrendered himself to his pursuers, and upon giving security for his good conduct and declaring his submission to the Confederate Government, he was released from custody. Col. Connelly F. Trigg, chairman of the chief committee in the Union Convention at Knoxville and Greeneville, of May and June, feared with good reason that he would be arrested. He therefore made his escape speedily but with difficulty through the mountains into Kentucky. Other lawyers, known to have been friends of the Union, were admitted to the practice of their profession before Judge Humpl reys, upon their submission to the Confederate Government.

During this time, General Zolicoffer, whose camp was on the Kentucky border, made a visit to Knoxville, and by his direction, as it was understood, the soldiers who guarded the town and also the requirement of an oath of allegiance for ingress and egress, were withdrawn. The general condition of things, however, was so disturbing and offensive to Union men throughout East Tennessee that their departure from the country became more frequent. Among their leaders who had not yet gone away, the person most obnoxious to the Confederate authorities was the Rev. Wm. G. Brownlow. He had been from the beginning of their *de facto* government in the State a thorn in their flesh. Through his weekly journal, the *Whig*, he had annoyed them with complaints of acts of oppression and violence, and a bold use of the freedom of the press, which left no room for doubt of his loyalty at heart to the United States, yet gave no occasion for his arrest and punishment. These ills threatened him so strongly about the middle of October, that he felt compelled to suspend the publication of his newspaper. In the number issued on the 21st of that month, he informed its readers of the indictment impending over him before the grand jury of the Confederate court at Nashville, and that he could probably "go free by taking the oath" which the authorities were "administering to other Union men," but his "settled purpose" was "not to do any such thing." He spoke of "the wanton outrages upon right and liberty" suffered by the people of East Tennessee "for their devotion to the Constitution and laws of the Government handed down to them by their fathers and the liberties secured to them by a war of seven long years of gloom, poverty and trial;" and concluded with his expectation of "exchanging with proud satisfaction the editorial chair and the sweet endearments of home for a cell in the prison or the lot of an exile." Both these were not far distant from him. Entreated by friends to be absent for a time, he went with Rev. Jas. Cumming, an aged Methodist minister, into Blount County.

Informed that Confederate cavalry were searching for him with deadly intent, he and others—members of the Legislature, preachers and farmers—fled into the Smoky Mountains that separate North Carolina and East Tennessee. There, in Tuckaleeche and Wear's coves, they were encamped for days in concealment, but were at length driven by close pursuit to disperse in pairs, and he, with Rev. W. T. Dowell, went to a friend's house six miles from Knoxville. From thence Brownlow addressed a letter on November 22, by Col. John Williams to Gen. W. H. Carroll, asserting his innocence of all complicity in the bridge burnings; that he had kept the pledge he with other leading Union men had given Gen. Zolicoffer, "to counsel peace," and he claimed protection under the civil law. To this, Gen. Carroll, on November 28, replied that Mr. Brownlow should meet with no personal violence by returning to his home, and if he could establish what he had said by letter, he should have every opportunity to do so before the civil tribunal, were it necessary: *Provided*, he had committed no act that would make it necessary for the military law to take cognizance. Gen. Crittenden had succeeded to the chief command at Knoxville, and to him, eight days before the above named letter of Gen. Carroll, the following was written:

CONFEDERATE STATES OF AMERICA,
WAR DEPARTMENT, RICHMOND, Nov. 20, 1861.

To Major General Crittenden:

DEAR SIR—I have been asked to grant a passport for Brownlow to leave the State of Tennessee. He is said to have secreted himself, fearing violence to his person, and to be anxious to depart from the State.

I cannot give him a formal passport, though I would greatly prefer seeing him on the other side of our lines as an avowed enemy. I wish, however, to say that I would be glad to learn that he has left Tennessee; and I have no objection to interpose to his leaving if you are willing to let him pass.

Yours, truly,
J. P. BENJAMIN,
Secretary of War.

This advice was obeyed by the transmission of the following:

> HEADQUARTERS, KNOXVILLE, TENN., Dec. 4, 1861.
>
> W. G. BROWNLOW, ESQ : The Major General commanding directs me to say that upon calling at his headquarters within twenty-four hours, you can get a passport into Kentucky, accompanied by a military escort, the route to be designated by Gen. Crittenden.
>
> I am, Sir, very respectfully, your obedient servant,
>
> A. S. CUNNINGHAM,
> Acting Adj't General.

Before the expiration of the allotted time, Mr. Brownlow, accompanied by the Hon. John Baxter —who had originally applied at Richmond to Secretary Benjamin, for the passport—reported in person to General Crittenden. It was then arranged that he should depart for Kentucky on the 7th, in charge of Capt. Gillespie and cavalry company. But on the 6th he was arrested by the marshal upon a warrant issued by Commissioner Reynolds, and based upon the affidavit of District Attorney Ramsey, that Brownlow was a traitor to the Confederate States. Application to bail the prisoner was made by his friends and a large sum in good bond was offered, but these were refused, and he was sent to jail. In it he was confined until the last of December, when upon representation of his dangerous illness to Capt. Monserrat, then Commandant of the Post, made by his family physician, Dr. O. F. Hill, he was removed to his own house. The District Attorney had the case of the prisoner taken up in court, and read to the Commissioner a letter from Secretary Benjamin to the Attorney of some length, personally historical and explanatory, concerning the promise of a passport to the offender, upon his surrender. It concluded with the words:

> Under all the circumstances, therefore, if Brownlow is exposed to harm from his arrest, I shall deem the honor of the Government so far compromitted as to consider it my duty to urge on the President a pardon for any offense of which he may be found guilty; and I repeat the expression of my regret that he was prosecuted, however evident may be his guilt.

Thereupon the District Attorney entered a *nolle-prosequi* in the case, and Commissioner Reynolds ordered the prisoner's discharge. He was instantly arrested by the military authorities, and a guard of soldiers placed around his house day and night. For the greater part of January and February his bodily illness continued, partly owing no doubt to mental anxiety and troubles in the midst of enemies, some of whom cordially hated and annoyed him. From the threatenings that surrounded him, the apprehensions they naturally awakened, and the vexations of his life in custody, he was delivered by the obedience of Major Monserrat to an order by telegraph from the Richmond Secretary of War, authorizing him "to send Brownlow out of Tennessee." On the third of March, the irrepressible friend of the Union departed on his journey for another and, certainly for him a better country, than that in which he sojourned and where he had with singular determination and zeal waged an angry contest against odds. Defeated at home, he left it with strong hope of the coming time when the cause which he had deeply at heart should be there victorious and he among the victors. His departure at the time, and in the manner adopted, could not do otherwise than afford a sense of relief not only to him and his friends, but also to many of his enemies. In this latter class were some who would have been gratified had he been sent to jail at Tuscaloosa or even to the gallows, for their passions against him as the persistent "very head and front" of offence to them, were kindled to white heat. And the *Register* of the town expressed their mind, in declaring the action of the Secretary of War as "worse than a crime—a blunder," and that the authorities had "been outwitted and over-reached diplomatically" by giving a "pledge to convey Brownlow within the Hessian lines." Besides, they feared that the results to the Confederate supremacy in East Tennessee of his influence and work north of the State, would be as that journal predicted, disastrous. It was with delays and difficulties he reached Nashville; but after a journey of two hundred miles, requiring twelve days, on the fifteenth of March he was delivered by his military Confederate escort within the Federal lines at that city. There he was heartily welcomed. Among those who greeted him were his former East Tennessee compatriots, Andrew Johnson, then Military Governor of the State, Horace Maynard and Connelly F. Trigg. They and he were glad to meet again on soil of the United States where, under its protection, they were free.

For a long time previous, less conspicuous Union men had been leaving East Tennessee for Kentucky in smaller or larger companies. The stream of departure was sometimes feeble, at others strong, but always continuous. Among those who left in the earlier part of that time was R. L. Stanford, M. D., of Sullivan County. His compulsory expatriation resembled that of many that occurred. On his return to East Tennessee, a Surgeon of the United States Army under General Burnside, in September, 1863, he gave substantially a narrative of his escape that shows the dangers to single refugees:

In 1861 his Union sentiments made him very obnoxious to many of his neighbors. One day, returning home from visits to patients, he found on approaching it, that he had to pass through an array of armed men on both sides of the way. He braced up his nerves and rode between the threatening lines with his hat off and bowing to the right and left as he proceeded. No one of his enemies, who were also his neighbors, was willing to take the responsibility of being the first to fire upon him; and unhurt, he passed the gauntlet. That night he concluded, from written warnings, that it was prudent he should obey the order given him to leave the country. In his journey next day to Kentucky by way of Cumberland Gap, he was accompanied by Rev. Mr. M., a Methodist minister. At night they halted at a wayside inn, north of the Clinch Mountains, where a few Confederate officers soon arrived. One of them (Col. David Cummings) and Dr. Stanford being acquaintances, they held a friendly conversation while imbibing moderately of the drink, stronger than water, set before them by the landlord.

"Doctor," said the Colonel, "let me ask where you are going?"

"To tell you the truth, Colonel," replied the Doctor, "I am going over the mountains to buy some cattle of these Kentuckians to feed our people."

During the colloquy Colonel C. made a significant motion to his fellow-officer, not unobserved by the watchful refugee. The Methodist minister being of a timid nature, had meanwhile taken a seat at the farther end of the long front porch, with his hat pulled over his ears to avoid recognition. Soon night fell, supper was announced, and while it went forward Dr. Stanford, feigning illness, rose from the table and went down the road he had just traveled until a covert of bushes was reached. He knew that the two Confederate officers would shortly pass by on their way from Cumberland Gap to Bean's Station in the great valley of East Tennessee, and from weary waiting in concealment he was at length relieved by the sound of their horses' feet approaching. When arrived opposite the spot where he hid, they halted, and the owner of a cabin across the way obeyed their summons to its door. Frightened at first by the thought that he was about to be discovered, he soon dismissed all anxiety upon over-hearing the conversation that ensued between Col. Cummings and the man of the house, to whom the former gave a letter for delivery to the army messenger who would pass by the next morning to Cumberland Gap.

At a very early hour the next day, the two refgees resumed their journey. When they were entirely beyond hearing upon the road, the physician said to the minister: " I think it probable that Col. Cummings has left a letter to be sent to the Gap for our arrest there. If the messenger carrying it overtakes us on the way, I shall instantly shoot him." At that early period of the war, people generally were unaccustomed to the pre-meditated destruction of human life, and some of them at least were slow to think of it as wearing any complexion but that of bloody murder. It is not surprising, therefore, that the face of the Christian minister, on hearing the deadly intention of his companion, should have lost its usual color. " He turned as white as a sheet."

Arrived at Cumberland Gap without adventure, Dr. Stanford met with a Confederate Lieutenant—his personal friend—who had joined the army under constraint. The young man, knowing the mind of the refugee, gave him in conversation without the camp and under the pledge of secrecy, the word and sign by which he might pass the sentries on the road over the Gap.* The minister earnestly dissuaded him from attempting to cross the mountain, and failing in this effort, lay sleepless throughout the night, tossed with fears of ills that would befall them on the morrow. Breakfast over,

---

* NOTE.—The youthful officer was soon after killed in battle for the Confederacy.

the Doctor rode unconcernedly on his way without any interference from the sentinels, while the minister, abandoning the enterprise, stood and watched his companion's progress in ascending the mountain gap.

Once safely beyond interruption, the refugee put spurs to his horse and rode swiftly forward. By and by, with the mountain fairly left behind, he checked his horse and fell into reflections upon his home—his wife—his children. Should he ever see them again? Perhaps not—certainly not soon—probably not for years. And then, what would be his personal future? The perils which ordinarily attend human life are doubly increased to one adventuring as he was among strangers at a time when the whole country was involved in violent conflict. Gathering together the reins that hung loosely on his horse's neck, and lifting up his head he saw just before him a company of armed men. "Ah, then," was his thought, "I am to be foiled after all, and taken back a prisoner to the Gap." Rallying courage, he rode forward, asked for a drink of water, and was told to help himself with a gourd from the spring near by. The men looked at him with curious and suspicious eyes. One of them said to him bluntly:

"What are you: Union man or Confederate?"

"Now, gentlemen," said he, "that's hardly a fair question. As you are decidedly in the majority, it seems only right that you should first tell me what you are."

He was answered with a smile, but was also assured that their question could not be met with such evasion. He then boldly said he was for the Union.

"So are we," they replied. "These rebels have come and taken possession of the Gap, and we Kentuckians have met here to see what they are after."

From that friendly encounter the refugee went forward without molestation to his journey's end, volunteered in the service of the United States army and was appointed a surgeon.

On the 20th of January, 1862, the battle of Fishing Creek, or Mill's Springs, Kentucky, was fought and the victory won by General Thomas, of the United States army, produced a strong, disturbing sensation among the Confederates at Knoxville. For this there were good reasons. The battlefield was not far distant; it was the first fight of any importance that was at all near the town; the Confederate chief Zolicoffer and his subordinate Generals, Crittenden and Carroll, had been successively in command at Knoxville, and many of their troops had been stationed there at different times. Upon their defeat, they went according to the rule with Buonaparte's soldiers upon their defeat at Waterloo: *sauve qui peut;* and some of them in the pell-mell flight were not slow in reaching Knoxville. The tidings they carried created intense excitement, anger and fear. At first the blame of the defeat was attributed chiefly to Gen. Crittenden and his inferior in office, Gen. Carroll, both of whom, it was alleged, were drunk on the eve of the occasion. The story ran, that Zolicoffer, who was slain in the fight, had opposed the attack upon the Federal army, and that being overruled, he had entered on it reluctantly. All the reproaches visited upon Crittenden and Carroll grew out of, or were plausibly justified by, their reputation for using spirituous liquors to excess. When the agitation subsided, the Fishing Creek tales were found to be untrue. Gen. Crittenden, from being cursed as an inebriate and almost suspected as a traitor, became an object of friendly sympathy as a victim of ill luck in war. Popular opinion is always capricious and prone to undue elation or depression in prosperous or adverse circumstances. The wrath to which calamities move the thoughtless and passionate must be vented upon somebody, and it is apt to turn upon him through whose well known frailty the calamity may easily have been incurred. The intemperate man has to suffer for a time at least, on occasions of ill to which he is a party, from the quick presumption in people's minds that his vicious indulgence stands as an open door to all blunder and disaster.

The fall of Fort Donelson on February 1, 1862, had been followed by a panic at Nashville that was ludicrous in some of its scenes and incidents. It spread, feebler and with less extravagant display, to other places in Tennessee. The small migration of families to Georgia from Knoxville immediately on the heels of the disaster was really needless, for the Fort was more than two hundred miles distant, with the Cumberland Mountains intervening. Governor Isham G. Harris and the Legislature felt compelled to flee from Nashville. He took up his residence at Memphis and assembled there a quorum of the Legislature, which passed an act calling the State militia between the ages of eighteen and forty-five into active military service. The Governor took steps promptly to enforce the law, but in East Tennessee the preliminary measures were not very effective. In many instances the people refused to attend muster at their regimental parade grounds, where, indeed, they had not been used for many years to assemble for military training. It was not long before many men sought refuge in Kentucky from the conscription. They left their homes in companies of ten, fifty or a hundred, starting at night, sometimes concealing themselves during the day and resuming their journey under cover of the darkness, and at length passed over the border, rejoicing that they were free from the strong hand that would force them to fight against the United States. With the joy they felt at their deliverance was mingled an earnest purpose to return, attended by powerful friends, to their beloved land and restore it to the nation.

A body of refugees numbering six or seven hundred, assembled early one day at Blain's Cross Roads, Grainger County, and took up their line of march for the mountains on the northern frontier. More than half safely escaped from the Confederate cavalry which pursued them, but over three hundred, who had in the morning been unintentionally separated from their companions, were taken prisoners. Cowardice was imputed to them by ready censors for surrendering at once to a force numerically inferior. But they were surrounded by their enemies in an open field—they were comparatively unarmed—had no able and efficient leader nor any military training—and were mostly of immature age. As these young men, with weary eyes and feet, were marched under guard through the streets of Knoxville on their way to jail in the South, for the crime of trying to escape enforced service in arms against the United States, an observer who loved the Union might be pardoned if his throat choked with a throb of pity from his heart and his cheek flushed hot with righteous indignation at the violence. How many of the prisoners, most of whom were only just old enough to be included in the conscript law, ever saw their homes again it is impossible to say. Probably some died in a Georgia prison or on the way to it. Some probably in utter hopelessness were persuaded to wear the grey, and died in the Confederate service. Some may have escaped at one time or another to within the Union lines. It is doubtful if more than a few of them ever returned.

"Parson Brownlow," as he was often called, made this entry in his Diary for 1862, while he was in prison:

SATURDAY, MARCH 1.—Thirty Union men, well dressed, were arrested by the cavalry who found them leaving for Kentucky to

ESCAPE OF REFUGEES.

avoid the draft ordered by Governor Harris. Seventeen of them agreed to join the Confederate army to keep out of jail.

But a Sabbath past they brought twenty Union men out of jail, arms tied behind them with strong ropes, and marched them with bayonets to the depot, cursing and insulting them, and sent them off to Tuscaloosa to be held as prisoners of war." * * * To have seen them coming out of the jail yard and entering the street would have brought tears from the eyes.

Brownlow, two days afterwards, started for Nashville, and the work of arresting refugees had then only begun.

Mr. Edward J. Sanford, at the time a young man, was, as he is now, a citizen of Knoxville. His narrative of the escape made by him and others through the mountains, from the conscript law, is interesting in itself.* It is still more so, as illustrating the privations, dangers and sufferings through which men of like principles and decision with him, had to pass at that time, in going from East Tennessee to a land of liberty, under law and in harmony with their conscience and will. There did not appear to be any hope of deliverance coming to them from without. It is true that early in March, 1862, the 2nd Regiment of East Tennessee Infantry, accompanied by one company each of the 1st Regiment, East Tennessee Infantry, and Monday's Kentucky Cavalry, all commanded by Col. J. P. T. Carter, adventured from Kentucky through Big Creek Gap in the Cumberland Mountains into Campbell County, East Tennessee. They found the Gap blockaded by the Confederate troops, but managed to pass it, attacked a force at Sharp's Church in the neighborhood and routed it, wound-

* See Appendix: Note K,

ing, killing and capturing a considerable number of the men. The raiders' cavalry went down the valley to Jacksborough, where they encountered the scouting party of Capt. James Gibson. In the fight that ensued, Capt. Gibson was slain and Capt. Winstead, of the Sappers and Miners, was taken prisoner, but no important results followed the adventure. Col. Carter without delay retreated into Kentucky, and at that date no other like military expedition was even expected.

CHAPTER XI.

GENERALS KIRBY SMITH, J. E. JOHNSON AND BRAGG—REFUGEES INVITED HOME BY PROCLAMATION — MRS. BROWNLOW, HER CHILDREN AND MRS. MAYNARD EXILED—GENERAL CONDITION OF THINGS RESULTING FROM SECESSION.

> "Faults are easier look'd in, than redress'd:
> Men running with eager violence,
> At the first view of errors, fresh in quest;
> As they, to rid an inconvenience,
> Stick not to raise a mischief in the stead,
> Which after mocks their weak improvidence.
> And therefore do not make your own sides bleed,
> To pick at others."
> DANIEL.

IN the spring of 1862, the authority and power of the United States throughout East Tennessee, were thoroughly supplanted by those of the Confederate States. Any benefits, however, which might result from the substitution to that region and all its people did not presently appear. There was no violence going on within its borders, except that inflicted by Confederate soldiers; and the actual strife between hostile armies was far away. The general condition of things was most deplorable. As a large majority of the able-bodied men had fled or were fleeing under the impulse of patriotism and duty to another State, that they might stand beneath the folds and uphold the staff of the American flag, many fields were left untilled. The fruits and grains gathered in by farmers from their labors in 1861, had been or were being consumed by the military who occupied the country, and no just expectations were indulged of an ordinary harvest in 1862. The outlook, indeed, in every respect of the people's welfare was discouraging. One conclusion it favored—that secession, as a remedy for real or imaginary ills, resulted for the time in greater evils.

About this date Gen. E. Kirby Smith was appointed to the supreme command at Knoxville. He had been at the battle of Manassas, and was reported as wounded, but not seriously. He was reputed to have firmness, decision of will and other qualities of character required by his office, and also of as great humanity and kindness as consist with the vigorous conduct of war. A marked contrast in his favor was observed between his general bearing at the town and that of some Confederate officers who had chief command there. In scholarly attainments he surpassed them all, in personal morals he was without reproach, and his manners were quiet and unpretentious.

It will bear mention in this connection that two distinguished Generals of the Confederate army—Joseph E. Johnson and Braxton Bragg—briefly tarried on their way at different times in the town. There were little incidents in their respective visits that afterwards entered into the talk of the citizens and were thought to be characteristic.

Gen. Johnson ranked very high in people's esteem for both modesty and ability, and had the credit of being a natural, as contra-distinguished from an artificial, man. During his stay he was called on by an aged colored woman who had nursed him in childhood. Some men would have been indifferent or repellent to the hearty greetings she gave him in presence of stern warriors: but her words of love and blessing made way through his coat of mail, and to the surprise of by-standers, filled his eyes with tears.

Gen. Bragg, from his hotel, summoned a Swiss tailor, who was of like political sympathies, to come and take his measure for a new suit of clothes. The civilian, perhaps thinking the call too peremptory, or desiring to honor his own vocation, declined to obey. The officer's demand for the tailor's attendance was then repeated, accompanied with the statement that "General Bragg never went out to be measured for clothing." The undismayed citizen again refused, and bade the messenger say that he "never went out to measure people for clothing." And the warrior who commanded regiments and brigades of soldiers was compelled to surrender to one man, whose only weapons were a pair of shears, a needle and a tailor's goose! *"Inter arma, leges silent," sed non sartori.*

Gen. Kirby Smith had too clear intelligence not to see that it was expedient or even necessary to do whatever was possible to recover the losses already incurred and to prevent any further losses in the able-bodied male population of East Tennessee, and to promote the greater cultivation of lands. Therefore, on April 18th, 1862, was published from headquarters, Knoxville, this

PROCLAMATION.

The Major General commanding this Department, charged with the enforcement of martial law, believing that many of its citizens have been misled into the commission of treasonable acts through ignorance of their duties and obligations to their State, and that many have actually fled across the mountains and joined our enemies under the persuasion and misguidance of supposed friends, but designing enemies, hereby proclaims:

First. That no person so misled, who comes forward, declares his error, and takes the oath to support the Constitution of the State and of the Confederate States, shall be molested or punished on account of past acts or words.

Second. That no person so persuaded and misguided as to leave his home and join the enemy, who shall return within thirty days of the date of this proclamation, acknowledge his error, and take an oath to support the Constitution of the State and of the Confederate States, shall be molested or punished on account of past acts or words.

After thus announcing his disposition to treat with the utmost clemency those who have been led away from the true path of patriotic duty, the Major General commanding furthermore declares his determination henceforth to employ all the elements at his disposal for the protection of the lives and property of the citizens of East Tennessee—whether from the incursions of the enemy or the irregularities of his own troops—and for the suppression of all treasonable practices.

He assures all citizens engaged in cultivating their farms, that he will protect them in their rights, and that he will suspend the militia draft under the State laws, that they may raise crops for consumption in the coming year. He invokes the zealous co-operation of the authorities and of all good people, to aid him in his endeavors.

The courts of criminal jurisdiction will continue to exercise their functions, save the issuance of writs of *habeas corpus*. Their writs will be served and their decrees executed by the aid of the military, when necessary.

When the courts fail to preserve the peace or punish offenders against the laws, those objects will be attained through the action of military tribunals and the exercise of the force of his command.
(Signed)   E. KIRBY SMITH,
Maj. Gen. Comm'dg Dep't E. T.

Five days after the issuance of the above proclamation there was published as follows:

TO THE DISAFFECTED PEOPLE OF EAST TENNESSEE.

HEADQUARTERS DEPARTMENT OF EAST TENNESSEE,
OFFICE PROVOST MARSHAL, April 23, 1862.

The undersigned, in executing martial law in this Department, assures those interested who have fled to the enemy's lines, and who are actually in their army, that he will welcome their return to their homes and their families: they are offered amnesty and protection, if they come to lay down their arms and act as loyal citizens, within the thirty days given them by Major General E. Kirby Smith to do so.

At the end of that time, those failing to return to their homes and accept the amnesty thus offered, and provide for and protect their wives and children in East Tennessee, will have them sent to their care in Kentucky, or beyond the Confederate States' line, at their own expense.

All that leave after this date, with a knowledge of the above acts, their families will be sent after them.

The women and children must be taken care of by husbands and fathers, either in East Tennessee or in the Lincoln Government."
(Signed)   W. M. CHURCHWELL,
Col. and Provost Marshal.

It is obvious from the preceding documents, that the Confederate authorities were uneasy over the prospect of a diminished harvest from the soil the ensuing season; and not only for political reasons, but to avoid a scarcity of food because of the departure of many farmers, they would be glad to have them return home.

The men thus invited to return, made no answer from beyond the mountains which walled in their beloved land on the north. It was like whistling to the winds to call them back. And they continued to go until they were thirty thousand strong —wearing the blue. As to the threat that after thirty days, unless they recanted their faith in the Union, came home and swore to be loyal to the Confederate States, their wives and children should be sent after them at their own expense, it was a mere *brutum fulmen*, and if it ever reached their ears they treated it with indifference or perhaps with derision. Its fullfilment belonged to the category of human impossibilities. The expulsion and march of an army of women and children from East Tennessee over mountains and rivers into Kentucky who could be counted by tens of thousands, would have sent a thrill of amazement akin to horror throughout enlightened Christendom. It is not to be supposed, however, that the Confederate authorities intended to carry into effect the threat of such retaliation. Nor does it appear that the threat emanated from or was approved by the Major General commanding the Department of East Tennessee. He did, however, authorize the order of the Provost Marshal for the compulsory removal from Knoxville *via* Norfolk, Virginia, beyond the Confederate lines of the wives and families of two prominent Union men —Hon. Horace Maynard and Rev. William G. Brownlow. In those cases special reason for the harsh measure was assigned. The following letter was sent from headquarters addressed to—

Mrs. W. G. Brownlow, Knoxville:

MADAM—By Major General E. Kirby Smith I am directed most

HON. HORACE MAYNARD.

respectfully to inform you that you and your children are not held as hostages for the good behavior of your husband, as represented by him in a speech at Cincinnati recently, and that yourself and family will be required to pass beyond the Confederate States' line in thirty-six hours from this date. Passports will be granted you from this office.

     Very respectfully,
       W. M. CHURCHWELL,
        Colonel and Provost Marshal.

April 21, 1862.

At Mrs. Brownlow's immediate written request the time of departure was extended a few days, and on April 25th, she and her family, being a party of four adults and four children, were conducted by way of Norfolk out of the Confederacy. With these exiles were sent Mrs. Horace Maynard and family, whose expatriation could not of course be covered by the plea of Mr. Brownlow's utterances in Cincinnati: but although Mr. Maynard was not inculpated by that alleged offence, or a like one from his own lips, he was highly obnoxious as a Union leader who had gone to the enemy.

Mrs. Brownlow was a native Tennesseean, and Mrs. Maynard, born in Massachusetts, had resided in the town for some twenty years. In the pending conflict their sympathies were naturally and properly with their husbands, but they had stood entirely aloof from active politics, and no charge of misdemeanor in word or deed was made against them. Mrs. Maynard, a lady of superior culture and fine sensibilities, was sickened in the enforced departure from her home by its excitement and worry, and a hemorrhage of her lungs ensued:

but her spirit was bravely equal to the emergency, and when the appointed hour came she was ready for the journey under military escort.

As the war advanced, shops and mercantile houses in some instances were closed, but as a rule, they kept open doors with diminished stocks. A few new shops were established and traders found employment not unprofitable. Prices gradually increased until they became very high. Many articles in frequent or habitual use by the people could not be had at any price, or if at all, only in the smallest quantities. Coffee, which formerly could be bought at from 14 to 16 cents a pound, became scarce soon after hostilities began, and before long sold at one dollar a pound. Salt, almost a necessary of life, could only be obtained with difficulty, and its price of $2\frac{1}{2}$ and 3 cents a pound, rose to 30 cents and more. Brown sugar advanced from $12\frac{1}{2}$ cents to 75 cents a pound. Common calicoes, before sold at $12\frac{1}{2}$ cents a yard, increased eight fold in price by retail. Men's ordinary apparel shared in the upward movement of values, especially shoes of all kinds, which sold by and by, for from ten to twenty dollars a pair, and boots, which went up to twenty dollars and more.

The great increase in prices of dry goods and groceries induced a corresponding advance by producers in those of grain, meat, poultry, vegetables and fruits. Provision for their own maintenance demanded of the farming class that what they had to sell should be valued higher.

At the beginning of the troubles gold and silver

passed out of general circulation. Next the notes of the various banks chartered by the State gradually disappeared. Numbers of people hoarded these notes as a provision for possible exigencies, and they were valued in exchange at twenty-five per cent. more than Confederate notes. The banks themselves were ready enough to pay out the latter notes to customers, and by doing this withdrew much of their own paper from circulation. Gold was sold for Confederate notes at a premium of one hundred per cent. or more.

By the necessities of the times the question of sustenance was of general consideration. As the rate of interest and salaries of civilians continued the same, they who depended for maintenance upon income from loans or upon stipends for regular services, suffered from the derangement in all affairs. Debtors who before had such strong reluctance to pay their just obligations, that their hearts fainted in the endeavor, became wholly metamorphosed. They manifested a cheerful zeal to settle their debts, which would not let them await the coming of the creditor. For they could pay in depreciated bank notes, or better still, Confederate notes were plentiful and could be used in liquidation. A citizen of well known loyalty to "the South," especially one of prominence, could probably refuse them in payment of debts, but such a refusal by others might lead to unpleasant consequences. It might diminish one's reputation as a friend of the Confederacy, or worse still, if that reputation were already damaged, subject him to the reproach visited upon all "Lincolnites, tories and traitors." Nevertheless, the pecuniary disadvantage of taking a depreciated currency, which was going down all the time, as a valid tender, was too plain to fail of its influence. The unwillingness and refusals of people to be paid in Confederate notes, at length attracted the attention of the authorities, and it was ordered, in the spring of 1862, that persons refusing to receive such notes should be held guilty of political offense and be punished accordingly. The order sufficed to correct the growing tendency, as no instance of an arraignment for violating it was publicly known.

The civil law courts were still held, but with imperfect sessions, except the County Court, which met regularly on the first Monday of each month. Justice, in a capacious robe, with bandaged eyes and a pair of balances in hand, had been thrust into the back-ground. And its imitation, dressed in regimentals, with stern visage and wielding a sharp sword, stood in the front. In the sphere of ordinary legal proceedings dullness reigned, but the Confederate tribunals and the courts martial derived a stiff business look, without any pleasant animation, from the trial of offenders for disloyalty or treasonable practices.

From an early period of the troubled conditions, the State Deaf Mute Asylum was appropriated to use as a hospital for sick soldiers. The climate in winter was too cold for those who came from Alabama and other Gulf States, and they suffered much from the inclemency of the weather in 1861 and 1862. The mortality in hospitals that winter was great—two or three patients dying daily for a considerable time.

After the battle of Fishing Creek, January, 1862, the buildings of East Tennessee University were taken by the military for the lodging of wounded men, and afterwards the Male Academy was turned by them into a guard house. These diversions of school property to uses of the army, seriously interfered of course with the work of educating boys and young men. And yet the loss incurred in that way was not very serious, because the number of students in the disordered state of things had severely diminished. The army had absorbed some of the older youth into its ranks, some borne on the fierce currents of excitement, drifted off one way or another, and many were demoralized from study by the abnormal social conditions. One of the University professors had been for years a most successful teacher of boys. He hailed from north of Mason and Dixon's line, and before the secession of Tennessee in June, 1861, had expressed his Union sentiments in letters to friends who dwelt in the *taboo-ed* region beyond the Ohio River. As the State was then still in the Union, all letters from it by mail should have been transmitted to their destination without previous disclosure of their contents, but this was forbidden by patriotic zeal for the Confederacy, to which the State was bound by a military league. Of the intercepted communications to a distance written by Union citizens, were some by the professor. Then there went to him in writing anonymous threats of personal indignity and injury, and the circumstances of the case appeared to justify the fears they excited in him. After seeking judicious advice and not being willing to contend with the wrath of his enemies, he shortly departed for Ohio and left goods and chattels behind him, which were afterwards seized and confiscated.

Another of the professors—a clergyman of the Presbyterian Church—became an officer in the Confederate army. Another, who was a native of the county, moved with fear of being forced to serve in that army, and loving the Union, fled the country to Washington and only returned upon the advent of Gen. Burnside into Knoxville. The President of the University—a clergyman of the Protestant Episcopal Church—thought that some such unwelcome advent would occur in 1862. In the earlier part of that year, therefore, he made a prudent arrangement with his associates to teach the few students who remained until the session's end, and departed for a quiet home in North Carolina. Not long afterwards the doors of the institution were closed to the work of education for four years. Schools for the instruction of children continued in the town to a limited extent, but their usefulness and success were lessened by the prevailing anxieties and excitements.

The public worship in the several Christian Churches was conducted without interruption. In several of them politics were introduced into the prayers to God or in the preaching to men from the pulpit, or in both. After Confederate troops occupied the place, the chaplain of a regiment would now and then preach in a church that was strongly in sympathy with the Confederacy. The pastor of one of the churches kept aloof in his sermons from the chief topic of the day, but often made the success of the Confederacy a subject of petition in his public devotions. The pastor of another was less reticent, and expressed his political sentiments with much warmth and frequency from the pulpit, in both prayers and sermons. The minister of a third church, in 1861 became involved in local strife connected with the great conflict of the time, to the partial hurt of his usefulness. His successor was a stranger, and adhered more closely to the usual line of clerical duty, but it was understood that he heartily sympathized with the friends of secession. They were largely in the majority among church-goers, and all these ministers were esteemed and beloved by the great body of their respective peoples. The war therefore, occasioned no break in the substantial unity of their churches, nor any material decrease in the attendance of worshippers. Than these, another church was less fortunate. Its rector entertained Union sentiments, to which some of its more influential families were strongly opposed. He was also in disagreement with the bishop of the diocese, not personally, but officially, as the latter had set forth in July, 1861, by request of the Diocesan Convention, a form of prayer for the success of the Confederacy which the rector felt he could not in good conscience use. The bishop, while manifesting all fatherly kindness to the non-conforming minister, decided that he could make no exception to the rule of obedience. He was then asked for and gave the rector a letter dimissory to Bishop Smith, of the Diocese of Kentucky, which was forwarded and accepted. The minister was disabled by an accident from following the letter in person as he intended, and the rectorship, which he had before resigned, was filled by a clergyman from the neighboring town of Loudon. The priest of the Roman Catholic Church was unknown in connection with the troubles. His successor at a later period, "Father Ryan," was quite a young man, of delicate physique, but of a ready mind, lively imagination and rhetorical power. He had espoused the cause of the Confederacy with fervid enthusiasm, and used his talents zealously in its behalf. His published poetical effusions were often inspired by devotion to the "Sunny South" and its flag. Sometimes they were filled with his thoughts of the wrongs it had suffered, and have been no little admired and praised by many of its friends. It showed the mastery of political over religious as well as other sympathies in the war, that among those who attended upon his discourses were men who in times of peace would not, because of their religious prejudices, enter the door of a Roman Catholic Church.

Many citizens, because of their political sympathy or distrust of the outcome, abstained from keeping actively along with the current of affairs through 1862 into 1863, under the reign at the locality of the Confederate. Government. They merely subsided into quiet and retirement. Deploring the country's condition and observing the progress of events with more or less interest, they yet gave their thoughts and time to ordinary duties, content to await whatever the future might develop. To people of truly Christian character, the habitual surroundings of pageantry, clamors and clashes of war were disagreeable: and for the promotion of a higher life in the soul, they turned to seek "water out of the rock of flint." Their religious principles became firmer and stronger, and they themselves more like their Master in the spirit of His mind. On the other hand, the vicious and profane were emboldened to greater wickedness, and the wicked dispositions of some could only be checked by military discipline. It is not to be disputed also, that some professed Christians were demoralized by the war and fell away from their uprightness. History repeats itself. The results just named are like those which have followed all great calamities to human society in the form of civil wars, pestilences and famines.

Evidently a revolution had not only been attempted politically, but was actually progressing in other respects. Its fruits thus far were so ill and sour as to confirm the opinion of some that it had better have been unborn or stifled in its birth; better that the evils which it was proposed to remedy had been patiently borne with, and so far as they really existed, peacefully removed. In the time to come, its life might be short or long, and its consequences prove it for better or worse, but one thing was certain: a most disagreeable change of present conditions had occurred. Old things had been displaced and new ones substituted. Citizens who preferred that the former order were restored, found their hopefulness to that end beset with discouragements. These very differently affected the minds of Union men. All along the way since the spring of 1861, they had been like an unorganized army retreating before a closely pursuing foe. Sooner or later, some had weakened and fallen; some had turned aside and lain down to sleep; some still trudged on, but lagged behind their companions. And all these had previously made up their minds to be captured. At length the number of staunch friends of the United States left by refugees through the mountains was largely diminished.

Among the country people there had been absolutely little submission of mind to the power over them as a *de jure* government, and the spirit of patriotic adventure was strong. In more than a few instances it incited them to toilsome and hazardous ridings over the mountains into Kentucky, and back again with news concerning the war which could not otherwise be had, except as it might be stintedly published from Richmond after being distilled in Confederate alembics. The presumption is, that as opportunity served, not only was general news carried by these messengers, but also valuable information relative to military situations and movements. Among Union women there were heroines in action, equal to their grandmothers in the first settlement of the land when the Indians were a terror. *

In April, 1862, tidings brought to East Tennessee of the battle of Corinth, like those elsewhere circulated at first in the South, were exaggerated. "The slaughter of the Yankees," as reported, "was enormous," and the number of Confederates killed and wounded was very small. Great rejoicings followed over the victory said to have been won by Gen. Albert Sidney Johnston, but these soon abated, for what reason Union citizens could not tell. They had their suspicions that the actual results differed materially from the extravagant statements that had been boastingly made, but their incredulity did not rest upon knowledge of any facts. Former experience had taught them not to give credence to such statements, but to discount them largely on the score of military policy in time of war, and even more on account of the intense party bias which prevailed in Confederate circles. After the evacuation of Corinth by Gen. Beauregard, the demonstrations of the Federal forces towards East Tennessee, which had begun before, became more threatening. They compelled the Confederate troops at Bridgeport to retire, made indecisive attacks upon them at Chat-

* See Appendix Note L.

tanooga and Cumberland Gap, and harassed them in East Tennessee into frequent and forced marches. Finally General Kirby Smith evacuated Cumberland Gap under military necessity, and the Federal army under Gen. G. W. Morgan occupied his fortifications.

In July, 1862, Gen. John H. Morgan, of Kentucky, who had considerable fame as a partisan Confederate officer, having been defeated at Lebanon, Tenn., reorganized his command and made Knoxville his starting point for a new expedition. He passed into Kentucky, capturing and destroying, engaged the Federals in battle at Cynthiana, and at length withdrew from that State before a superior force. One year later he again entered Kentucky from Sparta, Tenn., just west of the Cumberland Mountains, and went upon his well known raid into Ohio and Indiana. Afterwards he again appeared in East Tennessee, and one night, when asleep in a private dwelling, exceptionally well provided, at Greeneville, he was surprised by a party of United States soldiers. They had been informed as to where he lodged, and in his attempt, partially dressed, to escape through the garden of his hostess, a soldier fired upon and killed him.

The ordinary routine of things at Knoxville was enlivened in the summer of 1862, by the arrival of some forty United States soldiers who had been taken prisoners by Col. Forest, in the military adventure and surprise he accomplished at Murfreesboro. They bore their adversity with fortitude and unlessened devotion to their country. Horses and wagons captured at the same time, accompanied them and with the prisoners presented a spectacle of military trophies that drew a crowd of triumphant beholders. Some of these spectators made then their safe and nearest approach to the destructive war, which they had rejoiced that others should carry on with danger and hurt. The captured men were sent to Georgia. An exhibition by authority—less creditable than the show of prisoners and horses—was that of the private correspondence seized at Murfreesboro, which was distributed the next day among soldiers and citizens and read on the streets.

About the middle of August, 1862, Gen. Kirby Smith, having collected forces sufficient for the purpose, made a forward movement into Kentucky, crossing the mountains at a gap considerably west of that named Cumberland. Soon after he departed, Col. W. M. Churchwell, Provost Marshal, died of disease that was probably contracted through exposure the previous winter at Cumberland Gap.

CHAPTER XII.

NEWS AND LITERATURE IN THE CONFEDERACY—A MIXED DINNER PARTY AND ITS CONVERSATION—CARTER'S RAID AND WHAT BEFELL A RECRUITING OFFICER—AN UNTERRIFIED YANKEE CITIZEN OF GEORGIA—SANDERS' RAID—DEATH OF PLEASANT MCCLUNG.

> "Young men soon give, and soon forget affronts;
> Old age is slow in both."
> ADDISON'S *Cato*.

> "A wise man * * * examines if those accidents
> Which common fame calls injuries, happen to him
> Deservedly or no. Come they deservedly?
> They are no wrongs then, but punishments:
> If undeservedly and he not guilty,
> The doer of them first should blush—not he."
> JONSON.

IT is not advisable to follow closely the course of events at the locality during the next winter and spring, for the most of them were not important or interesting enough to be chronicled. Men and things settled down into a state of comparative quiescence under the new Government. While with some there was glad acceptance of the existing power, others, silently submitting to it, looked out, hopeful of soul for its overthrow, and secretly listened for news of victories to the United States armies at a distance. Tidings of all occurrences beyond the limits of the seceded States were meagre in quantity and obtained with difficulty, except so far as the few newspapers still published in the South, gave them. These papers had dwindled away in size, and of course had little room in their columns for news from the United States and from foreign lands, after printing matter of local interest. If any news from outside were published, which was thought to bear seriously upon the fortunes of the war, its proportions had to be shorn and its color changed to suit politic requirements. The *Richmond* (Va.) *Examiner*, with its very able editorials by Mr. Daniel, was more in circulation than any other journal from a distance, and some persons counted themselves happy in the opportunity to peruse it. There was an independence in its tone that reminded Union men of former days of the Republic, and its zest was enhanced to their mental palates by its occasional fault-finding with those in authority. At length its dimensions were reduced by the necessities of the times to one-half sheet of very indifferent paper. If, as was sometimes the case, a few newspapers were smuggled into the town from the North by the underground railway *via* Kentucky, and came into the hands of a Union citizen, they were counted as worth their weight in gold. He first devoured their contents in secret, then passed them covertly to a friend, and so they would continue their rounds among hungry readers. In like manner would be circulated any important news received by the "grapevine telegraph." Such eagerness among Union men for information from without, was no doubt largely due to their hope of deliverance, but it was partly owing to their desire to know something of what was going on in the great world beyond the limits of the Confederacy. They felt like men in a prison, and to this day many of the current events in that world for more than two years are blank in the knowledge of persons in the South, who had been accustomed to keep pace with journalistic columns.

As for current literature and science, periodicals and new books, they found no access at all to the place from abroad. The only volumes recently published, copies of which had circulation were, "A Strange Story," by Bulwer, and a translation of Victor Hugo's "Les Miserables." These had been re-printed at Richmond, and were remarkably inferior in their mechanical execution. The paper on which they were printed and the typography vied in poverty and unhappiness. The covering was of wall-paper with very large figures, the mutilation of which, in adapting the binding to its use, added to the grotesque appearance of the books.

News was still given by authority. The community would be told of a battle somewhere, in which many "Yankees" were killed, wounded and taken prisoners, and the Confederate losses were relatively small. These reported victories, with their great disparities in results, occasioned, as did the news from Corinth, much open joy on the one hand and secret incredulity on the other. They who doubted and still clung to the Union, although reduced in numbers, were not so crushed in spirit as to sulk, Achilles like, in their tents, but they sought one another's company, listened to news from the United States, brought in by adventurous runners, discussed the situation and probabilities, and encouraged each other to steadfastness. Sometimes the national heavens wore to them an intense gloom, relieved by but few dim rays of hope. But at one time their hope grew very bright, only to suffer a fatal eclipse. No occurrence of the war gave the Union people of East Tennessee such disappointment as the failure of General McClellan's Peninsular campaign. In their imaginations, "Little Mack" was the hero of the epoch, the Alexander who would cut the Gordian knot of the rebellion, the American Cæsar who would shortly capture the insurgents' capital and proclaim to the nation, "*Veni, vidi, vici.*" And when they learned the campaign's result, they did so with more grief and discouragement than was felt elsewhere in the land, because of their isolation from sympathy and their unfriendly environment.

In the great majority of instances, friendly social intercourse between people of hostile opinions had ceased, but there were exceptions to the rule. Early in May, 1863, a civilian who was firm in his devotion to the Union, but strong also in his attachment to personal kinsmen, and equally free in manifesting both, had a number of invited guests to dine with him one day. News of the death of Gen. Stonewall Jackson had but just arrived, and the sorrowful event was a topic of conversation at the table. The hero who had recently departed, has been since the war ended, an object of reverent admiration to some people who cared nothing for or detested secession, as well as to all who sympathized with it. While the bloody conflict was going on, the godliness which was a strong trait in his character, seemed to sanctify altogether in the view of some minds, the cause for which he fought so bravely and skillfully. They would, no doubt, have stoutly rejected the dogma of works of supererogation. But the religious merits of General Jackson appeared to more than counterbalance with them all religious demerits of others who sought with him to dissolve the Union. In the conversation just mentioned, pertinent expressions were given of esteem for the deceased and of regret for his death. After these had been spoken a young man at the table exclaimed:

"I have no doubt that General Jackson is now commanding a legion of angels in heaven!"

This sentimental climax to the panegyrics before uttered, somewhat startled its hearers, and seemed to forbid any remark that might even imply dissent. The prevailing silence was broken by one of the company relating an anecdote of the Rev. David Nelson, who had been for years a doctor of medicine. From being a downright religious sceptic, he had been converted to the Christian faith, had become a prominent Presbyterian minister in East Tennessee, and was the author of a book entitled, "The Cause and Cure of Infidelity," which once had a very extensive circulation. He was in Washington City during the presidency of Andrew Jackson, who, hearing of his presence in the city, sent him an oral invitation to visit him at the White House. The two had been well known to each other in former years and were personal friends, but Dr. Nelson said, in narrating the incident, he had found after becoming a Christian minister, little or no benefit to result from his social visits to men in high places of the State or Nation. He therefore did not make the proposed visit. The President then sent him a written request to go and see him, and Dr. Nelson went. General Jackson had lost his wife by death, and the affliction had been the means of leading him to serious reflection and to faith in Christ—to baptism and membership in the Presbyterian Church. As a consequence, the conversation that ensued between him and his reverend visitor, was of a religious nature. Dr. Nelson, in speaking afterwards of the interview, said:

"I talked with General Jackson. I think he is a true Christian. Yes, I think when he dies he will go to heaven. But he will be no bigger than a rat! There's my old colored man—a preacher. He will be soaring away up in heaven, while General Jackson will be crawling along on the floor like a rat."

This recital was followed at the table by a silence as deep and universal as that which went before it. Whether the guests highly valued Dr. Nelson's opinions that degrees of blessedness obtain in heaven and that high and low positions will in some instances be reversed up there, is by no means certain. But they appeared to think that the story entailed a moral which lay in its application, that the subject was exhausted and the conversation might be discreetly diverted to another topic.

In December, 1862, Gen. Samuel P. Carter made a military raid into that portion of East Tennessee lying nearest Virginia. He was a native of one of the most eastern counties of Tennessee, which bears his surname, and he belonged to a prominent and influential family. He had been for years an esteemed officer of the United States Navy, but in 1862, was detached from it and assigned to duty with the land forces in Kentucky which might operate in East Tennessee. There, it was probably thought, his nativity and name would prove collateral aids to his services. This particular enterprise was brilliantly executed, but he was compelled by the gathering of superior hostile forces to withdraw from it speedily. A compend of his report of the expedition is appended.*

A very young man, son of Wm. Harris, a worthy merchant of Dandridge, Jefferson County, fled to Kentucky in the summer of 1862, from the conscription. He became a volunteer in the United States Army and was made captain in the East Tennessee troops, was sent by the Colonel of his regiment to obtain recruits in Sevier County, East Tennessee, crossed the mountains for that pur-

*See Note M.

pose with General Carter's command on its raid, left it at Union Railroad depot, and was betrayed and captured in Washington County. From there he was brought to Knoxville and tried by court martial as a deserter from the Confederate army, was found guilty and sentenced to death. Gen. Burnside communicated from Kentucky to the Confederate Government that Captain Shade T. Harris was an officer of his army, for whom he held Captain Battle, of the Confederate States Army, as hostage, but no exchange of the men was effected. Subsequently Captain Battle was released at Nashville through some misunderstanding or mal-administration, Harris being still detained. His friends claimed that he was a United States soldier. Perhaps prompted by the feeling that a Christian minister who was a Union man would more heartily advise with and prepare him for approaching death, his father requested a minister who bore that reputation to visit the prisoner. Authority to do so was promptly granted upon application, but the reverend man was rather surprised to be attended on his errand by two soldiers "armed to the teeth," as though he had not only dangerous propensities but Sampsonian strength. This formidable guard, with its superfluous watchfulness, kept close to the minister's person while he read the Word of God to the prisoner, prayed with and counselled him. The jail was crowded with inmates and the miserable food that waited to be scantily dished out to them lay thrown together in a box on the way from the main door.

One result of the visit was, that with consent of the authorities, a quantity of good, wholesome bread from the baker's went that day to regale the prisoners. The ministerial visit, with a reduced military escort, was now and then repeated, and the condemned youth was exhorted to cherish a spirit of forgiveness to his enemies, as a duty, because of God's forgiveness through Christ. He professed to do this. The fatal day drew near. A coffin was prepared for the body of the alleged culprit. His father learned from Richmond that a reprieve had been granted, and visited the recently appointed Commandant of the Post at Knoxville, who in reply to an inquiry concerning the respite from President Davis, said he did not know, and told an Aid to look and see. Several pigeon holes were examined, and the official document was at length found! No doubt King David was right when he said to the prophet Gad, "I am in a great strait: let us fall now into the hand of the Lord: for his mercies are great: and let us not fall into the hand of man."*

Throughout the winter of 1862-3, and the next spring, the current of life in the community, with its mingled civil and military elements, flowed on in wonted channels. The occupancy of the town by Confederate troops and the conduct of their affairs made the most prominent and engrossing feature on the face of things. There were soldiers on the streets, and sick or dying soldiers in the hospitals. Courts martial were held, and stories,

* See Appendix: Note N.

PREVALENT DULLNESS AND INFLATION.   197

true or false, of military movements and skirmishes, of battles, victories and defeats, were frequent topics of conversation. Men bought and sold, Confederate notes and bonds went down in value, and gold went up. Purchases of different commodities in trade and of real estate, were made in sums of money, nominally large and really small. Some men seemed to prosper in their financial operations, in like manner with the speculator, of whom an admiring friend said, " He is rich—that is to say, he is not rich, but he has all the sensations." But there was no firm foundation in pecuniary affairs and many of the superstructures were chaffy.

In general, things appeared to be permanently settled. There was so much of ordinary routine in their daily movement, so little of jarring or eruption about it, that men, if disposed, might easily think that the Government under which they lived had a long, indefinite future before it. To some observers, however, the uniformity in the movement, like that in the soldiers' dress and march, had too much the look of being imposed by mere power and of wanting in healthy freedom. After all that might be said favorably of the social condition, one had to admit that it was too dull and monotonous to suit rational beings, and needed an infusion of vitality from some source or other. To observers whose spirits revolted against their surroundings, and were fed with the hope that

" Springs eternal in the human breast,"

the state of society suggested its comparison to

that of the inhabitants of a remote locality in a great empire, where insurrectionists temporarily held power and things went on among the people under a prevailing sense of suppression. They were compelled to silence but were still resistful of mind to the power that held them down. They had faith that the surrounding night would sooner or later disappear before the light of day, bringing

> "Stern and imperious Nemesis,
> Daughter of Justice, most severe;
> * * * * *
> Whose swift, sure hand is ever near."

During this period of a more quiet Confederate rule over the region, there was an occasional escapade of persons from the Gulf States through East Tennessee to the North. Secretly a system had been perfected by which they and other refugees were directed from point to point and supplied with means of conveyance by resident citizens—well known to each other and their special friends—whose names were never exposed as helpers in such a work. One of this class of travellers was Mr. B., a native of Connecticut, but for many recent years a respectable, peaceable citizen of a State south of Tennessee.

At the advent of the war, knowing that he had the esteem generally of his neighbors, he did not think of being disturbed during its progress, in the quiet pursuit of his lawful business. After the conflict had fairly begun, the passions of men made them sharply sensitive to the presence of one, whose antecedents formed a ground of suspicion that he was not "loyal to the South." He belonged by birth to the hated race of "Yankees," and although he was discreet of speech and well behaved, it was supposed that he could not well enough love the production of cotton by slave labor, to be allowed in the town at such a critical time. Therefore he received in writing an anonymous warning to leave the country, but he refused to heed it. Another was sent to him with the same result, and yet another. At length he was threatened in an open and positive way, that forced him to answer with emphasis. "They told me," said Mr. B., speaking with a decided nasal twang, "they told me I must leave or forfeit my life, and I told them *I would forfeit my life!*"

He was evidently such a man as Hosea Biglow would admire. George Borrow says, "When threatened by danger, the best policy is to fix your eye steadily upon it and it will in general vanish like the morning mist before the rising sun; whereas, if you quail before it, it is sure to become more imminent."

The result of that policy by Mr. B., was that without further molestation, he was permitted to continue his residence in the town. Long afterwards, he chose to depart with a young man as companion, and passed through Knoxville to Morristown, where Mr. N. would provide them conveyance over the mountains into Kentucky.

One afternoon in June, 1863, agitating news spread from the military to the people. Col. Wm. P. Sanders, of the United States Army, was said to be marching upon the town with a formidable force, to be already not far away from it, and would arrive on the morrow. The cry, "To arms!" went everywhere. Messengers upon the streets summoned citizens to shoulder their guns and aid the military in resisting the invader. "To the front! to the front!" And away men sped under a strong sense of duty. The tradesman left his store, the laborer his toil, the mechanic his shop, the lawyer his office and even the clergyman his study. Young and more mature men, and boys, obeyed the call, in some instances as if eager for the fray.

A noble spirit is that of patriotism. Who is there of such base metal, as not to be prompt in defending his home, his city, his native or adopted land? That arrant coward, John Falstaff, thrice pronounced "a plague upon all cowards!" And the sentiment, put into rude or elegant phrase, has the common consent of mankind. There is "a common and indeterminate courage," which Edmondo De Amicis says "in Europe is considered with chivalric reciprocity, the property of all armies." Bishop Stephen H. Elliot (eminent scholar and gentleman) said that the late civil war proved one thing—that there are few men not brave enough to fight. Much rarer is *moral* courage, as it is immeasurably superior in kind. Physical courage has more of its roots in the animal nature and is liable to great heats and fury. Moral courage, having its roots in the conscience and being trained by the reason, has firmness and composure. Nor is all patriotism alike. It differs in scope and expression. That which is narrow and tied down to a section is apt to have a concentration of energy, which gives a certain fire and dash to its courage. The patriotism that includes the whole country in its arms, may because of breadth, have less flaming intensity, but has more substantial capacity for calm endurance in heroic action.

On June 14th, 1863, by order of Maj. General Burnside, then commanding the Department of the Ohio, Col. Sanders (Fifth Kentucky Cavalry), started from Mount Vernon, Kentucky, for East Tennessee, with a party of fifteen hundred men, which included the First East Tennessee Regiment under Col. R: K. Byrd. He passed *via* the neighborhood of Huntsville, Scott County, East Tennessee, and Montgomery, Morgan County, and leaving Kingston and Loudon in succession to his right, made some captures at Lenoir's, and moved up to Knoxville at daylight on the 20th. General Buckner was in command of the Confederate Army in East Tennessee. He was absent that day, having gone the previous morning to concentrate his forces at Clinton, but all possible preparations were made to repel Col. Sanders. Afterwards it was stated that he had no intention to assault the town, which if he had taken he could not have held. He himself officially reported that he "made demonstrations against Knoxville so as to have their (Confederate) troops brought from above." An engagement followed upon his appearance before the town between the two hostile parties, chiefly with a Confederate battery planted on Summit Hill, southwest of and overlooking the railroad depot, and a United States battery on elevated ground opposite, near the junction of Fifth Avenue and Crozier streets, North Knoxville. Few injuries resulted to either side. Most of the shells thrown by Col. Sanders' guns, missing their mark, flew over the town harmlessly enough, except in frightening the women and children with their whizzing through the air. But the casualties from one of the shrieking missiles were serious to the Confederates. It first mortally wounded the captain of a company of citizen volunteers, then struck and killed a sergeant who on higher ground was nearly prone with the earth to avoid harm, and finally exploded, killing a Lieutenant from Florida, who with other convalescents from the army hospital in the Deaf Mute Asylum close by, sat on a fence to see the fight.

The Captain of Volunteers was a young man of specially amiable and genial qualities. His bravery and vivacity of spirits led him into heedlessness of danger. As he stood upon the hill-top that morning, nigh to the Confederate earth-works and artillery, and saw his fellow-soldiers drop for safety into the ditch at the same moment with the flash of Sanders' guns, he exclaimed, standing upright: "Don't be afraid; there's no danger!" Instantly a shell hit him, and his mutilated body was tenderly borne to a kinsman's house in town. Surgical aid was summoned and could mitigate his sufferings, but not save his life.

A non-combatant minister of the gospel, having removed his invalid wife to a friend's house less exposed to the flying shells, was seeking the same refuge for his infant child. As he walked, he met a brother minister, who had just taken part in the fight. The contrast, one bearing in his arms a musket and the other a child, was almost comical, and provoked a smile from the Quaker-like professional. He repressed it in presence of the grief he quickly encountered, as he met the wounded Captain's wife and children.

"O, Mr. ———," she cried aloud, throwing her arms aloft into the unsympathizing air, "they have killed my husband! Come and see him!"

This he did, and administered such consolation as our holy religion affords for sufferers. The dying young man was a sincere Christian believer. It was noted that only the Sunday evening before, with his family around him at home in the country, he had sung, with a heavenward aspiration of spirit, the grand old hymn, on whose winged words of divine promise and human faith many a devout heart has often risen into the Christian empyrean:

"How firm a foundation, ye saints of the Lord."

As his life ebbed fast away, his right hand now and then pressed that of the kneeling minister, in sympathy with the supplications offered to God. Soon the end came, and his dying breath went forth in prayer. Among his petitions to the King invisible, was one of "forgiveness to those who killed him."

No doubt he meant the enemies with whom he did battle that morning; but were there not others, positively, although remotely in time, accountable for his death? Who inaugurated that bloody war —whether it were rightly named civil or infernal? Did it come down from the sky above or leap up from the deep beneath, fully matured, as Minerva sprung forth from the head of Jupiter, in complete armor, with lifted spear and clashing weapons? Or was there some gigantic national wrong against humanity, that clamored for righteous adjustment, and would not sleep until it found redress? Was it begotten of enthusiastic philanthropy? Or of an unholy love of lordship? Of zeal for freedom and hate of oppression? Or of ambition to cut the Nation in two and create one with slavery for its corner-stone? Was it evolved from the heart and brain of William Lloyd Garrison and Wendell Phillips? Or from those of Jefferson Davis and Robert Toombs? Did the first gun fired on Fort Sumter, whose echoes went sounding through the land and sent the patriotic pulses of the people bounding to the quickstep of marching battalions, begin the biggest strife the world has known? Or were its seeds sown in earlier decades, when men, women and children of barbaric Africa, cruelly crowded in slave-ships, were freely imported to American Colonies and States, to be forever an inherited "bone of contention?"

"*Forgiveness to those who killed him?*" Let the question in all its bearings of responsibility for his death, be referred for answer to the Son of Man, whom God has appointed to judge the quick and dead! Meanwhile, let thy dismembered body, O, Pleasant Miller McClung, sleep on in the quiet grave of thy early manhood, until the morning of the resurrection of the dead! Then shalt thou meet those for whom thou didst pray forgiveness. And surely, thy unstudied petition was so like one that passed from the pale lips of the Man of Sorrows when expiring on the cross, that it must have gone up through Him to the throne of eternal grace. Sleep on, then, until that coming day! Multitudes, equally brave—wearing the blue or the gray—fell on sleep in the same mighty conflict. In many and crowded cemeteries the grass grows on lowly mounds over them, the white and pulseless marble glints in the shine of the sun as it rises and sets, and the birds sing their peaceful requiem in the air. And shall they not—a grand army, hundreds of thousands strong—come again to life? What if some are in unmarked graves? What if some graves have headstones that bear the sorrowful word, "Unknown?" *God knoweth!* And they shall rise again, for He has said it. But if, in the generations hereafter, "Columbia" is indeed "to glory arise," O ye, her sons, heed well the lesson taught by the war between her children in '61–65. "The beginning of strife is as when one letteth out water, therefore leave off contention, before there be quarreling."

In this Republic the avenues to employment are so many and wide open, that some measure of success awaits all who have capacity and diligence. Justly enough, a poor and obscure lineage does not prevent the rise to eminence or wealth of him who is worthy, nor are they to be attained by the son of rich or notable parents, who has no merit of his own. "Parson Brownlow," in writing once for the public about some of his enemies to whom he attributed aristocratic pretensions, compared them to "turnips, the better part of which is under ground." Still, wisely enough, men generally even under Democratic institutions, count an honest and industrious ancestry of some worth. By common consent, sons are to be commended who copy the virtues and good conduct of their fathers. One of the guests at a dinner party in Knoxville given to Gen. Burnside, said to him: "Andrew Johnson deserves great credit for having risen from poverty and obscurity to honorable distinction in the country." The General was expected to reply in just the same strain of sentiment. His answer was: "Yes! but so does every man who inherits superior advantages and uses them wisely and faithfully." And there are strong temptations to idleness and improvidence besetting the young man who is born to affluence and favorable opportunities, which it is meritorious in him to overcome, and with which the poor boy has never to struggle.

The genealogical facts concerning the young Captain who met his death on Summit Hill during the "Sanders raid" are interesting, for he was the only living man in whom met lines of descent from two persons distinguished in the earliest history of Tennessee and Knoxville. He was the great grand-son of William Blount, Governor of the Territory south of the Ohio, from 1792 to 1796, and also of James White, founder of Knoxville, (the capital of the Territory) and fellow-worker of Blount in the organization of Tennessee.

Col. Sanders, after one hour's passage at arms with the Confederates under the command *pro tem.* of Col. R. C. Trigg, took up his line of march eastward and burned the bridges at Strawberry Plains and Mossy Creek. He captured stores and prisoners at several places, and was finally compelled to withdraw hastily to Kentucky. His enemy pressed him closely on all sides, and to avoid capture, he had to pass the mountain by an unfrequented gap, (Smith's) through which there was no road, but only a bridle path, to follow. Reports made by the respective parties in the conflict, are appended in a condensed form.*

When the excitement occasioned by Sanders's visit had passed away, Knoxville returned to its former quiet condition and remained so for two months.

Meanwhile, the United States forces which held Cumberland Gap were in turn compelled by their adversaries to evacuate it, because of insufficient supplies.

*See Notes O. and P.

CHAPTER XIII.

Gen. Buckner's Retreat—A Citizen's Adventure—Gen. Burnside; His Welcome; His Expedition — Cumberland Gap; Its Surrender—An Eccentric Farmer—Military Movements in East Tennessee—Fight at Blue Springs—Affairs at and near Loudon—Burnside and the People.

> "Now is the winter of our discontent
> Made glorious summer by this sun of York;
> And all the clouds that lowered upon our house,
> In the deep bosom of the ocean buried."
> Shaks.: *Richard III.*

Gen. Buckner had been for some time at Knoxville in command of the military department o Kentucky, Middle and East Tennessee, North Alabama and Southwest Virginia. His personal presence was commanding and adapted to fill the popular notion of a grand army officer. The attention of citizens was attracted and their criticism challenged by his imposing appearance, as he rode without escort upon a splendid charger through the principal street. His reputation was that of a true gentleman and a soldier of superior merit. The public esteem had been drawn to him, by his conduct at the fall of Fort Donelson, in comparison with that of his companion-generals, especially Floyd.

MAJ. GEN. A. E. BURNSIDE.

Late in August, to the surprise of civilians, he departed westward with his troops, crossed the Tennessee River, twenty-nine miles distant and burned the railway bridge behind him. Something important had happened or was expected, but the people in their ignorance could only wonder as to its nature. The retreat left them unprotected from roving, lawless bands, which the war had spawned. One of these came into the town at night and despoiled stables of horses. A citizen was roused from sleep by their near prowling. Hastening to his stable, he came upon thieves who quickly decamped. They had brought to the spot a valuable horse just stolen by them from a near stall. They left it behind in the hurry of flight, but took away the horse whose owner had alarmed them. Without intending a deed of disinterested benevolence by interfering with the rogues' work, he had saved his neighbor's property, losing his own. The next day steps were taken to form companies of armed townsmen for defence against marauders. Before any thorough organization to that end was made, an unexpected event occurred.

It was the 2nd of September, 1863. A worthy Swiss immigrant of the town at the beginning of the war espoused the side of " the South" with all the fervor of his naturally ardent disposition. His friend, "native and * * to the manner born," was a decided Union man, and because of his sentiments, met with various troubles during the Confederate supremacy at the place, but the true-hearted Switzer was steadfast in his friendship, at the risk of losing *caste* with his own party. In the afternoon of the day, he had concluded a visit to the Unionist and was walking homeward, when to his astonishment he saw three men on horseback and in blue uniforms, four hundred yards distant, galloping towards him as if for life. "Halt!" they shouted. But not heeding their call, he turned and ran to the room of his friend, crying out as he entered it, "The Yankees are coming!" Instantly the family assembled, and as quickly the soldiers in blue were at the door. They were advance riders of the army under Maj. Gen. Burnside, and being on the lookout for hostile soldiers in the town, they had pursued the Switzer in the belief that he was one. Through an upper window his friend looked out upon the troopers in the yard, but they saw in the company gathered above, the man whom they had followed, and immediately one of them, with face white from excitement, raised his pistol and pointing it upward at the group exclaimed, "There he is now! Stand out of the way, ladies!" The native citizen stepped forward and said. "Don't shoot! I am a Union man." The pistol was at once lowered, but the soldiers kept their ground and must needs be talked with. The Switzer bravely said in his imperfect English, that he would go down stairs and give himself up, but his companion would go before, and opening the front door, he assured the eager troopers that the man they supposed to be a Confederate soldier, was only a citizen at the house as a visitor. They were at once pacified, made apologies and rode away.

The United States army had indeed arrived, and to look upon it, the delighted Union man sought without delay the principal street. At the end of two squares he found the way barred by a sentinel. In the halt thus imposed upon all persons, he was entertained by the outspoken displeasure of the company—chiefly ladies of the neighborhood—at the incoming of the "Yankees." One of them—a truly amiable, but for the time deeply offended matron—gave free vent to her feelings until the current of her thoughts was diverted at the suggestion of a bystander, that the town might well be thankful for the protection the United States army afforded it from robbers. Only a few nights before they had stolen from her a valuable pony. This recollection turned her resentment from "Lincoln and his hordes" to the source, as she thought, of all present woes to the country. "If it had not been for South Carolina," she complained, "we should not have had all this trouble!"

Gen. Burnside, on his arrival, established his headquarters in a large mansion recently vacated by its owner, which stood near the principal street and had a spacious front yard. From its covered porch a large United States flag was lifted up, and in its drooping folds the welcoming crowd wrapped themselves with beaming faces. Expressions of joy from the people rung upon the air. They hailed the General as their deliverer from a hated power and the oppression it inflicted; and also as the representative of their beloved nation, clothed with its authority and armed with its sword. Some of them were so glad that they scarcely knew what to do with themselves. In the overflow of their emotions they could have clasped him in their arms, or, if opportunity had served, have drawn him in a carriage with their own hands all over the town, that everybody, men, women and children, might look upon him. Meanwhile he bore himself with dignity and gentleness. Briefly he addressed them with words suited to the occasion and full of friendly sympathy. Then, his attentive hearers, elated with joy as with new wine, were eager for more discourse. An adjournment was made to the courthouse, and from its front several citizens addressed the assembly in the open air.

The expedition of Gen. Burnside into East Tennessee had been conceived in his mind at least six months before it was made. He took command of the department of the Ohio, at Cincinnati, March 25, 1863. It included Indiana, Ohio, Michigan, Illinois, Kentucky (excepting west of the Tennessee River), and "all of East Tennessee that he might at any time occupy." At that date Gen. Pegram, with a formidable cavalry force, had marched from East Tennessee across the Cumberland River, had driven the United States forces to the north of Kentucky River, and had taken possession of Danville and its vicinity. In a few days, by direction of Gen. Burnside, Gen. Gilmore compelled Gen. Pegram to retreat; and afterwards at Somerset, with the co-operation of Gen. Manson, commanding a part of Gen. Boyle's forces, completely defeated Pegram, and made the Cumberland River again the dividing line. Central Kentucky was for the next month free from hostile forces. Early in May, upon the organization of the troops in that State into the Twenty-third army corps, under Gen. G. L. Hartsuff, Gen. Burnside at once commenced to make preparations for moving into East Tennessee. On June 3d he left Cincinnati to take command in person of the troops which were organizing for that movement, and which consisted of the two divisions of the Ninth army corps under Gen. Wilcox and a portion of the Twenty-third corps under Gen. Hartsuff. On arriving at Lexington, Ky., he received an order to send the Ninth corps to Gen. Grant, and in consequence, the expedition to East Tennessee had to be deferred. After Col. Sanders returned to Kentucky from his raid, "preparations were still continued" by the General, "in the hope of being able to spare sufficient force to go into East Tennessee." But they were disturbed by the approach of the rebel General, John H. Morgan, with a large cavalry force, about the 1st of July, on his memorable raid through Kentucky and Indiana into Ohio, which resulted in his surrender near Steubenville, and the capture altogether of 3,000 men—three-fourths of the troops with which he had entered Kentucky. While the United States soldiers were absent in pursuit of Morgan, a considerable force of rebel cavalry under Col. John S. Scott, went from East Tennessee, crossed the Kentucky River and approached the Ohio, evidently with the view of assisting Morgan on his expected return. They were soon driven out of Kentucky with heavy loss, by Col. Sanders' cavalry after it came back from the pursuit of Morgan.

Then preparations were again begun by Gen. Burnside for a movement into East Tennessee. As the troops were worn and scattered by their recent fatiguing services, it required much labor and time to perfect the organization necessary for that purpose. He appointed Gen. J. D. Cox to take charge in his absence of the District of Ohio, Gen. Wilcox of the District of Indiana, and Gen. Boyle of Kentucky, all of whom he considered "officers of great skill and determination." On August 10th, he left his headquarters at Cincinnati to join the column that was to march into East Tennessee. It consisted of the Twenty-third army corps, commanded by Gen. Hartsuff, and on the 20th was located as follows, viz.: White's division at Columbia, Ky.; Hascall's division at Stamford; Carter's division at Crab Orchard; Graham's cavalry at Glasgow; and Woolford's cavalry at Somerset. As ordered, Gen. Hartsuff moved his commands as follows: Hascall's division to Kingston, Tenn.. by way of Somerset, Chitwood, Huntsville and Montgomery; White's division from Columbia to Montgomery, Tenn., by way of Creelsboro and Albany, Ky., and Jamestown, Tenn.; Graham's cavalry to join White by way of Burksville, Albany and Jamestown; and Woolford's cavalry brigade to guard the supply and ammunition trains that were with Hascall's division. Carter's cavalry brigade, which Gen. Burnside's headquarters accompanied, was to move by way of Mt. Vernon, London and Williamsburg, Ky., over the Jellico Mountains to Chitwood, Huntsville, Montgomery and Kingston, Tenn., except such portions as might be detached. These forces were directed to meet at such times and places as not to interfere with each other's movements; and the whole work was performed with wonderful promptness and accuracy, considering the great difficulties in the way, of steep, rugged mountains, bad roads and short forage.

At Williamsburg, a cavalry force under Col. Byrd, of the 1st Tennessee Regiment, was detached for the purpose of making a demonstration on Knoxville, by way of Big Creek Gap, and at Montgomery a cavalry force was detached with orders to pass through Winter's Gap and occupy Knoxville. The main body of the command moved on the direct road to Kingston, which point the advance reached on the 1st of September. Col. Foster arrived at Knoxville September 2nd, captured several engines and cars, which he sent up the railroad to Morristown, Greeneville and near Jonesboro, and took also large quantities of supplies. Little resistance was met with by the Federal troops, throughout their entire march from Kentucky—the enemy in all cases retreating before them. Their main body, with Gen. Burnside in person, moved forward from Kingston and reached Knoxville on the 3rd. In his opinion, "nothing could be better than the conduct of the officers and men of the Twenty-third corps; from the time it left Kentucky, their labors were most difficult, but were performed with the greatest accuracy and efficiency." The mountainous route by which the army traveled was long and fatiguing, but it was the only one possible. At the end of the journey the army was, he said, "in the midst of friends;" it "found the people generally loyal and disposed to do all in their power for its comfort and welfare." At the same time it was more than two hundred miles from the Ohio River, and one hundred and fifty miles from the nearest point where the mountains and ridges that traverse Southeastern Kentucky give place to the fertile and garden-like "blue-grass region." From beyond those highlands, supplies for the army must be transported in wagons drawn by mules, whose mongrel nature, hardy as it is, was so unequal to the roughness and toil it had to bear in the work of transportation, that the number of their dead bodies lying on sides of the road over the mountains might be named Legion. It was currently estimated, as aggregating from first to last, ten thousand. Although the army occupied Knoxville and other important points in East Tennessee, it had not exclusive possession of that region. The great body of the population was friendly, but there were hostile troops in several directions.

Before leaving Kentucky, Gen. Burnside had organized a division of new troops under Col. De Courcy, to move down upon the north side of Cumberland Gap, and if possible, occupy that position. On his own arrival at Knoxville, he learned that the Gap was still occupied by the enemy. He directed Gen. Shackelford to proceed to its south side, and if within his power, capture the garrison. Gen. Shackelford on arriving there, communicated with Col. De Courcy on the north side by courier, and ascertained that the position was too strong to be carried by the small force under his command. Gen. Burnside, upon being informed of this fact, started at once for the Gap, with Col. Gilbert's brigade, and after a march of 60 miles in 53 hours, reached it on September 9th. Dispositions were made to assault the place, but before the next morning, he demanded of Col. Frazer, who was in command of the garrison, that he should surrender. The demand was complied with, and nearly 2,500 men were delivered over to the United States, together with all the material and armament of the fort. Shackelford's and Gilbert's brigades returned to Knoxville, and Col. De Courcy's division (then under command of Col. Lemert) was left as a garrison at the Gap.

As the Commander-in-chief was drawing nigh to that place on the 9th, with Gilbert's brigade, he was given an illustration, somewhat extravagant in its manner, of the joy inspired among the loyal people of East Tennessee by his coming, and of the respectful affection they had for him personally.

An eccentric farmer, son of a learned judge at Knoxville, resided in the autumn of 1863, near the Gap. Amusing stories are yet current of his unaffected oddities. He was a man of much simplicity of character, of high, impulsive temper, of great frankness, a warm and steadfast friend, a strong hater, quick to speak his mind, and in his earlier mature years, a ready fighter. It is related of him, that having once quarreled with a neighbor who bore the not uncommon name of John Smith, he contracted sometime afterwards a bodily illness that brought him nigh to death's door. Some of his friends advised, in view of the probability that his end was at hand, that he should be reconciled with his enemy. To this he consented, and accordingly John Smith was sent for, and without delay, arrived. The two adversaries "made friends"—shook hands and parted in strong doubt of another meeting between them on earth. But the sick man reflected that he might get well, and in his great candor, he called out from the bed to his former enemy, who was about leaving the room: " I say, Smith! you understand. This is all very well if I die; but if I get well, it goes for nothing!"

He was a Union man during the war, from the crown of his head to the soles of his feet. Nothing else could have been expected of one who was accustomed to espouse a cause with his whole soul, who had always been an intense Whig in politics, and whose love of country was both unalloyed and fervent. Hearing that the Commander-in-chief of the United States army was drawing near Cumberland Gap, he went forth to meet him, and falling down upon his knees in the highway, he expressed aloud to the General, by words and gestures, his thankfulness, love and joy. It was with some astonishment, mingled with gratification, that Gen. Burnside witnessed this exhibition of patriotic feeling, to which he made a kindly response. And afterwards, whenever others told of the incident, his amused memory would light up his face with a broad smile, which was instantly restrained, as if by a feeling of respect for the honest enthusiasm that had expressed itself so oddly at the Gap. He seemed to think that the occurrence had its serious as well as its funny side.

Before leaving Cumberland Gap, he received the following dispatch:

HEADQUARTERS 21ST ARMY CORPS,
CHATTANOOGA, Sept. 10, 1863, 2 A.M.

MAJ. GEN. A. E. BURNSIDE,
    Commanding Department of Ohio—Tennessee River:

SIR—I am directed by the General commanding the Department of the Cumberland to inform you that I am in full possession of this place, having entered it yesterday at 12 M. without resistance.

The enemy has retreated in the direction of Rome. Ga., the last of his force, cavalry, having left a few hours before my arrival. At daylight I made a rapid pursuit with my corps, and hope that he will be intercepted by the center and right, the latter of which was at Rome. The General commanding department requests that you will move down your cavalry and occupy the country recently covered by Col. Minty, who will report particulars to you, and who has been ordered to cross the river.

    (Signed)   T. L. CRITTENDEN,
                    For Maj. Gen. Commanding.

This information relieved Gen. Burnside from all apprehension concerning Gen. Rosecrans. It also fixed his determination to occupy all the important points above Knoxville, and if possible, reach the Salt Works near Abingdon, Va. Sufficient forces were left at Kingston and Loudon.

Col. Byrd, who was stationed at Kingston, was ordered to occupy Athens, and if possible, Cleveland, thus communicating with the cavalry of Gen. Rosecrans, as requested in the above dispatch, and as directed in another soon afterwards received from Gen. Halleck at Washington, as follows:

> Hold the gaps of the North Carolina mountains, the line of the Holston River, or some point (if there be one) to prevent access from Virginia; and connect with Gen. Rosecrans, at least with your cavalry.

A heavy force under the Confederate General Jones, was then holding points in the upper part of East Tennessee Valley, which, by the above order, Gen. Burnside was to occupy. Col. Foster's brigade had been doing excellent service in keeping that force in check. Gen. Hartsuff was directed to send at once all his infantry (except Gilbert's brigade), and also Woolford's cavalry up the valley. Col. Carter's cavalry brigade was already well advanced in that direction. On the 16th, at night, Gen. Burnside received another dispatch from Gen. Halleck, sent on the 13th. It read:

> It is important that all the available forces at your command be pushed forward into East Tennessee; all your scattered forces should be concentrated there; move down your infantry as rapidly as possible towards Chattanooga to connect with Rosecrans.

Early on the morning of the 17th, Burnside sent orders by telegraph for the Ninth corps and all other available troops then in Kentucky, to join him at once. He also gave instructions for all the troops then in upper East Tennessee and not in presence of the enemy, to retrace their steps down the valley towards Rosecrans. The same day he received another telegram from Halleck, dated the 14th, as follows:

> There are several reasons why you should reinforce Rosecrans with all possible dispatch. It is believed the enemy will concentrate to give him battle; you must be there to help him.

Burnside then repeated his order concerning the troops up the valley. Having already started to take command of them in person, and efficiently to promote the purpose of their movement, he proceeded beyond Jonesboro to near the Watauga River. When arrived at the extreme advance of his command, he saw no way of extricating it from its situation, except by attacking the enemy's position at Watauga bridge. A cavalry brigade under Col. Foster was sent around on the morning of the 23rd, to threaten the enemy's rear, who on that night burnt the bridge and evacuated the position. Immediately Burnside set in motion all the United States troops, except a small portion of cavalry, on the way to aid and relieve Rosecrans. The following day he returned to Knoxville.

His movements were watched from Richmond. On the day when he received Halleck's telegram of the 14th, a close observer at that city wrote: "It is said the enemy is evacuating East Tennessee, concentrating, I suspect, for battle with Bragg." *

It may easily be seen that it was impossible that the obedience promptly given by Burnside to Halleck's order, could avail in helping Rosecrans, as intended. The United States troops, which were in the upper country of East Tennessee, according

---

* See "A Rebel War Clerk's Diary at the Confederate States Capital," Vol. 2, page 46.

to instructions before given to Burnside, were from 150 to 200 miles distant from Chicamauga, where Rosecrans was to do battle, and they could not travel so far in the very short time before that battle began, even if they were moved towards the spot as rapidly as possible. Afterwards, when Rosecrans had established himself in Chattanooga, many dispatches passed between Halleck and Burnside, in reference to the latter's going to strengthen and assist Rosecrans, and some misunderstandings occurred in regard to the purport of those dispatches. Gen. Burnside, in his report to the War Department, gives the underlying reason. He says: "I was averse to doing what would in any way weaken our hold in East Tennessee, and he (Halleck) was anxious lest Rosecrans should not be able to hold Chattanooga. He (Rosecrans) was not disturbed at Chattanooga, and we held our ground in East Tennessee, so that what occurred in no way affected the result."

By the 30th of September, the whole of the Ninth army corps arrived, numbering about 6,000 men. Previous to that date, Gen. White's division had been sent to Loudon, Col. Woolford's cavalry had reinforced Col. Byrd, and they were instructed to connect with Rosecrans' cavalry; Gen. Carter held Bull's Gap, which was then the most advanced position of the United States troops up the valley, and Col. Haskell was in support at Morristown. Many of the men were suffering from want of clothing, for there was great difficulty in getting sufficient supplies across the mountains, and the temperature of the air was frosty. On October 5th, Gen. Wilcox arrived at Cumberland Gap with four new regiments of Indiana troops. He was ordered to Morristown, and thence to Bull's Gap, and to him Col. Haskin's brigade was directed to report from Morristown. Gen. Burnside had determined to push his advance farther up the valley, and with this purpose he sent the Ninth corps, under Brig. Gen., R. B. Potter, in that direction, together with all the cavalry under Gen. Shackelford, except Byrd's and Woolford's brigades. A junction of all these forces was made at Bull's Gap, where Gen. Burnside arrived in person on the 9th, and on the following morning an advance movement was ordered. At Blue Springs, between Bull's Gap and Greeneville, the enemy was found in heavy force and in a strong position between the wagon road and the railway to Greeneville. The United States cavalry occupied him in skirmishing until late in the afternoon. Col. Foster was sent, with instructions to establish his brigade in the rear of the enemy, on the line over which the latter would be obliged to cross in retreating, and at a point near Rheatown. An attack from the front was delayed until sufficient time had passed, probably for those instructions to be fulfilled. After 5 P.M , Gen. Ferrero's division of Gen. Potter's command, moved forward in the most dashing manner, driving the enemy from his first line, and compelled him to retreat that night. Gen. Burnside pursued early in the morning, driving his foes again beyond the Watauga River, where he directed the United States cavalry to hold them. Col. Foster's brigade met with serious difficulties upon its special errand, chiefly in rough roads, and did not reach its intended point of establishment in the rear ground and check the enemy in his retreat by night on the 9th, but it joined the pursuing forces next morning.* The cavalry was left in the advance, supported by Col. Haskin's brigade of infantry at Jonesboro, Gen. Wilcox was left at Greeneville, and the Ninth corps returned to Knoxville.

Nothing of importance occurred in the region of this fight until the 1st of November, when the outposts at Kingsport and Blountville were driven in, and in consequence the road from Kingsport to Rogersville was left unguarded. A heavy force of the enemy under Gen. S. Jones moved down that road, surprised a brigade of United States cavalry under Col. K. Garrard at Rogersville, and completely routed it. Col. Garrard, with his shattered forces, retreated to Morristown, and as the strength of the force which attacked him was unknown to Gen. Burnside, he prudently directed Gen. Wilcox to fall back to Bull's Gap and hold that position. From that time until the 17th of the month, operations were confined to cavalry fighting, skirmishing and foraging.

West of Knoxville, on the south side of the Tennessee River, below Loudon, the enemy were

---

* NOTE.—The Comte de Paris charges "guilty neglect" upon Foster: that while he halted his column under the pretext of allowing his men time to rest, he sent on the road to Henderson's Mill the Fifth Indiana Regiment, through which the Confederate troops easily opened a way.—*The Civil War in America*, Vol. 4.

very active during the early part of October. On the 19th of that month, Gen. Burnside had directions to report to Gen. Grant, commanding Division of Mississippi, concerning the situation and operations of his forces. This he did, and at the same time sent a flag of truce through Col. Woolford's lines, whose headquarters were at Philadelphia, Tenn. The enemy's cavalry took advantage of the flag, made an attack upon Col. Woolford, and captured from 300 to 400 of his men and some mountain howitzers. On the 28th, the forces at Loudon were moved to the north side of the Tennesee River, and the pontoon bridge was taken up and transported to Knoxville. There it was thrown across the Tennessee, and proved of immense service during the siege. The indications at that date were that Bragg was sending a considerable force against Burnside. The latter reinforced Kingston with Col. Mott's brigade of infantry, left Gen. White and his command at Loudon, and posted Gen. Potter with the Ninth corps at Lenoir's, about five miles east of Loudon. All the available cavalry force at Knoxville was thrown on the south side of the Tennessee River, with instructions to guard it down to the junction of Little Tennessee and Tennessee rivers opposite Lenoir's. And in order to enable the United States forces to communicate with each other, Gen. Potter was instructed to build a pontoon bridge over the Tennessee just above the mouth of the Little Tennessee. That was done with great expedition, under superintendence of Col. O. E. Babcock. Some correspondence was carried on between Generals Grant, Halleck and Burnside as to the proper points to be occupied in East Tennessee, and a visit to Burnside's headquarters followed from Col. Wilson, of Grant's staff, by order of his chief, accompanied by Hon. Chas. A. Dana, Assistant Secretary of War. Burnside gave them his reasons in full for desiring to hold Knoxville in preference to Kingston. They concurred with him in that conclusion. They all agreed it would be proper to recommend that both places be held, if possible, but certainly Knoxville. At that date it was definitely known that Longstreet was moving against Burnside.

Sometime before, Gen. Shackelford had been ordered to report from upper East Tennessee at Knoxville, to take command there of all the United States cavalry, and on the approach of Longstreet, Haskin's brigade was ordered to that place. This left Gen. Wilcox, with his new division, with some newly recruited North Carolinians, and also Foster's division of cavalry, composed of Graham's and Garrard's brigades, in the country above Knoxville. The whole command in that region, though it consisted of good men, was in bad condition, for want of almost everything that was needful. Burnside, when he learned certainly that Longstreet was advancing towards him, directed Wilcox to arrange for the march of his command to Cumberland Gap, in the event telegraphic communication between him and Gen. Burnside's headquarters should be broken. On that night,

November 16, it was cut off, at the same time that the siege of Knoxville was about to begin.

The United States Army under Gen. Rosecrans had been saved on the 20th of September by the firmness of Gen. Thomas. It was then shut up in Chattanooga by Gen. Bragg, who reported to Richmond that he expected its "speedy evacuation" of that place, "for want of food and forage." Whether Bragg thought that, as he said, he held his enemy at his mercy, and therefore could weaken his own force for a distant purpose, or whether, as Gen. Grant thought probable, the movement of troops to that end was ordered by Jefferson Davis, in default of his endeavor to reconcile a serious difference between Bragg and Longstreet, a heavy force, including cavalry, was detached from Bragg's army and sent under Longstreet to capture Burnside.*

The United States General who was the intended victim of that undertaking was not blind to the possibility that his military occupation of East Tennessee would shortly be brought to an end by a hostile force from the southwest. The bare thought of such an event deeply grieved him, not only as a disaster to the Federal Government, but also as a great calamity to the Union people of East Tennessee. A short time before Longstreet's march upon Knoxville began, Burnside in private conversation with a citizen-friend, spoke with

---

* Gen. Grant, in his "Personal Memoirs" (see Vol. II., page 49) puts the force with which Longstreet left Chattanooga "to go against Burnside at about fifteen thousand troops, besides Wheeler's cavalry, five thousand men." For Longstreet's mind as to the situation, see Appendix, Note R.

strong feeling of the possibility that he would not be able to continue to those people his protection. Had they known that not without reason he thought such a contingency existed, they would have been as deeply pained as he was, at the idea of his departure. He had been among them only about ten weeks, but in that brief time he had won their hearts. He had made good use of his opportunities to establish the military supremacy of the United States, to extend its area in East Tennessee and to hold it in possession against enemies. He had also, without putting aside the dignity becoming his official position, manifested the kindly sympathy he sincerely felt for the Union people who had suffered for more than two years under Confederate rule, he had permitted a healthy freedom of approach to his presence, had listened when at leisure to their griefs and wrongs, had now and then, as his public duties permitted, partaken of their hospitalities, and in a word, had in various ways showed that he was their friend. Everywhere he was looked upon with respect and affection. Even among citizens, at heart hostile to the flag he defended, were some who admired and liked him. They could not well be otherwise than content with him, for he visited them with no needless severities and his judgments were reasonable. His native magnanimity of soul would have lifted him above seeking revenge for his private wrongs suffered from the conflict, but he had no such wrongs. The bitterness and animosities which he found the war had produced among neighbors in East Tennessee, met with no favorable response from his own heart. He could not fully understand them, and spoke of their existence with mingled surprise and regret.

In the same connection he related that in his recent march from Kentucky, he pitched his tent at the base of the mountain on the Tennessee side. By and by, a number of the mountaineer Unionists gathered not far off, and soon, a few of them stepped out from the company and approached the General as a committee. They said to him, "General, we want you to give us authority to go down here into the valley, and carry off the hogs and cattle we find there." This request the General refused in few words. "But," they said, "that is the way they have treated us. And we will not make any mistakes. We will carry off only the cattle and hogs of the rebels." The General replied, "That is not my way of carrying on war;" and the petitioners withdrew very much disappointed.

General Burnside was buoyant with hope that the Union of the States would not only be preserved, but be stronger and better from the triumphant conclusion of the war in its behalf. He once expressed an opinion, which did not show great sagacity as a worldly-wise politician. It was the reflection, at the moment, of his own generous, magnanimous spirit, rather than a deliberate conclusion of his judgment from careful weighing of future possibilities. In conversation with a few friends concerning the ruinous losses by citizens generally of personal property, he ventured the prediction that "when the war is over, everybody will be paid."

Business at head-quarters was necessarily alive and active. Gen. Samuel P. Carter was Provost Marshal General. His office was a place of many affairs, and was visited by various applicants and their friends. There were citizens from near at hand and from a distance, who wanted to take the oath of allegiance to the United States, some of whom had been before of doubtful loyalty, and who desired, when they had passed through that process of political purgation, to carry home with them an official certificate of their title to the protection by the United States Government, of their persons and property. There were men from town and country who wanted to "go North" on business, or to get away from the strife, its turmoils, uncertainties and troubles, or to leave for Europe. There were men under arrest to be dealt with, or recusant citizens to be allowed the freedom of the town on parole or to be held as hostages, and others still who invited by their belligerent and dangerous speech a compulsory trip for themselves to Camp Chase or preferably into the Confederate lines. Then there were men of known loyalty, who had complaints to make, or claims to be adjusted, or this, that or something else done or prevented or remedied. Citizens who had influence with the military authorities, were kept busy in the service of their Confederate friends and neighbors. To some of such workers it was a labor of love, but probably not to all. Instances occurred, if rumor were true, of ten dollars each being charged for introducing people to General Carter. There were also orders to issue, official reports to receive, and troops to be sent here and there. Sometimes Union citizens, overflowing with patriotic zeal, had news to tell at headquarters, which they thought to be important. If now and then their zeal outstripped their discretion, it was little wonder that the information they carried should be lacking in accuracy. No doubt such instances of unintentional but hurtful mistakes were rare, for military life and discipline forbade their repetition even by civilians. One case was visited with a reprimand to the offender that was justly severe upon him and amusing to others.

Late one night a strong partisan interrupted the serenity at headquarters with the exciting statement that the Confederates had marched upon Maryville, in Blount County, 17 miles distant, where were only a few United States soldiers. Quickly a sufficient body of cavalry were summoned from their beds into their saddles and dispatched to repel the invading force. The alarm proved to be false; no Confederate troops were found in or near Maryville. The next day, General Burnside, on meeting his deceived and deceiving informant, said to him, "Mr. ———, you bring me a great deal of news. Now, I don't want you to bring me any more, for *the average is bad!*"

It has been said that all religion springs from a

sense of dependence upon the Supreme Being. We may doubt the truth of the postulate, but certainly all true religion includes that sense, and it had its proper place in the mind of Gen. Burnside. While his personal and social conduct in East Tennessee was upright and blameless, he was not forgetful of Him who "doeth according to His will in the army of heaven and among the inhabitants of the earth," and to thoughts of whom, the responsibilities of his position, its difficulties and dangers tended to move him more actively. He once said to a friend during that period, that he "loved sometimes to retire to his own room, there to lift up his mind and heart to God, and to give himself to quiet meditation." The impression made by his conversations, his reverent participation in the worship of God and hearing of the gospel, was that without much knowledge of religious doctrine, he accepted in faith the truth of Christianity.

Immediately after his first arrival at Knoxville, Burnside sent to a certain Christian minister, who because of his Union sentiments had been excluded for precisely two years from his pastoral charge, a written invitation to fill the unoccupied pulpit of his own church on the next Sunday. The request was complied with—the day being the 6th of September. By one of those curious coincidences which have been noticed to occur at different times in similar religious services, when the portion of the Psalms for that morning came to be responsively read, the minister unexpectedly to himself and to the surprised attention of some in the congregation who knew all the facts of the case, began, as prescribed, with the words:

"I will magnify thee, O Lord; for thou hast set me up, and not made my foes to triumph over me."

CHAPTER XIV.

GRANT AT CHATTANOOGA—PERIL OF BURNSIDE—THEIR CO-OPERATION—LONGSTREET AT LOUDON—BURNSIDE RETREATS AND IS PURSUED—BATTLE OF CAMPBELL'S STATION—MILITARY CONDITIONS AT KNOXVILLE—ESCAPE OF LEADING UNIONISTS.

> "Once this soft turf, this rivulet's sands,
>   Were trampled by a hurrying crowd,
> And fiery hearts and armed hands
>   Encountered in the battle cloud.
> Ah! never shall the land forget
>   How gushed the life-blood of her brave:—
> Gushed, warm with hope and courage yet,
>   Upon the soil they sought to save."
> WILLIAM CULLEN BRYANT.

The departure of Longstreet from Bragg against Burnside, taking with him twenty thousand men, or more, including 5,000 cavalry under Wheeler, occurred on the 4th of November. It was very soon known at the United States headquarters at Chattanooga and at the White House in Washington. Grant was eagerly desirous to extend relief to Burnside, but it was not in his power. That end would have been gained by inflicting a defeat upon Bragg, against whom he could not move until joined by Sherman, who was then on his way with reinforcements from Memphis to Chattanooga.

Before Longstreet started on his expedition, dispatches were constantly coming to Grant from the alarmed authorities at Washington, urging him to "do something for Burnside's relief;" calling attention to the importance of holding East Tennessee, saying that the President was much concerned for the protection of the loyal people in that section, &c., &c. To this statement in Grant's Personal Memoirs, he adds: "We had not at Chattanooga animals to pull a single piece of artillery, much less a supply train. Reinforcements could not help Burnside, because he had neither supplies nor ammunition sufficient for them: hardly, indeed, bread and meat for the men he had. There was no relief possible for him, except by repelling the enemy from Missionary Ridge and about Chattanooga."

After Longstreet's movements began, the Washington authorities were still more solicitous for the safety of the United States army at Knoxville, and were importunate by telegraph with Grant to "do something" to succor it. He was disposed to do all he could for that purpose. On November 7th, he ordered Gen. Thomas to make "an attack on the northern end of Missionary Ridge with all the force" he could "bring to bear upon it, and when that is carried, to threaten and even attack, if possible, the enemy's line of communication between Dalton and Cleveland." This was with a view to "force the return of the (Longstreet's) troops that had gone up the valley." But Thomas with his chief engineer, William Farrar Smith, and chief of artillery, Brannan, looked carefully over the ground, on which the proposed attack would have to be made. They became convinced that it was not feasible, and Smith so reported to Grant at once, and the order was countermanded. In his official report Grant says: "After a thorough reconnoisance of the ground, "it was deemed utterly impracticable to make the move until Sherman could get up. * * * I was forced to leave Burnside for the present to contend against superior forces of the enemy." Longstreet on November 13th was still at Loudon, which he could reach by railroad. Grant thought that probably he tarried so long at the latter place in obedience to orders, the point being eligible for the reason, that if necessary, he could speedily return to the support of Bragg, or otherwise proceed to Knoxville, 29 miles distant, by the common highway. His presence at Loudon was definitely known at the last named date.

On the morning of the 14th (Saturday), Gen. Burnside left Knoxville, accompanied by his visitors, the Hon. Mr. Dana and Col. Wilson, by the Hon. Horace Maynard and others, to Lenoirs, five miles east of Loudon, where they parted from him. He found that Longstreet was building a bridge from the west to the east bank of the Tennessee River, at Hough's Ferry, just below Loudon, and had thrown a force across in advance of the main body of his army. Burnside sent Gens. Potter and White to drive it back, which by nightfall they did, the day being consumed in skirmishing. He had previously proposed by telegraph to Grant that he, Burnside, should draw Longstreet on to Knoxville, so as to separate him at a greater distance from his base, and prevent him from going as quickly as he might from Loudon, to give help to Bragg, if needed. The suggestion was approved by Grant, who in reply dispatched to Burnside on the 14th, that Sherman would be ready to move from Bridgeport towards Chattanooga by the following Tuesday, 17th, at furthest. Grant's dispatch continued: "If you can hold Longstreet in check until he, Sherman, gets up, or by skirmishing and falling back, can avoid serious loss to yourself, and gain time, I will be able to force the enemy back from here and place a force between Longstreet and Bragg that must inevitably make the former take to the mountain passes by every available road to get to his supplies."

General Grant estimated at its true worth the advantage he would derive in his intended battle of Missionary Ridge, from the absence of Longstreet and his veteran soldiers. He has written that "the victory at Chattanooga was accomplished more easily than was expected by reason of Bragg's making several grave mistakes," and the first of the three, he proceeds to state, was "sending away his ablest corps commander with over twenty thousand troops."

General Burnside in his official report, says in connection with a recital of his first encounter with Longstreet near Loudon: "Knowing the purpose of Gen. Grant as I did, I decided that he could be better served by drawing Longstreet farther away from Bragg than by checking him at the river, and I accordingly decided to withdraw my forces and retreat leisurely towards Knoxville, and soon after daylight on the 15th the whole command was on the road." His object was attained. As he retired, his adversary pursued, except that Longstreet sent Wheeler's cavalry by way of Maryville to seize the heights on the south side of the river, opposite and commanding Knoxville. Wheeler surprised and captured at Maryville, the Eleventh Kentucky. Gen. Parkes with a part of the 23rd corps, and a body of cavalry under Gen. Sanders had been left at Knoxville to protect it. Sanders checked the progress of Wheeler and fell back upon the heights south of the river, where he and Parkes defeated Wheeler, who retreated to join Longstreet by way of Louisville. To that village, Longstreet had tried to have boats towed up the Tennessee River, but the current was too rapid.

New life was given the United States troops at the front by Burnside's coming to them. As he went forward, he passed by a large body of them, near Lenoir's Station. "Under his slouched hat," says one of his observers, "there was a sterner look than there was wont to be." "There is trouble ahead," said the men: but the cheers which rose from regiment to regiment, as, with his staff and battle flag he swept past, told the confidence which all felt in "old Burnie." Their strong trust in him was also shown when he arrived near Loudon and took the chief command. One of them relates:

"Notwithstanding the continued rain and the heavy roads, the presence of our commander produced a noticeable change in the spirit of the troops. An hour before, the men were deliberately covering themselves with mud, as if that were an appropriate mourning for their departed hopes, and their guns seemed naturally to seek a reverse position. But now they were all animation, and a slip here and a fall there, was made the cause of laughing, notwithstanding the rain. I think the secret of it was, that we reposed in our leader an almost perfect confidence resulting from long and tried associations. Few corps commanders have ever won the affection of their men as Burnside did."

The retreating march on the 15th was made with difficulty. Clouded heavens in the morning, soon gave forth heavy rain, followed by a cold north wind. The roads were almost impassable. Regiments of infantry had often to pull the artillery with ropes from out of the deep, stiff mud in which it stuck. Now and then, horses were held fast by the tough, clay soil, until a detail of men came to their deliverance. Soldiers lost their shoes in it, and on running back to recover them were greeted by the merry laughter of their companions. At Lenoir's, the army halted for the night of Sunday. The air was bitter cold. To avoid observation only one fire was allowed to each company. The hours of darkness passed away in broken rest and petty alarms. In the early morning, one hundred wagons, whose mules were needed to draw the artillery, and also as much of the supplies—bacon, coffee, sugar—as the soldiers could not carry, were burned. Officers' baggage, books —everything that could not well be transported— were destroyed. The trains were started for Knoxville, guarded by the 79th New York Highlanders. Then a number of military divisions and the artillery, moved forward to the village of Campbell's Station, eight miles distant. A brigade guarded the rear, and at one time was severely pressed by its enemies, until it turned and drove them back. In the struggle, Col. Smith of the 20th Michigan was killed at the head of his regiment after most able conduct.

Not far west of Campbell's Station another highway from Kingston forms a junction with the road they traveled. It was believed that Longstreet would try to reach that point first, in order to cut Burnside off from Knoxville. Therefore, the latter sent Gen. Hartraupt with his division and Col. Biddle's cavalry, in advance to the fork of the roads. They were successful in anticipating their foes, and held the point of junction until all the United States troops and their trains had passed, but not without some fighting. Among their losses by death, was one specially lamented, that of Lieut. P. Marion Holmes, of Charlestown, Mass., a member of the Bunker Hill Club, who bore on his person its badge, engraved with the line,

"*Dulce et decorum est, pro patria mori,*"

quoted by Warren just before the battle of Bunker Hill. He is described as "frank, courteous, manly, brave; one who had won all hearts."

While that contest was going on, Col. Loring reconnoitered the ground near Campbell's Station and Gen. Potter planted his artillery there. Gen. Burnside also proceeded to dispose his troops at the village for battle, as he felt it to be necessary to check his enemy in order that his own trains might get to Knoxville. His infantry was drawn up in line between two ranges of hills nearly a mile apart. Gen. Ferrero's division, Ninth corps, was placed on the right of the road. Gen. White's division, Twenty-third corps, held the centre, and Gen. Hartraupt's division, Ninth corps, was on his left. The batteries were chiefly on the right of the road, only one of the five being on its left. At noon Longstreet's troops advanced out of the woods to the attack in two lines of battle, with a line of skirmishers in front. As the whole field of action lay exposed, the panorama was very interesting for its scenic effect. When the Confederate troops had emerged from the forest, their heavy and well-dressed ranks went forward rapidly with colors flying. Benjamin's battery on Burnside's right and Roemer's battery on his left, opened fire upon them immediately with shot, which tore gaps in their ranks, but their line closed up, and they still advanced. Then the batteries, with accuracy, poured forth shell, which broke them up so badly that nothing else could be done but to fall back, which they did in confusion. The Confederate batteries were brought into service and played with some precision upon the Union infantry, and an artillery duel ensued that made the very hills tremble.*

Under cover of the smoke and the woods a strong column moved against and pressed a brigade of Burnside's right, which changed its front, and by its resistance, with the aid of double charges of canister shot from artillery at short range, his enemy's column was checked, and retreated.

Longstreet then maneuvred to turn the Federal left. As there was some high ground on that hand, commanding Burnside's position, which he saw his enemy was endeavoring to occupy, and he could not, for lack of men, extend his own line to prevent the threatened movement, he moved his troops and established a new line upon a ridge nearly three-fourths of a mile to the rear. This was done under a heavy artillery fire from his enemy, but with no disorder. It was about 4 P. M. Quickly a fierce attack was made upon the new line, not in front, but flank and rear, at the extreme left. That was handsomely repulsed. His enemy went back in disorder, and did not renew the fight. The United States troops were much elated by their success against odds, Burnside having had only about five thousand men in the battle, and his adversary from two to three times that number.

* NOTE.—" Near one of the batteries, when the wind would lift the smoke a little, we could distinguish a pair of (high) boots that resembled Burnside's boots, and judging from an occasional glimpse of an old soft felt hat which seemed to be nearly above them, we knew that somewhere between the two, our commander had his headquarters established.—WILL. H. BREARLEY."

He states in his official report: "Our loss in killed, wounded and missing was about three hundred, and that of the enemy must have been very severe, as he was the attacking force."* The "Rebellion Record" extols the military maneuvres of both armies for skill and beauty—as showing admirable discipline. Although comparatively an insignificant fight, "it certainly will rank among those contests in which real generalship was displayed. Every motion, every evolution, was made with the precision and regularity of the precision on a chess-board." The result was decisive. Burnside's line of retreat was saved, and he was given the few precious hours that were absolutely necessary to further fortify, and so, to hold Knoxville.

To that town, fifteen miles distant from Campbell's Station, the United States troops moved off silently, as soon as night fell.

During the night before at Lenoir's, following upon a day of weariness and anxiety, neither officers nor men had slept. No one could speak to his fellow, and in the thick darkness through the long, long night, they lay on their arms waiting for the morning, which ushered in a day of hard fighting. When that was ended, their soldierly patience and power of physical endurance were subjected to the additional test of marching over very muddy roads for another dark night. Some of them fell asleep from utter weariness as

---

* Charles F. Walcott's History of the 21st Regiment Massachusetts's Volunteers states the Union troops at six thousand, and their losses twenty-six killed, one hundred and sixty-six wounded and fifty-seven missing. The Rebellion Record, Vol. VIII, gives the rebel loss as one thousand killed and wounded.

they walked, but without losing their places in the ranks. About four o'clock on the morning of Monday, November 17th, they reached their destination. In the night, General Burnside arrived at his headquarters.

In the afternoon of the preceding Saturday startling rumors were circulated in Knoxville, that a considerable body of Confederate cavalry had appeared on the south side of the river opposite the town, and had attacked Col. Woolford with success, capturing a portion of his regiment. It was said, "they are rapidly moving upon the town," "they are already at Rockford, only nine or ten miles away and still coming." At the same time Gen. Shackelford could be seen with his staff upon Gay Street, riding towards the pontoon bridge, which had been transferred from the Tennessee river at Loudon, and thrown across it at Knoxville. Placed by Gen. Burnside in command of all the cavalry, the reason of his then taking the field was the arrival of Gen. Wheeler, sent by Gen. Longstreet from Loudon to take possession of the heights on the south side of the river opposite Knoxville. Considering the importance and peril of Gen. Shackelford's errand, he appeared to a citizen observer, cool and calm to the point of indifference. Readers of romantic fiction and lovers of American chivalry, are accustomed to associate with their ideas of the warrior and hero a gay, prancing steed, of fiery temper and proud head. The horse he rode was a gentle, well-conditioned pacer, with a short tail, and the *tout*

MAJ. GEN. S. P. CARTER.

ensemble of such a quadruped, capable of serving equally well any and every member of a family. The chief of cavalry himself, as he rode along the street, was composedly smoking one of the short-stemmed pipes which were extensively used by the soldiers. As the conflict on the south side ended in possession of its hills being retained by the Federal troops, the unpleasant fears Union citizens felt concerning the capture of the town were shortly dispelled: but with the morrow similar apprehensions were aroused among a few leading public men upon being informed of Longstreet's advance with his main army and of Burnside's retreat upon Knoxville.

General Saml. P. Carter was of course advised of those movements and was strongly impressed, as well he may have been, with the imminent danger there was, that the United States army with only 12,000 men, would be unable to hold the town against 20,000 men including cavalry. In his regard for the safety of certain prominent Union citizens, he sent them word of the disastrous contingency shortly ahead, and, if they chose to escape the consequences of its occurrence, that he would provide them an escort as far as expedient on their way to the more favored clime of Kentucky. At such a time, men whose active locomotion may deliver them from imprisonment that might end in death, are apt to

"Stand not upon the order of their going,
But go at once."

Their dislike to travel night and day by wretched

roads, over mountains and unbridged rivers, and their sensitiveness to ridicule for imputed cowardice, are not strong enough to overcome their love of personal liberty and life. Many or all of them who received the Provost Marshal General's message—some of whom were of less note but still liable to violent treatment if they were captured—speedily took their leave of home and its comforts and were conducted by Capt. A. J. Ricks, eight miles to the picket lines. Among the refugees were John Baxter, William G. Brownlow, Samuel R. Rodgers, Thos. A. R. Nelson, O. P. Temple, John M. Fleming, Samuel Morrow and M. M. Miller of Knoxville, and John Netherland and Absalom A. Kyle of Rogersville. It was after nightfall and raining heavily when they started, and their transit on horseback through the darkness upon a road shortly before traveled and reduced to mire by 6,000 or 7,000 hogs that had been brought in to supply the army, could not fail to attract attention from people of the country through which they passed.* Despite all perils and difficulties the journey was at length safely accomplished.

The company thus delivered from impending harm, might have been joined at the start by some other citizens of less prominence, had they been included in the message and given an opportunity to depart.

One of that description had been informed in succession by his personal friends of both parties, that

* See Appendix: Note S.

it was intended, if the town fell into the hands of Longstreet, to seize and hold him as hostage for a contumacious enemy of the United States whom Gen. Burnside had found it necessary to send to Camp Chase. He gave no heed to the warning, because he rested in his strong impression of the town's security from enemies, but this mental persuasion was disturbed on the afternoon preceding the exodus of noted public men, as just related. Passing along the street in utter ignorance of events then transpiring between the hostile armies not far from Loudon, he met a fellow-citizen of capricious loyalty, who had been known as a "Southern man" during the Confederate *regime*, but was understood to have publicly thanked the Lord upon the advent of Gen. Burnside's army, for "bringing in our friends." In the conversation that ensued on the street, the person of versatile opinions indulged in such fault-finding with the United States Government, its policy, &c., as to suggest a strong suspicion that he was adapting his sails to a contrary wind. Acting upon this conjecture, the citizen who had been forewarned of his danger if the town should change its masters, went immediately to the house of Gen. Carter, and found his staff in a state of unusual excitement. In reply to his question, "What is the matter?" the visitor was told, "Longstreet is marching upon Knoxville with, it is said, 20,000 men. Burnside is retreating from Loudon, fighting as he comes. We do not know what is going to happen." Said the citizen, "I have been told that I had better get out of the town in the event it is to be captured. Should anything more of importance occur, I shall be glad to know it." After night, a few hours later, two gentlemen called on him. They were aides, one of whom said, "We have been sent by Gen. Carter to say, that you must leave town for Kentucky early to-morrow morning."

After a night's deliberation, though very loth to leave home, wife and children, he decided that the direction of his military friend called for some obedience, and with reluctant mind and slow hands he made preparations for the journey. These were not completed before the second morning, but when all was ready he decided, before starting, to say "good-bye" to Gen. Burnside. Near a large gate that opened from the street upon a wide yard in front of headquarters, the Commander-in-chief was found about to mount his horse. His brows were knit, stern determination sat upon his face, and his whole soul seemed to be wrapped in earnest self-communion. The fighting had begun west of the town between his troops and Longstreet's and he was on the eve of starting to the front. The citizen saw at once that then was not the time to speak. He was content to keep at a distance and thoughtfully contemplate the man to whom the moment was evidently a supreme one. Perhaps it was a critical one in the destiny of many people in the region for whose defence the General had been appointed.

The civilian may be forgiven, if as he stood and

looked at the man of war going forth to conflict, he should be reminded of Job's words descriptive of the war horse:

> "He goeth on to meet the armed men,
> He mocketh at fear and is not affrighted,
> Neither turneth he back from the sword."

As the citizen stood and looked, there came upon him the irresistible conviction that Burnside would hold the town! Immediately turning upon his heel, he went home and sent to the stable the horses which were waiting to take him to Kentucky.

CHAPTER XV.

SIEGE OF KNOXVILLE—ITS DEFENDERS AND DE-
FENCES — COL. SANDERS — HIS DEATH AND
FUNERAL—PROGRESS OF THE SIEGE—BURN-
ING OF NORTH KNOXVILLE.

> "Flag of the free hearts' hope and home,
> By angel hands to valor given;
> Thy stars have lit the welkin dome,
> And all thy hues were born in heaven;
> Forever float that standard sheet!
> Where breathes the foe but falls before us,
> With Freedom's soil beneath our feet,
> And Freedom's banner floating o'er us."
> JOSEPH RODMAN DRAKE.

From Campbell's Station, Gen. Burnside, on November 16th, sent instructions to Capt. Orlando M. Poe, chief engineer of the Department of the Ohio, who was at Knoxville, to select lines of defence for the town, in readiness for the troops to occupy positions. This order Poe was able, from previous and frequent examinations of the ground and his familiar knowledge of the army, to fulfil quickly. Before leaving Kentucky he had organized an engineer battalion from the 23d corps, and by great efforts had brought over the mountains engineering tools.

Knoxville is situated chiefly on a hill, about two hundred feet high on the north bank of the Tennessee river. The hill, at its top, has a wide table land, and is separated on the east and west by creeks from even higher hills that rise up from the river. In the valley immediately on the north, runs the road of the East Tennessee, Virginia and Georgia Railway Company, beyond which the town was then but partially extended.*

Capt. Sims', 24th Indiana, and Henshaw's battery (the first of six and the second of two James' rifle guns), and also four brass six-pounders, occupied Temperance Hill on the east side of First Creek, supported by Chapin's Brigade of White's Division, and Riley's Brigade of Hascall's Division of the Twenty-third army corps. Shield's battery, six twelve-pound Napoleons, and part of Wilder's, occupied Mabry Hill, which is higher and farther east than Temperance Hill. These were supported by the brigades of Cols. Hoskins and Casement, extending from Bell's house on the northern base of Mabry Hill to the river south of it. One section of twelve-pound howitzers was planted on Flint Hill, nigh to that point on the river manned by soldiers of loyal Tennessee regiments. On the west of the main town and Second Creek, Roemer's battery of four three inch rifle guns, occupied College Hill near the river, supported by Morrison's brigade of the First Division, Ninth army corps. At the fort on the hill top northwest of College Hill, were placed Benjamin's battery of four twenty-pound Parrotts, and Buckley's battery of six thirteen-pound Napoleons, sup-

*Appendix: Note T.

ported by Humphrey's and Christ's brigades, of the First Division, Ninth army corps. The ground occupied by this Division extended from the river near the mouth of Second Creek around to the point· where the East Tennessee, Virginia and Georgia Railway crosses Second Creek, northwest of the older town, and was under the command of Gen. Ferrero. Gitting's battery was on Vine street, overlooking the railroad depot on the north, and between it and First Creek was the Fifteenth Indiana battery of three three-inch rifle guns—these two batteries being supported by the Second Division, Ninth army corps, (Gen. Hartraupt's), extending from Second to First Creek and parallel to the railroad.

On the south side of the river were Shackelford's cavalry and Cameron's brigade of Hascall's Division, Twenty-third army corps, the latter supporting Koukle's battery of four guns and two sections of Wilder's battery (all three-inch rifles). Riley's brigade was held in reserve in the streets of the town.

The defences at first raised by the troops were simply ditches four feet wide and deep, with the excavated earth embanked on the outside; except the more formidable structures on Temperance Hill and those held by Lieut. Benjamin's battery built by the engineer battalion. Fatigued as were the soldiers who had been at Campbell's Station, they as well as others, labored with energy upon the entrenchments throughout the whole day and night of November 17th, and would then have

PREPARATIONS FOR A SIEGE.

been compelled to cease, had not Col. Sanders, with his cavalry on the Kingston road, and Col. Pennybaker, with his mounted regiments on the Clinton road, held Longstreet's forces in check. Capt. Poe says: "The hours in which to work, that the gallant conduct of our cavalry secured us, were worth to us a thousand men each." The next morning two hours of rest were given them, and were used in sleep by the men without delay on the ground where they stood. At the same time Gen. Burnside, in consultation with Capt. Poe and Col. Sanders, was informed by the first that the rifle pits would be ready for defence before the end of many hours, and by the other, that with his cavalry, "seven hundred strong and in good fighting trim," he could hold Longstreet at bay until that time had expired. For another day and night the men persevered in labor with ready wills and hands. The suggestion by one of their officers that the alternative of effective resistance to the enemy would be a visit to Libby prison, served as an incentive to both industry and heroism. Many of them had been without rest but for two hours in a hundred, and it was necessary for their relief that contrabands and citizens should be pressed into service. The former did heartily the tasks assigned them, the difficulty of which in some instances may be inferred from the fact that places for the guns of Benjamin's and Buckley's batteries could only be cleared by four hours diligent labor of two hundred men. Of the citizens who had to work on the entrenchments, they who were loyal to the United States did their duty cheerfully, but "many," according the Chief Engineer, "were rebels, and worked with a very poor grace, which blistered hands did not tend to improve."

In the afternoon of the 18th the skirmishing between Sanders' dismounted cavalry and Longstreet's advance, two miles west of the town, was concluded by a fire of artillery upon Sanders, which compelled him to retreat after he had successfully resisted—with rail fences as shields—the charges of his powerful foe. At the close of the contest he received a mortal wound, reeled upon his horse and falling, was caught in the arms of his men and taken to a house in town. In full possession of his mind, there was no disturbance of its calmness by the answer of the surgeon to his question as to the nature of his wound. Death had no terrors for him. "He had done his duty and served his country as well as he could." That was all in few and simple words he had to say. The following day, being informed that the end of his life was nigh at hand, he asked for a Christian minister, and then that he should be baptized in the faith and name of Jesus, the Son of God. The Rev. Mr. Hyder, chaplain of the post, complied with this earnest desire, and a writer in the *Atlantic Monthly** relates that, "then the minister in prayer commended the believing soul to God, General Burnside and his staff, who were present, kneeling around the bed. When the prayer

*Major Burrage, of the 36th Massachusetts Regiment.

was ended, General Sanders took General Burnside by the hand. Tears dropped down the bronzed cheeks of the chief as he listened to the last words which followed. The sacrament of the Lord's Supper was now about to be administered, but suddenly the strength of the dying soldier failed, and like a child he gently fell asleep." To this pathetic recital its author appends the quotation from the sayings of Him who spake as never man spake: "Greater love hath no man than this, that a man lay down his life for his friends."

It was found impossible to assemble the chief officers of the United States army by day at the funeral of their slain companion. Longstreet's troops had advanced to the ridge for which they fought and planted themselves within rifle range of the defences on the northwest, and the town had become fairly besieged, north, from the river above to the river below. Lines parallel with and in cannon range of Burnside's, had been established, and redoubts had been thrown up for batteries, which on the third day opened a continuous fire that met with prompt answer. There was need of constant vigilance and alertness upon the long line of defences, and those in command could not prudently leave their posts of duty in day-light.

In the afternoon, a resident minister of the Gospel was requested by General Burnside to attend after nightfall the funeral of the officer, whose wound unto death had signalized the beginning of the siege and thrown a dark shadow upon the spirits of his companions. They gathered together at their commander's headquarters, and among them was the Chief Engineer of the Department, who was a personal friend of the deceased—his only class-mate at the siege—who spoke of him as a "most gallant, chivalric soldier and noble gentleman." To Capt. Poe, Gen. Sanders had communicated the premonition he had, that death awaited him in battle on the day he fell. And with the Captain, he had left on going to the field, some personal treasures, among which were a few letters from one who he had hoped would in the future be his bride. He was yet young, his age being 28.

As the party of mourners passed down the street to the hotel where the body lay, Gen. Burnside spoke of the extraordinary personal daring of the departed man. With sad emphasis he said, "I told Sanders not to expose himself, but he *would* do it." Upon reaching the hotel, the company's number was increased by waiting friends, and after religious offices a procession was formed upon the silent street. There was no plumed hearse, drawn by well-fed horses, but kindly hands of brother-soldiers to bear the dead, at the end of

"The path of glory that leads but to the grave."

A sort of weird solemnity invested the darkened scene. Its features were in such strong contrast with those which might be expected in the fitness of things it would wear. No funeral strains of martial music floated on the air. Its quiet was not even disturbed by the dull thumping of the solitary drum and the heavy tread of armed soldiers. It seemed as if War, disrobed of its pomp and pageantry, had taken its departure and its absence was supplied by heaven-born Peace, clothed in plain and simple attire, disdaining through profound grief all trappings of woe. An observer might fancy that the army, which with dauntless courage refused to surrender to men in superior force, had now surrendered to God, and that its chieftains, having yielded up their swords, were marching along the way into captivity.

But yet, not all is peaceful. For hark! there comes the sound of booming cannon. And every little while it again peals forth upon the hushed air. From the presence of these night obsequies, War is gone, but he lingers near and bids defiance to the encroacher on his domain. Little heed, though, do the mourners give to his hoarse notes. And the heavens appear to sympathize in the grief, for their face is covered with mist as with a veil, and hanging low in the western sky, a young moon sheds her dimmed luster on the scene, and from above all, the loving eye of One looks down, without whose notice, although He rules the army of heaven, not a sparrow falls to the ground.

At the head of the procession went the Commander-in-chief and the minister. By their side walked the Medical Director of the army,[*] bearing a lighted lantern in his hand. Said the clergyman:

"I am reminded of the lines on 'The Burial of Sir John Moore.'"

[*] Dr. Jackson, of Pennsylvania.

Gen. Burnside quickly replied, striking his hand on his thigh, "I have thought of them twenty times to-day."

That lantern did duty at the grave, as the body was committed, " earth to earth, ashes to ashes, dust to dust," in hope of the resurrection of the dead. When all was over, the General said to the minister a thoughtful word concerning the event, inevitable, awaiting all men; and then every one went his way, some to watch and some to sleep: but probably few of the company could forget the burial of Gen. R. M. Sanders, in the likeness of its circumstances to the "Burial of Sir John Moore."

> "Not a drum was heard nor a funeral note
>   As his corse to the ramparts we hurried,
> Not a soldier discharged his farewell shot
>   O'er the grave where our hero we buried.
>
> We buried him darkly at dead of night,
>   The sod with our bayonets turning,
> By the struggling moonbeams' misty light,
>   And the lantern dimly burning.
>
> Few and short were the prayers we said
>   And we spoke not a word of sorrow,
> But we steadfastly gazed on the face of the dead
>   And we bitterly thought of the morrow.
>
> *   *   *   *   *   *   *   *
>
> But half of our heavy task was done,
>   When the clock struck the hour for retiring,
> And we knew by the distant random gun
>   That the foe was sullenly firing.
>
> Slowly and sadly we laid him down
>   From the field of his fame, fresh and gory,
> We carved not a line, we raised not a stone
>   But we left him alone in his glory."

On the morning of November 20th the defences were thought to be capable of resisting any probable foe, but during that entire day and night, the work of strengthening them was continued. Indeed such labor was prosecuted for a considerable period of time, in which the besiegers were also busy at work for a contrary purpose. All that skill and toil could effect was done to hold the town. First Creek was successfully dammed at the Vine Street bridge, and a dam that made a strong obstacle was built across Second Creek where it passes through a tunnel under the railroad. In front of the rifle pits, a *chevaux de frise* was formed of pointed stakes, bound together by wire, and nearly five feet high, and at one place two thousand pikes, captured at Cumberland Gap, were used for a like purpose. In front of the stakes thick branches of trees were firmly set in the ground. The besiegers occupied a large brick dwelling house a short distance west of Fort Sanders, which the adult children of the Hon. Wm. B. Reese, Sr., deceased, had been compelled to vacate. The sharp-shooting carried on from it became at length so annoying that at night on the 20th, the Seventeenth Michigan regiment was sent to destroy the building. One might have supposed from the loud voice of the Colonel in giving orders and the ringing cheers of his men, that a small army was approaching the house, and in a great fright the inmates ingloriously fled without firing a gun. The dwelling and barns were burned to the ground. On that day, there was a repetition of the firing from a battery Longstreet had planted upon the Tazewell road, and which had thrown the first shells into the town—without harm at either time. For several days there were constant sharp-shooting, skirmishing and cannonading without important consequences.

It was believed by some that had Gen. Longstreet attempted with concentrated forces to take the town upon his arrival, he would have succeeded, but the judgment of mere civilians upon the subject is of little or no account, and competent military strategists would probably differ in opinion concerning it. There can be no doubt that his delay in a vigorous and determined assault increased the hazard of defeat, by giving Burnside time and opportunity, which he took care to improve, for adding to the strength of his defences. Perhaps Longstreet felt that he had Burnside in a trap from which there was no reasonable hope of escape, and that instead of sacrificing men in capturing him by violent conflict, he would compel the surrender of the United States army by starvation. To all appearances the Confederate commander had plenty of time to that end. Armed help could not come to the besieged, except from Gen. Grant at Chattanooga, whose predecessor had not long before sustained a *quasi* defeat at Chicamauga, who was confronted by a powerful foe, and who, Gen. Bragg, from his own advantageous position, thought was at his mercy. Could Longstreet have fore-seen the complete rout of Bragg at Missionary Ridge, no doubt he would more actively have prosecuted his undertaking at Knoxville, but alas! for the shortness of human prevision. Important events in the womb of the near future, military as well as civil, are foreknown but by Him who only is wise. As Longstreet could not anticipate the serious disaster to the Confederate arms at the battle of Chattanooga, he sat down before Knoxville with composure and wariness, and rather toyed with his supposed victim than contended with him as an equal adversary.

And really, the investment of the town was so closely maintained, that a surrender of the besieged army, because of starvation before relief could be had from any quarter, seemed within the range of probabilities. The amount of its supplies when the siege began was very limited. Cattle and hogs were at once slaughtered and salted down, but there were in the commissary department only one or two days' rations for the whole army. Only quarter rations were at first issued. Within a few days these were wholly stopped, as all that could be served were needed by the hospitals, and no sugar or coffee could be had. Possession was taken of the mills for Government use. Citizens were living upon plain food in reduced quantities, but these were necessarily drawn upon to meet the army's necessities. The larders of people who sympathized with the Confederacy had especially to suffer. In some cases Union families befriended their neighbors, who in the exigency would otherwise have been put to great straits. A Union man might be troubled by the thought that he was giving "aid and comfort to the enemy," by keeping under his bedstead a sack of flour for a Secessionist who had a wife and five children to feed (of which there was an instance), but his troubled mind would easily find refuge in the thought that he was obeying the teachings of humanity. A spirit of fear was widely diffused, under the influence of which money as well as provisions, were temporarily transferred for safety from one person to another. The fright was greatest in respect to cash, at the beginning of the siege, when not only small sums thus changed hands, but a place of secure deposit for large ones was eagerly sought. A citizen was surprised by a night visit, the object of which was to leave with him a hundred thousand dollars, belonging to a stranger who the next morning had sufficient nerve to decamp to Kentucky, carrying the money with him.

By the pontoon bridge over the river, free access was had by Burnside's troops to a portion of the country that was intensely loyal to the United States, including the southern side of Knox county and the whole of Sevier County. Some of the people of that region voluntarily furnished supplies to the besieged; and foraging parties from the army were sent out, who returned with corn, wheat, &c. By these means, conducted by Capt. Doughty, spoken of by the commander-in-chief as "a most excellent officer," the commissary department was enabled to issue during the siege after its first few days, bread made of mixed flour, meal and bran, but then only in half and quarter rations.

Even for this bread, corn on the cob, eaten in some instances unroasted, had to be substituted several times late in the siege. Soldiers often ate at once the small piece of bread which was their whole allowance of nourishment for twenty-four hours. Some of them, whether from a prudent regard to the returning excesses of hunger, or to keep up the fiction of three meals a day, divided their bread into as many parts, which gave them a single mouthful for each meal. This scanty fare was increased on occasional days by a piece of fresh pork.

The besiegers wisely thought it important to deprive Burnside of his supplies from south of the river, and for that purpose to destroy his bridge. Therefore Confederate soldiers were sent a few miles up the Tennessee to Boyd's Ferry—a point near its junction with the French Broad River, for the construction of a raft, which floating down would carry away the pontoon. News of this intended feat was conveyed to headquarters. Townsmen understood that one of the patriotic and courageous women, who never failed in East Tennessee to serve the United States upon opportunity, from her home in the country saw the hewing down of timber and building of the raft, then adroitly she made her way by night through the Confederate lines with information to Knoxville, at the risk of liberty and life. In consequence, on the 22d, at the General's order, Lieut. Col. Babcock and Capt. Poe constructed a boom, by stretching an iron cable 1,000 feet long across the river above the bridge. Begun at 5 P. M., it was finished at 9 A.M. the next day, and three days later upon renewed alarms, a second boom was laid, of long timber fastened with chains, on the surface of the water.

On the 23d, after night had fallen, the Second Division, Ninth army corps, (Gen. Hartraupt), was attacked and forced to fall back through that part of the town lying north of the railroad. In this retreat, houses that were occupied, or in danger of being so, by Confederate sharp-shooters, were set on fire and burned. For that purpose the Federal troops made some gallant sorties. Among the buildings destroyed in the course of the general battling in that quarter, were dwellings of citizens. In a few instances families were able to save some of their household goods, to which work officers and men contributed help when it was possible, but on the night of the 23d, little or nothing could be done in that way. The railroad machine shops, numbering eighteen or twenty buildings, and a former Confederate arsenal containing a large quantity of war material, shared in the conflagration. The flames that with crackling noise wrapped many houses in their glowing arms, the billows of smoke brightly spotted with huge sparks and burning fragments of wood, the crash of breaking timbers and falling roofs, the explosion of shells in the arsenal, the firing of guns by the contending armies which the light of the flames made conspicuous, and their defiant shoutings at each other in tumultuous anger, altogether combined to form a remarkable scene. To a lively imagination, it might seem a panorama of the infernal region—that the roar of guns was the music of its orchestra, and that evil spirits joined in the *melee*, were struggling for the mastery in the smoky air above the blazing houses and fighting men. The conflagration lasted nearly all night.

Next morning the ground from which the Union army had been driven was recovered by Lieut. Colonel Hawkes of the Twenty-first Massachusetts.

The 24th witnessed a brave sally of the Second Michigan Volunteers upon the enemy's advanced rifle pits north of Fort Sanders. They were at first successful, but not being properly supported, were finally repulsed, with some loss. On the night of the same day, a pontoon bridge was thrown across the river below the town, upon which a portion of Longstreet's forces passed over, and on the 25th they made a desperate attempt to seize the heights commanding Knoxville, but Gen. Shackelford, reinforced by Col. Riley's brigade, encountered and defeated them. Failing in that object, they planted a battery upon a high bluff close to the river's southern bank, more than a mile distant from Fort Sanders, but partially commanding it and also the nearer earthworks on College Hill.

The 26th was thanksgiving day, and Gen Burnside issued an order for its observance, not in customary feasting, which was impossible, but by gratitude to God; and he recalled to his men's minds the trials of those who established the Republic, as an encouragement to endure their own hardships. And indeed they had need of fortitude, for not only were they hungry, but the weather was cold—the overcoats and blankets of many had been cast away at Campbell's Station, with their tents—and their resource for warmth was to crawl, when off duty, into holes which they dug in the bank, back of the trenches. Still as they ate their bits of bread, their thoughts were turned to loved ones at home, and their hearts might be thankful. After dark, important positions were made stronger in front with telegraph wires stretched from stump to stump.

On the 27th Longstreet kept up active firing chiefly with artillery, but Burnside's army was silent. Early that evening there was much cheering by the besiegers and music from their bands. In the night men were employed in chopping down trees, clearing the way for a battery on the south-side river bluff, two thousand yards and more from Fort Sanders. The signs of their taking positions in the front for attack were so strong in the afternoon that the Federal soldiers stood in the trenches awaiting it.

Both armies were hard at work on Saturday, the 28th. The battery of six guns on the river bluff opened fire upon Roemer's battery between Fort Sanders and west of College Hill, but did no harm. About 11 o'clock at night, which was cloudy and very dark, the enemy attacked and drove in the pickets in front of Fort Sanders, captured many of them and occupied their lines about one hundred yards away from the Fort. The fighting was hot, and lasted two hours. Capt. Buffum, with a fresh detail, established a new line of pickets and by hard work, new pits were thrown up before day. There was skirmishing all night long, and a slow cannonading from the enemy's guns, principally upon Fort Sanders. The hours of darkness seemed long to Burnside's men, for they had to stand in the trenches, with no extra clothing to protect them from the cold.

Evidently, Fort Sanders was to be assaulted. Longstreet had had his arms around Knoxville for ten days, and had closed its doors to all messages from Burnside's friends. Grant had sought to send encouraging words from Chattanooga to the besieged commander, but could only dispatch them to Gen. Wilcox at Cumberland Gap, in the hope that by some means or other they might be transmitted to Knoxville. And now, the Confederate commander determined to come into close wrestle with his adversary and bring the siege to a triumphant conclusion.

CHAPTER XVI.

HOSPITAL NEEDS—A SCENE AT HEADQUARTERS — INCREASED DESTITUTION — ASSAULT ON FORT SANDERS — LONGSTREET RETREATS — SHERMAN'S APPROACH — BURNSIDE GIVES HONOR TO HIS ARMY.

> "Hark! to the call of the bugle horn,
> Or the quick rattle of mustering drum!
> Swift to the summons at even or morn,
> Bronzed and bearded the gallants come.
> Balls from the rifle-pits *plug* about,
> Great guns boom from the big redoubt,
> And the angry hiss of the burning shell
> Screams through the fire of smoke and hell.
> 'Who's for the trenches? We must have it out;
> Now is the time, lads, to try the redoubt.'
> Belted with fire and shrouded with smoke,
> Girdled with rifle-balls as with a wall,
> Yet with a yell from the trenches they broke,
> Plunging through rifle-balls, hell-fire and all."
> REV. WALTER C. SMITH,
> In "*Hilda Among the Broken Gods.*"

To a peace-loving civilian, not enlisted in the fray, it seemed on the 28th of November, that there had been enough of wounds and blood-shed during the siege to have satisfied any but a very ruthless soldier. Such were not those who engaged in strife at Knoxville, but war has its inexorable demands, and the soldier cannot refuse them. Therefore must sanguinary scenes be enacted on the morrow at Fort Sanders, at the sight of which the cheek of such a civilian might well grow pale with horror. All that happened on the preceding ten days would not compare with it. It was shocking to hear, at the first of the investment, the noise of musketry and artillery, knowing that it came from fellow-countrymen engaged in killing each other, and shocking to listen to the groans of wounded soldiers, borne along the streets in ambulances from the field of battle, and one's pity was deeply moved at seeing strong men prostrate in hospitals, with features sharpened by pain or pallid with the touch of death, but if one would learn greatly more of the evils of war, let him wait for the morrow and study the lesson it teaches.

At one time during the siege the hospitals in use became over-crowded and others had to be provided. One afternoon a Union citizen who was thought to have considerable influence with the United States military authorities, was visited by Judge A., who said:

"Mr. B., they are about to take the house of the Rev. Mr. C. and use it as a hospital."

"I am very sorry to hear it," replied B.

The Rev. Mr. C. had a wife and children, and might well be commiserated, if he and they should be turned out of doors in such sharply cold weather.

"I wish," proceeded the Judge, "you would see Gen. Burnside, and if possible, prevent it."

"Certainly," said B.; "will you not go with me?"

The Judge consented and they started for headquarters, but upon reaching the first street corner, the Judge stopped.

"Mr. B.," said he, "I have not much influence with the authorities. I wish you would undertake this matter alone."

"Very good," was the reply; for B. knew that his companion, although a worthy citizen and eminently learned in the law, was of doubtful reputation for loyalty to the United States, and as a good name in that last respect was of chief importance in the enterprise, he concluded that the Judge might as well withdraw.

Upon being admitted to headquarters Mr. B. found the Commander-in-chief engaged. Seizing the first good opportunity, he said:

"General, I learn from Judge A. that the house of the Rev. Mr. C. is about to be taken and used as a hospital."

"We do not take the houses of ministers of the Gospel for army purposes. Judge A. has been to us this morning and obtained exemption of his own house from that use." And then, calling with a loud voice to his adjutant, who was at the other end of the large room, the General said:

"Col. Richmond! send word to Dr. Jackson to take Judge A.'s house and use it for a hospital."

Mr. B., at this unexpected result of his interposition in behalf of the clergyman, was secretly perturbed. If he had known that the Judge had only a short time before applied successfully for the exemption of his own house, he could have

A SCENE AT HEADQUARTERS.

refrained from naming him. As it was, the Judge had been brought to grief by the intercession.

General R. B. Potter stood near and listened to the colloquy. His countenance wore an air of martial severity that was adapted more to repel than encourage further mediation. Mr. B. had, however, a "happy thought," and summoning up courage, he said:

"General, Doctor Jackson, I know, has already taken possession of a suitable building for a hospital and has never used it."

Promptly the General called out again, "Col. Richmond! you need not send that message to Dr. Jackson. Send him word to come and see me."

Whatever passed in their interview, neither Judge A. nor the Rev. Mr. C. was disturbed.

The sufferers in hospitals were all from the army. Few citizens received injury from the besiegers, for Gen. Longstreet did not bombard the town. It was said that he refrained from doing so through the influence of citizens of Knoxville who accompanied his army. The only death in the town caused by the fighting was that of a child on the street, who was struck by a stray minnie ball. One death among Longstreet's men, which caused great grief to him and his military family was that of a young sharp-shooter, who was occupying the tower of the house* where Gen. Longstreet had his headquarters. Blood flowed profusely from the wound as the body was carried down stairs,

---

* Mr. Robt. H. Armstrong's, over one mile west of Fort Sanders.

and all efforts to remove the stains from the steps were unsuccessful.

The great scarcity of food was even more pinching for the horses and mules than for the soldiers. So difficult was it to find sufficient provender for them that many of them were taken across the river and turned loose. A number of horses, left tied in an open field, fed upon one another's manes and tails, and were finally reclaimed in a condition of ridiculous nudity. Towards the close of the siege, among the reports of general officers made to headquarters at night, was one from Gen. Manson of Indiana. In it was the statement that "the mules had that day eaten up the fifth wheel of a caisson." The official report of this exploit of stubborn animals, whose chief vivacity was supposed to be in their heels, lightened the social atmosphere for a moment of its cares, and provoked a round of laughter from the company, in which the Commander-in-chief heartily joined. Habitually, a spirit of cheerfulness prevailed at headquarters. At first they were established in a large and commodious mansion on the principal street; but a hostile shell struck near the house, and it was conjectured that his enemy had learned of Burnside's precise location from citizens of the town. Therefore, upon advice of friends, his office was transferred to a store-house, one hundred yards southward across the way. There, as the siege progressed, when the work of the day was over, he relaxed in pleasant conversation with his military family, the younger members of which occasionally joined in vocal music with spirit and effect. A favorite song of the party was Mrs. Howe's Battle Hymn of the Republic:

"Mine eyes have seen the glory of the coming of the Lord."

There, at night, Union citizens visited, to learn his mind concerning the military situation and draw comfort and encouragement from his frank and hopeful words. Nor were those known to have been "Southern sympathizers," but who gave no occasion of offense to the authorities, excluded from his presence during the day, when seeking it in their troubles. Men who indulged in open and persistent contumacy, he visited with restraint, but more obnoxious cases of that kind were chiefly sent by Gen. Foster after the siege within the Confederate lines.

To the scarcity of food for man and beast was added that of fuel. There was a general destruction of fences in the town to supply the necessity, which was specially urgent in the hospitals, where the cold hastened the death of more than one feeble patient. The celerity with which a company of soldiers, acting under orders, could pull down planks, wrest up posts, and carry them all away, was remarkable. The spectators stood amazed. Unionist owners were contented over their losses, knowing the army's need, and friends of the South who lost, grieved in silence.

Not the least trying quality in the existing condition to the minds of Union people, was the uncertainty of the result, so full to them of weal or woe. Their anxiety was lessened by emulating the confidence of the soldiers in Burnside. As for any quiet reflection upon probabilities, they had little or no opportunity to indulge in it. Even the returning hours of darkness did not bring stillness. The night of November 28th was especially disturbed. The noise from the fighting near Fort Sanders for two hours about midnight, was followed by cannonading from Longstreet, which shook the frailer houses of citizens and broke their sleep into fragments. Before 6 o'clock next morning, people looking westward from upper windows, could see the flashing of artillery on the river bluff beyond College Hill, which accompanied

THE ASSAULT UPON FORT SANDERS.

Its garrison consisted of Benjamin's battery, part of Buckley's, and portions of both the 79th New York and the 2nd Michigan volunteer infantry. The fort itself was a bastioned earthwork, built upon an irregular quadrilateral, fronting 125 yards each, on the north and south, 95 yards on the west and 85 yards on the east. The last named front was left open—to be afterwards stockaded; the southern front was about half and the northern nearly finished, and the one on the west was entirely so, except cutting the embrasures. The bastion angles were very heavy, the relief of the lightest one being 12 feet. The ditch of the fort was 12 feet wide and from 7 to 8 feet deep. On the parapet were laid bales of cotton, which a covering of wet hides prevented from ignition by the cannon.

The whole command of Gen. Burnside were on the alert during the night. Especially so was Lieut. Benjamin, with his two hundred and twenty men under orders to keep strict silence. Just as the sun rose, the National flag was unfurled above the fort, and as the music of the "Star-spangled Banner" was poured forth at the same moment by the Division band, the voices of the men also went up in cheer after cheer. Then the enemy began a furious fire from batteries on the north and west, 700 and 1500 yards distant, and from the battery across the river. This cannonading lasted for twenty minutes, injuring only one man, but it met with no reply from Burnside's batteries. Immediately a fire of musketry was opened by Longstreet, and at the same time a heavy column of troops, which he had concentrated in the night upon the ridge about 80 yards from the bastions, charged on them under cover of a fog, at a run. His order, issued after midnight, through Maj. Gen. McLaws, was as follows:

HEADQUARTERS, Nov. 29, 1863.

GENERAL: Please impress your officers and men with the importance of making a rush when they once start to take a position as that occupied by the enemy yesterday. If the troops once started rush forward till the point is carried, the loss will be trifling; whereas, if they hesitate, the enemy gets courage, or being behind a comparatively sheltered position will fight the harder. Besides, if the assaulting party once loses courage and falters, he will not find courage, probably, to make a renewed effort. The men should therefore be cautioned before they start at such a work, and told what they are to do, and the importance and great safety of doing it *with a rush.*

        (Signed)   J. LONGSTREET, Lieut. Gen'l.

The bastion against which the assault was specially directed, fronted to the north and was almost finished. Its relief was about 13 feet, which added to the depth of the ditch, say 7 feet, made a distance of 20 feet from the bottom of the ditch to the interior crest. This and the steepness of the slope presented grave difficulties to the assailants. Add to them the dampness of the morning, the nature of the soil, the obstacles placed in front of the ditch and the absence of scaling ladders, and the success of the storming party was, in advance, most uncertain. The columns formed by Longstreet were of his best men, and consisted of three brigades of Gen. McLaw's division: one of Georgians under Gen. Wofford, one of Mississippians under Gen. Humphrey, and the third composed of Generals Anderson's and Bryant's brigades, South Carolinians and Georgians, with others. They went forward as ordered, "with a rush"—impetuously, and with a yell. First they encountered the abattis which broke their lines; then the telegraph wires tripped up and threw headlong whole companies. In their confusion, Lieut. Benjamin opened upon them with canister from his triple-shotted guns, and at the same time, portions of Gen. Hascall's division, placed the night before by Gen. Ferrero on the flanks of the fort, made a cross fire upon the assailants. Although many of them fell because of the entanglements,

ASSAULT ON FORT SANDERS.

the weight of the column forced its advance forward. In two or three minutes a crowd plunged into the ditch, and a few tried to reach the parapet. The raking shot from the fort still poured swiftly down upon them. Shells lighted in hand and tossed by Lieutenant Benjamin into the struggling mass, helped in the work of its destruction.

A second brigade follows the first, to attack and be slaughtered, but some of the men, escaping the ditch and surviving the tempest of death, press on and upward. Some climb the embankment. Three battle flags are planted on its top and are instantly pulled down. An officer with his hand on the muzzle of a cannon demands surrender of the fort and is immediately blown to pieces. Others also demand it and are felled. A dozen courageous men get into the bastion, are surrounded and disarmed. Two hundred prisoners are taken and sent to the rear. The garrison has helpers in the defence and bravely they stand or move on steady feet. They are sons of Michigan and Massachusetts.* Hopeless of success the storming party retreat, and the defenders shout, "Hurrah! hurrah! hurrah!" Distant soldiers listen and are glad, for the Union is triumphant. The star-spangled banner still floats in the air where it was unfurled when the sun rose.†

* Wm. Todd in "History of Seventy-ninth Highlanders, N. Y. Volunteers," says that the Second Michigan was a part of the reinforcement, (page 383.) Chas. F. Walcott in "History of Twenty-first Regiment, Massachusetts Volunteers," page 289, states that the garrison was reinforced by five companies Twenty-ninth Massachusetts, two companies Twentieth Michigan and a brigade of the Twenty-third corps.

† The boast among the besiegers had been that they "had got Mr. Burnside and his pet corps into a trap."

The ground between the fort and the crest is strewn with the slain and with wounded men crying for help. The ditch is filled with them almost to the brim. Burnside tenders a flag of truce and it is accepted. Now bury the dead and care for the wounded. Bring up the empty ambulances and send them away full to the hospitals. See to the bodies of Confederate soldiers piled one upon another. Some are dead and some are dying. Others are injured but will survive. Pull away the corpses—ruddy-faced in battle a little while ago, now white-faced in death. Let the living men who are lying underneath have fresh air. How glad they are to breathe freely again and to be in the sunlight! Draw them forth, whether they are silent or groaning. What is that? One of them speaks. "O God," he cries, "this is horrible."* And so it is. Let us depart from the scene.

Finally, call the roll, and count the losses of the contending parties. The difference in numbers of their killed and wounded resembles that of the battle of New Orleans, between such losses in the armies of Jackson and Packenham. Of the United States soldiers, there were eight killed and five wounded.† Of the Confederate officers and men, there were probably seven hundred killed and wounded and three hundred taken prisoners.

---

*A fact. An intelligent eye witness of the scene, who served in the United States Army and numerous battles of the period, affirms that he never witnessed such a spectacle of human slaughter.

†Capt. Poe says in his report, four killed and eleven wounded.

The stands of arms captured were to be counted by the thousands.

On both sides the military conduct was heroic. Gen. Burnside said: "The gallantry of this defence has not been excelled during the war." He congratulated the division of Gen. Ferrero, particularly Lieut. Benjamin and the officers and men with him in the fort, upon "this great achievement." Pollard (Confederate) says: "Never, excepting at Gettysburg, was there in the history of the war, a disaster adorned with the glory of such devout courage as Longstreet's repulse at Knoxville."

There was during the assault and for some time after, sharp fighting on the south side of the river, but the Federal troops maintained their lines of possession. The attack upon them was at first slightly to their disadvantage, but it was finally repulsed with heavy loss to their enemy. Longstreet's defeat at Fort Sanders was discouraging. Gen. B. R. Johnson, who had just joined him, asked permission to renew the assault with two brigades he had brought with him from Chattanooga. He was refused.* Gen. Longstreet gave orders to withdraw his lines, for the purpose of returning to Chattanooga. Just then he was

---

*NOTE.—At a reception given Gen. Burnside, January, 1864, at Boston, by the Second Massachusetts Infantry, the General in the course of his speech, told how he asked a rebel prisoner four or five days after the attack on Fort Sanders why Gen. Longstreet did not make a second one. "Well," said the prisoner "General, I will tell you. Our men just swear that they are never going into that slaughter pen again, and when they won't go, the ball won't roll."
(See Chas. F. Walcott's History of the Twenty-first Regiment Massachusetts Volunteers.)

informed *via* Richmond of Bragg's defeat by Grant and he was ordered to retire from Knoxville and go to the succor of Bragg. As an attempt to obey the order would be worse than useless, with Grant's victorious army between him and the retreating General whom he was ordered to succor, Longstreet concluded to continue the siege in the hope of drawing Grant to the relief of Burnside, and so from the pursuit of Bragg.

For several days in the beginning of December, work was continued upon the defences of the town by the Federal army, and constant watchfulness was observed. Then, as well as previously, telegraphic wires connected headquarters and all the forts. Gen. Burnside observed constant personal vigilance; therefore an assault upon any point would be quickly known and met by him. The greatest precautions were taken. Skirmishers were supplied with cotton balls soaked in turpentine, which thrown blazing into the air would expose an attacking column. Rockets, to be used in like manner for the same purpose, were placed along the lines. Locomotives and driving wheels were fastened to the defences with ropes, by cutting which, they could be sent rapidly down hill to repel an assault. By the issuance of stored and captured arms, at least every other soldier had two guns at his post; but their chief want was the means, not of resistance to their enemies by force, but of sustaining life and strength. Rations were smaller every day, and in their hunger a single particle of food was so precious they were eager to adroitly make it their own.* On December 2d, Burnside had tidings by a courier from Grant of the battle of Chattanooga, and also a promise that Sherman should come to raise the siege of Knoxville. At noon of the same day a single gun was fired from Fort Noble which signalled this news, and the brigade stood in the trenches and gave three cheers for Grant and Chattanooga. The hope of early reinforcements buoyed up the spirits of the soldiers, but as their nutriment consisted of a little meal made of corn and cobs, with a bit of pork, or of eight ounces of flour for each man, the hope could not wholly disperse their gloomy thoughts about Libby prison and Andersonville.

On December 3rd, the enemy's trains were seen moving eastward, and at night Capt. Audenried, of Gen. Sherman's staff, reached Gen. Burnside's headquarters. Relief was actually on the way, and the movements of Longstreet's trains on the 4th indicated an early abandonment of the siege. In the afternoon, however, his skirmishers were unusually active and their fire was easily provoked. The besieged stood under arms all night in expectation of an attack, but the zealous shooting which had led them them to fear it, was intended to cover another sort of movement. The next morning a profound silence reigned all around the town outside its defences. The pickets of the 36th Massachusetts, under Capt. Ames, were the first to dis-

* NOTE.—One of them relates: "Whenever any of us could get off duty, we would stroll over to where the teamsters were feeding their mules; should the teamsters be gone, the mules invariably lost their rations. Frequently the kernels of corn that the mules and horses could not help losing, were picked up out of the dirt and eaten by the nearly famished troops."

cover that the besiegers had taken up the line of march. The First brigade began to cheer over the discovery, and this cheering was echoed all along the lines until the men almost lost their breath. Their hats were thrown away as they shouted, and when every man's head was re-covered he shook hands with every other man he met, and there was a general jubilee. Longstreet had moved off, as Burnside said, "in remarkably good order," and the few cavalry who could be mounted for pursuit were unable to make any impression on him.

On that day a letter came to headquarters with congratulations from Gen. Sherman, at Maryville, 17 miles distant, saying that he could bring 30,000 men into Knoxville the next day, but as Longstreet had retreated, unless Burnside specified that he wanted troops, Sherman would let his men rest and he himself would ride to see him. On the morrow, the distinguished visitor arrived in town and was hospitably entertained by the Commander-in-chief.* Their conference resulted in the agreement that Sherman's forces, with the exception of Gen. Granger's corps, should return to Grant at Chattanooga.

On Monday, December 7th, all available infantry were sent in pursuit of Longstreet and halted at Rutledge. The cavalry went to Bean's Station, but refrained from attacking him at Red Bridge, for want of sufficient strength. On the 11th, Gen. Burnside, in compliance with his previous sugges-

* Appendix: Note U.

tion, was relieved by Maj. Gen. Foster in command of the Department, and the following day he departed for Cincinnati. There, a few days afterwards, in a public speech, he gave all the honors he received, to his officers and soldiers. One of them has said: "These kindly words" they "will ever cherish; and in all their added years, as they recall the widely separated battle-fields, made forever sacred by the blood of their fallen comrades, and forever glorious by the victories there won, it will be their pride to say, 'We fought with Burnside at Campbell's Station and in the trenches at Knoxville.'" *

Burnside's departure from East Tennessee was witnessed generally with sincere and in some instances profound regret. He had the affectionate esteem of the people—which to every wise and good man, is of more value than admiration of his talents. His conduct of military affairs had been grandly heroic, and he was justly rejoiced over the behavior of his men. He wrote:

"I shall ever remember with gratitude and pleasure, the co-operation, devotion, courage and patient endurance of the brave officers and men of the Ninth and Twenty-third corps, who have served so faithfully and conspicuously in Kentucky and East Tennessee. During the whole siege, and in the midst of the most arduous labor and greatest privations I never heard a word of discontent or distrust from any one of them. Each man seemed anxious to do his whole duty, and to

* See Atlantic Monthly, for July, 1866

their perseverance and courage is due the ultimate success of the defence of Knoxville.

"The loyal people of East Tennessee will always be gratefully remembered by me for their hearty co-operation, efficient aid and liberal hospitality."

Chief Engineer, Captain Poe, has said:

"There is no language sufficiently strong which I can use to express my admiration for the conduct of the troops. From the beginning of the siege to the end, every man did his whole duty. The cheerful looks and confident bearing which met us at every turn, made it seem as though we were sure of victory from the first. It is doubtful whether any man within our lines had at any time after the first forty-eight hours, any fear of the result. All privations were borne, all hardships undergone, with a spirit which indicated as plainly as if written on the walls, that success would attend our efforts. The troops of the Ninth and Twenty-third army corps were chivalric rivals where duty was to be done. Never before had an engineer officer less cause to complain of the manner in which his instructions and directions were carried out."

In the same connection, he testified to the great value of the contrabands' services, in many cases voluntarily offered. "Nearly two hundred of them labored during the siege, and for the first week, regularly eighteen hours in the twenty-four. The amount of their work, performed both day and night, the whole time," he said, "was truly astonishing."

CHAPTER XVII.

Captain Poe's Conclusions—President Lincoln's Proclamation—Generals Sherman and Grant—Intercessions with Gen. Foster—Battle of Resaca—Influx of Refugees to Knoxville.

> "What is the end of fame? 'Tis but to fill
> A certain portion of uncertain paper."
> Byron.

> "No more shall the war-cry sever,
>   Or the winding rivers be red;
> They banish our anger forever
>   When they laurel the graves of our dead!
> Under the sod and the dew,
>   Waiting the judgment day;—
> Love and tears for the Blue;
>   Tears and love for the Gray."
> F. M. Finch.

Captain Poe, towards the conclusion of his official report to Gen. Burnside, has given a judicious estimate of the events just narrated. He says:

"The siege of Knoxville passed into history. If mistakes were made in the defence, they were covered by the cloak of success. That many were made in the attack was apparent to us all.* That the rebels made a great error in besieging, is as evident as it now is, that to accept siege at Knoxville was a great stroke of military policy. The

---
* See Appendix: Note V.

results of the successful defence are, the defeat of Bragg's army and consequent permanent establishment of our forces at Chattanooga, with tolerably secure lines of communication; the confirmation of our hold upon East Tennessee; the discomfiture and loss of prestige of the choicest troops of the enemy's service. * * *

Is there any man of that part of the army of the Ohio which was in Knoxville, who would exchange his nineteen days of service there for any other of the achievements of his life? Was there a regiment there which will not put Knoxville on its banners as they now bear Roanoke or Newbern, Williamsburg or Fair Oaks, Chantilly or South Mountain, Antietam or Vicksburg?"

The news of Burnside's successful defence carried joy to Washington and to all friends of the United States everywhere. The President issued a proclamation concerning it, in which he spoke of the retreat of the enemy from before Knoxville "under the circumstances rendering it probable that the Union forces" could not thereafter "be dislodged from that important position." He recommended that "all loyal people" should "on receipt of this information, assemble at their places of worship and render special homage and gratitude to Almighty God, for this great advancement of the National cause." Congress joyfully thanked Burnside and his army.

Maj. Gen. John G. Foster, Gen. Burnside's successor in command of the Department, was a wholly different type of man, and could not have sustained rivalry with Burnside in his characteristic lines of life and conduct. Nor was Foster at all emulous to excel him in that way. He sought to do his duty after his own fashion, and the fault-finding to a limited extent, with which his administration met, was largely due to the comparison civilians would silently make in their minds between him and his predecessor, to his depreciation, as the lesser of the two chief lights in their military firmament.

Gen. Sherman, who had arrived in town on December 6, remained only a few days. His freely active temperament was a subject of observation. He held himself in no severe restraint, such as a small official's sense of dignity would impose. A young Unionist who had been driven from his home to take refuge in Knoxville, had some skill in portrait painting, and desired to copy a portrait of the deceased Bishop Otey of Tennessee that hung in the parlor of the house then occupied as headquarters. When he applied to Gen. Foster for a loan of the picture, Gen. Sherman heard the request and springing quickly to his feet, said:

"Bishop Otey! I knew Bishop Otey. Let's go and see it."

When the company had gathered before the likeness, he added—

"I must have that picture. I shall present it to Bishop Otey's family."

The young artist, looking intently at the speaker, said, with great *sang froid*—

"What is your name?"

"Sherman," was the reply.

"*General* Sherman?" he persisted.

"Yes!" said the General: and asked,

"How long do you want the picture?"

Being told, he consented to the loan, and in all probability forgot entirely that he had made it.*

Shortly after Gen. Sherman's departure from the town, Gen. Grant visited it, and his reputation for unaffected simplicity of manner, was confirmed to those who formed his acquaintance. During an interview with him by a citizen, the conversation turned upon the siege. The visitor said:

"General, I understand that General Longstreet is loitering in upper East Tennessee."

"Yes," he replied, "I wish now that I had ordered Gen. Sherman to drive him out."

This frank admission of a failure to do what ought to have been done, showed at least, that his head was not turned by the laurels won at Vicksburg and Mission Ridge, and that he was not morbidly sensitive about the perfection of his military judgment. If he had then known the full extent of the ills to the people of upper East Tennessee which Longstreet's stay among them would inflict, the omission of the order to Sherman would have caused him greater regret; for that stay was prolonged for months. It was instrumental of much annoyance to the United

---

* Bishop Otey was at first in the troubles of 1860—'61, a decided Union man, but when actual hostilities began, he espoused the cause of "the South." Upon the occupation of Memphis by the United States forces, Gen. Sherman showed him kind and valuable attentions.

States troops at various points, and Longstreet's army, by living upon the country, contributed largely to bring upon its inhabitants the great destitution of food, from which they severely suffered in 1864-'65.

Gen. Foster had received a wound during the Mexican war, from the effects of which he still now and then suffered, and which furnished a convenient reason for his being refused to unwelcome visitors. Upon one very cold afternoon, two visits in quick succession were made to a citizen, by persons who sought his mediation with General Foster. First came a committee of Free Masons. A Kentuckian, who belonged to a Texas regiment, had been unavoidably separated from it at the time of Longstreet's retreat from Knoxville, and he had endeavored to rejoin it through the country south of the Tennessee river. In doing this, he had unfortunately for himself, worn, in part at least, the uniform of a Federal soldier, and had also entered in his diary that he had represented himself as one, in conversation with a woman. He was captured while hiding in a hay stack, was brought to Knoxville, tried by court-martial and condemned to death as a spy. Strong sympathy was felt for him by resident friends of the Confederacy, and this was shared by the Free Masons, of which fraternity he was a member. A committee of that order desired the citizen they visited to intercede with Gen. Foster to reprieve the prisoner until further proof of his innocence, which they believed to exist, could be produced.

They had scarcely gone, when a regimental officer from Mississippi made his appearance. Longstreet, in going eastward, had left in a hospital at the paper mill three miles northwest of the town, a number of wounded men, among whom were officers Moody and Smith. The former was suffering from heart disease, which did not, however, prevent his really distinguished presence upon the streets. His remarkable stature and aristocratic physique crowned with a planter's broad-brimmed hat, and his lordly bearing, combined to embody the idea which the natives entertained of "Southern chivalry," and to attract special attention. He was said to be withal, a cousin of the Rev. Granville Moody, of the United States Army, and known as "the fighting parson." The other Confederate officer was Major Smith, who because of his wounds, was still confined to his room in a private dwelling. On that day some rebel soldiers at the town had broken their parole, seized guns and absconded. In consequence, Gen. Foster had ordered that all other Confederate prisoners on parole should be arrested and sent to jail. This confinement Major Moody averred that he and Major Smith were physically unable to endure in such severe weather; and his request was that the citizen should intercede with the Commander-in-chief to still allow them liberty in the town. Equipped with this double errand, the citizen went on his way over the sleety pavements to that officer's dwelling and said to the orderly who opened the door:

"I wish to see General Foster."

"General Foster can't be seen; he is sick."

The citizen, at his own request, was then shown to the room of another United States Officer in the same house. There another visitor, General ———, had preceded him. He was evidently under the influence of potations from a bottle of strong drink that stood on the table near him, and soon the new comer's refusal to partake of his spirituous devotions was resented by him with maudlin freedom and profanity. By and by came a knock at the door, and who should enter but the veritable General, who just before had been announced as too ill to receive a visitor.

Not long before, Gen. Foster had sent copies of a Proclamation by President Lincoln, to be distributed among the soldiers of Gen. Longstreet. The latter thereupon had forwarded a sharp letter to Foster, rebuking him for discourtesy, and inviting him to transmit such documents directly to the commander, instead of seeking to circulate them privily among the soldiers of his command. To that letter Gen. Foster had prepared an answer, and he proceeded to read it to the owner of the room, not probably without expectation of the high encomium which that gentleman gave it.

When a suitable opportunity occurred, the citizen sought to fulfill his mission, first by repeating to Gen. Foster the statement of the committee of Free Masons, and conveying their petition for a short reprieve to the young Kentuckian.

"No!" was the General's reply, with knit brows

and emphatic tone, "he must die." And die he did the next day, on the gallows. Afterwards it was said that the execution might not or would not have taken place, had not Longstreet's army, early in its retreat, hung a Union man, and left on a tree by the way-side his lifeless body, placarded with offensive words. Information of the young Kentuckian's death, and of the Christian faith and hope with which he met it, was sent to Richmond, Ky., by a clergyman who was with him in his last days.[*] Although it was conveyed to his aged father and mother by their friend,[†] with all possible discretion, the sorrowful news almost broke their hearts. "But," the ruthless politician may ask, "must not war as well as law, have both its just and unjust verdicts? Must it not have its revenges as well as its wrath?" If so, then let it stop altogether its destroying marches and strife, and cease from breaking hundreds and thousands of good old loving hearts by the untimely death of their sons? Why not?

Concerning the second subject of intercession with Gen. Foster, the imprisonment of Majors Moody and Smith, he was so far lenient as to consent that they should not go to the common prison, but be confined in comfortable quarters. Meanwhile, however, Provost Marshal General S. P. Carter, in consideration of their physical condition, placed them again on parole.

Following upon the return of Generals Grant and Sherman to Chattanooga, the defences of the town were still further strengthened, and it re-

[*] Rev. Joseph H. Martin.   [†] Judge Daniel Breck.

mained without serious disturbances from enemies until the end of the Confederacy. Once quite an alarm was raised in consequence of a rapid movement of Wheeler's cavalry through the country and not far away from Knoxville, but the excitement soon subsided and order and peace prevailed as before. New conditions were attended by a hopeful vitality. Some of the officers stationed at the post during 1864-5 mingled freely in social intercourse with the citizens. Among these were Gen. Tilson of Maine and his staff; Gen. S. P. Carter, among whose aides was Capt. Thomas; Col. Gibson, Gen. Stoneman and Col. Ewing. Gen. J. D. Cox of Ohio impressed all who made his acquaintance, by his fine character and culture. An exhaustive list of officers worthy of mention would include Captains Whitman and Chamberlain of the Quarter-master's Department, Medical Directors Jackson and Curtis, and Dr. S. H. Horner.

General Schofield succeeded General Foster in chief command. He administered affairs judiciously and impressed observers as a serious person, who understood the value of method in conducting business, whatever its relations to human life.

Late in April, 1864, Gen. Schofield was ordered from his post to join Gen. Sherman's army in its famous march. Therefore, the Twenty-third army corps, under his command, leaving Strawberry Plains and Knoxville, arrived after a hard march and was concentrated May 2 on the Hiwassee River, near Charleston and Calhoun. That corps included several Tennessee regiments, viz.: the Third infantry, Col. Wm. Cross; the Fifth, Col. James T. Shelley; the Sixth, Col. Joseph A. Cooper;* the Eighth regiment, Col. Felix A. Reeve; and, soon after added, the first infantry, Col. R. K. Byrd.

The "loyal mountaineers" of Tennessee who enlisted in the United States army proved their courage upon various battle fields. No opportunity has heretofore occurred in this narrative, to say a word on that subject. The commendation which Gen. Burnside gave his troops, of course included the East Tennessee soldiers, who were a part of his command before and during the siege of Knoxville. The valor which animated them and their compatriots from the same region, was signally illustrated by the conduct of the above named regiments at the battle of Resaca. The army corps to which they belonged having been united May 2d, on the Hiwassee River, proceeded to the vicinity of Dalton, Georgia, before which place Gen. Sherman was arranging his lines for the first of the series of encounters with the Confederate army which he had on his way to the sea. Gen. Thomas on May 7th had a successful engagement at Tunnel Hill. Schofield's corps—of which the Third and Sixth Tennessee regiments were a part —came into position on Thomas's left, and occupied a steep ridge. On its side the men slept. The right wing and centre of Sherman's army had advanced so far that on the 9th Schofield was or-

---

* Soon after, for gallant conduct, made a Brigadier General.

GEN. JOSEPH A. COOPER.

dered to extend his lines farther to the left. An East Tennesseean, who was then a Union officer and an actor in the scene, relates that Gen. Schofield, "forming his divisions in two lines of battle, with his right resting at the base of the hills, moved down the valley in the direction of the Confederate lines, entrenched behind earthworks. As these two long blue lines moved forward under the eye of the soldiers who covered the crest of the hills to the north, their hundreds of flags floating in the breeze and their bayonets glistening in the bright sunshine, a band began to play 'The Star-spangled Banner,' and cheers rent the air from ten thousand voices. It was a most inspiriting pageant and filled the men with the wildest enthusiasm."*

Soon the skirmishing began, and was quickly followed by firing from the Confederate artillery, which continued during the afternoon, but did not prevent the Union column from moving slowly and steadily onward until when night fell, it was within a few hundred yards of the Confederate works. The losses of the day were not very heavy, those of the Tennessee regiments being perhaps a score killed and twice that number wounded. The men lay during the night with their cartridge boxes belted around them, greatly anxious of mind because of the nearness to each other of the hostile lines, and were compelled to feed upon such rations as were possible without kindling fires. The bayonet charge which they ex-

* Capt. William Rule.

pected to make early the next morning was not ordered, for Gen. Sherman determined to flank General Johnson's army and compel its surrender or retreat. To aid in that movement, Schofield's divisions were quietly withdrawn—a few troops, horse and foot, taking their place—and were marched to the rear, from thence to pass around the Union lines to the neighborhood of Resaca.

Gen. McPherson had preceded Schofield and taken position, and on the 13th the Second division of the latter's corps, commanded by Gen. H. M. Judah, and its Third division commanded by Gen. Jacob D. Cox, were formed into two lines of battle. The Confederate works were a few hundred yards distant, with a strip of woods intervening. For two hours there was skirmishing between the hostile forces. The Confederates, after being driven back, made a more stubborn resistance. Then at the word, "Forward!" the main line of the Union troops advanced with fixed bayonets. Soon they reached the crest of a ridge, in full view of their entrenched enemy and within range of his rifles. Twenty or more pieces of artillery opened fire upon them with grape and canister shot. The minnie balls they encountered fell thickly like hail-stones in a storm. Down the hill side to the assault they went at a double-quick step. Their cheers, as they went, rose clear and strong above the din of the battle. At almost every step one man in every ten of them dropped from the ranks, which still pressed forward and at the base of the hill entered an open field. There a creek, parallel with both army lines, stopped their way. The trees upon its banks had been cut down, and presented a tangled mass which forbid their progress. To attempt a passage through it under their adversary's heavy fire, would have been to incur a needless sacrifice of human life. Therefore they were ordered to fall back, and leaving many of their number up to their necks in the water of the creek, until night fell to their release, the survivors retreated across the ridge and re-formed.

The losses of the command were distressingly large. Of the two thousand men, First brigade, Second division, Twenty-third army corps, who went that day into action, between four hundred and fifty and five hundred were killed and wounded in fifteen minutes. In that brigade the Third regiment Tennessee lost one hundred and twenty-five: the Sixth Tennessee regiment was strangely preserved, its losses being only thirty.

The subsequent movements of Gen. Sherman's army resulted in the evacuation of Dalton by Gen. Johnson, and during the night of May 15th, his forces around Resaca were withdrawn. The Confederate army, being forced from its first stronghold of resistance in the Georgia campaign, on the next day moved southward. The bloody battle of Resaca has been thought to be interesting to Tennesseeans from the fact that in it "the valor of Tennessee soldiers on both sides was displayed, was fully tested and found equal to the emergency."*

At that date, the siege of Knoxville was fully numbered with the things of the past, and the possession of East Tennessee by the United States army had all the permanence possible in the circumstances. The country however, was in a sad condition. It had been the previous year, not only disquieted but impoverished, and in the winter of 1863-'64 there began an unexampled flood of immigration into the town from adjoining and eastern counties. It consisted not only of needy white people. Everywhere the negroes upon obtaining their freedom during the war, manifested a strong inclination for town life. On this occasion that disposition was sharpened by the hope of finding not only refuge from harm but necessary food. At first the stream of new, homeless, hungry population was small, but as confidence in the security and certainty of rest which Knoxville offered and of finding there the sufficient nourishment which could not be had at home increased, the tide of immigrants rose higher. It filled vacant tenements, and flowed into the rooms of the University buildings not already occupied by soldiers. The refugees came into town on railroad trains and lay all night on the uncovered depot platform, exposed to the inclemencies of the weather. The question which humanity as well as Christianity prompted was, what should be done with and for them. The calamity had many

* See Appendix: Note W.

and deep sources, and threatened to grow with the lapse of time. It would inevitably be fed more and more from the large impoverishment that extended over a wide region, and for which there seemed to be no remedy. Its evil results, thus brought home to the very doors of the people of Knoxville, might be overcome in their present magnitude; but how should they be met in the future when full grown in size? The only feasible method was to send forth supplies from there to meet and overcome it. The sole yet fatal objection to such a plan was the absence of means to carry it into effect.

But God is good, and His mercy is over all His works. He had already put it into the heart of one of His servants to begin an enterprise that would by His blessing bring help from a distance to the needy people, more than a few of whom were ready to perish.

At that date war had wrought its ravages for more than three and a half years. For a large part of that period, in some regions of the land, it had stayed the hand of the husbandman from industrious toil and prevented the fruits of the earth. In many instances the farmers' barns were no longer, as formerly, filled with plenty, for the words of Joel, so ominously read in churches on the Sunday after the Baltimore fight in April 1861, had proved truly predictive, and plough-shares had been turned into swords. Multitudes of hearts everywhere from Maine to the Gulf, and from the Atlantic to the far West, were now yearning for peace. Had not enough blood been shed, enough human life sacrificed upon the altar of Mars? Might not Americans cease now from destroying each other and brethren be reconciled? Perhaps the night of desolation and sorrow was well nigh spent and the day of peace about to dawn! And so it was, but men did not know it.

Soon kindly hands came in and healed where they could the wounds war had inflicted. They fed the hungry and clothed the naked, until by their industry they could feed and clothe themselves. It was a Christ-like work in which any man might be thankful to be engaged.

CHAPTER XVIII.

DEPLORABLE CONDITION OF EAST TENNESSEE—
WATAUGA SCENERY—LANDON C. HAYNES AT
A DINNER PARTY—NATHANIEL G. TAYLOR—
HIS WRONGS—HIS FEARS FOR THE PEOPLE—
HIS MISSION TO THE NORTH AND WORK AT
PHILADELPHIA—EDWARD EVERETT'S SPEECH
AT FANEUIL HALL.

> "Alas, poor country;
> Almost afraid to know thyself! It cannot
> Be call'd our mother, but our grave; where nothing
> But who knows nothing, is once seen to smile."
> MACBETH.

An intelligent observer of the condition of East Tennessee in the spring of 1863, did not need any supernatural gift of prescience to enable him to see that a dangerous scarcity of food would befall its people at no very distant day. This evil especially impended over counties where love for the Union was relatively strongest, and from which means of sustenance for Confederate troops had been more largely drawn. Twelve months had elapsed since Gen. E. Kirby Smith, in chief command at Knoxville, had the sagacity to foresee the ills that threatened the whole region because of the withdrawal of nearly all its able-bodied men from agricultural pursuits, and had thought it advisable to proclaim his promise that he would suspend the operation of the conscript law until men should cultivate their fields another season and raise crops of farm products.

Besides the more than thirty thousand men who were absentees northward—nearly all of whom had enlisted in the Federal army—and the unknown number who had been sent to the Southern prisons, some thousands were in the Confederate army. So that probably more than one-eighth of the entire population were withdrawn from all peaceful labor and chiefly from tilling the soil. As long before as 1861 and '62, the earth had very scantily yielded its fruits, because little work had been done in cultivating it. Even that little had been performed in the midst of excitements, agitations and disturbances, and was therefore defective in quality. Many Confederate soldiers had been quartered here and there throughout East Tennessee, or were in active movement over it from point to point. They had to be fed, and being imperfectly disciplined, they wasted much even of that they bought of their friends, and still more of that they took from Union people. The provisions and provender they ruthlessly seized, might be transported by them elsewhere or be wantonly destroyed on the spot. In the proclamation by Kirby Smith, April, 1862, was a clause following the invitation to Union refugees, which testifies of his good intentions to correct disorders committed by his own troops. In doing this, it bears witness also to their wrong doings and the need there was of protection from them being assured to all citizens. He said: "The Major-General commanding, furthermore declares his determination henceforth to employ all the elements at his disposal for the protection of the lives and property of the citizens of East Tennessee, whether from the incursions of the enemy, or the irregularities of his own troops."

The depleting causes continued during the year 1863. One who had good opportunity to be informed on the subject says, that in the summer of that year; "East Tennessee was full of parties marching and countermarching, skirmishing and battling, ravaging and devastating the whole country, which was far distant from reliable bases of supply. The young laboring men were in the armies; and what was left of the people's substance being wasted, the prevailing want pressed upon the brink of starvation and was brought to the homes of thousands who had never known hunger before. The present and prospective victims of the extreme destitution were women and children, old men and invalids." When autumn came, to be followed by winter, the out-look was ominous and distressing. Was there any way possible of mitigating the growing calamity? If so, how and from whence could help be had?

It will be remembered that the first permanent settlement in East Tennessee was on the banks of the Watauga River near the present Elizabethton; and that there, in 1780, the "Back-water men," as the British Colonel, Ferguson, called them, gathered under Shelby, Sevier and Campbell for their patriotic military expedition to King's Mountain. The natural surroundings of the spot are now attractive in summer. From the site of the Old Fort, which was built in early days for defence against the Indians on an elevation 300 yards south of the river, the eye may rest on the blue front of Holston Mountain, seven or eight miles distant. To the east is Lynn Mountain, three miles away; to the south is the blue outline of the Unaka and Roan mountains; in the south-west is the bold and craggy front of the Buffalo Mountain, that may easily be fancied to resemble an ancient castle of massive strength, and standing in solitude, its brow uplifted into the skies, impresses the mind of the spectator with a feeling of awe for its grandeur and majesty. And among all these mountains are pleasant vallies, through which flow the Doe River, Buffalo Creek, the Watauga River, Indian Creek, and twenty miles away, the Nolachucky River. The various features of the landscape combine to form a sublime and beautiful panorama.

At a dinner party given at Memphis after the recent war ended, to members of the Mississippi Bar, Gen. N. B. Forest, of Confederate memory, intended, it is said, to administer in pleasantry a sharp stimulus to the rhetorical powers of his friend, Col. Landon C. Haynes, who was present and had the reputation of being one of Tennessee's most brilliant orators. It was the habit of certain persons in 1861 and for some years afterwards, to speak contemptuously of East Tennessee because of its devotion to the Union. The habit seems not yet to have expired, seeing that not long ago a leading journal at the metropolis of the State could utter the historical solecism that the people of East Tennessee were descendants of men who were friends of Great Britain in the War of the American Revolution! Gen. Forest, merely to incite Col. Haynes to make an eloquent response, adopted a reproachful phrase, current among Secessionists, in giving this toast:

"Col. L. C. Haynes: our honored guest from East Tennessee—that God-forsaken country."

Col. Haynes was instantly on his feet, and in the spirit that dictated the lines:

> "Breathes there a man, with soul so dead,
> Who never to himself hath said,
> This is my own, my native land!"

spoke in his best style of voice and manner, as follows:

"Sir, I proudly plead guilty to the 'soft impeachment.' I was born in East Tennessee—on the banks of the Watauga—which in the Indian vernacular means 'beautiful river:' and beautiful river it is. I have stood upon its banks in my childhood, and looking into its glassy waters, beheld there mirrored, a heaven with moon and planets and trembling stars, and looking upward, have beheld the heaven, which the heaven below reflected. Away from its rocky borders, stretches a vast line of cedar, pine and hemlock evergreens, back to the distant mountains—more beautiful than the groves of Switzerland—reposing on a back-ground as perfect in grandeur as the cloud-lands of the Sierra Nevada of the far West.

"There stands the towering Roan, the Black, and the magnificent Smoky mountains, upon whose summits the clouds gather of their own accord, even on the brightest day. There I have seen the great spirit of the storm lie down in his pavilion of clouds and darkness to quiet slumbers. Then I have seen him awake at midnight and come forth like a giant refreshed with repose, arouse the tempest, and let loose the red lightnings that flash for hundreds of miles along the mountain tops swifter than the eagle's flight in heaven. Then I have seen those lightnings stand and dance like angels of light to the music of Nature's grand organ, whose keys were touched by the fingers of Jehovah, and responded in notes of thunder resounding through the universe. Then I've seen the darkness drift away, and morning get up from her saffron bed, and come forth like a queen robed in her garments of light, and stand tip-toe on the misty mountain heights. And while black night fled away to his bed-chamber at the pole, the glorious sun burst forth upon the vale and river where I was born. O, glorious land of the mountains and sun-painted cliffs! How can I ever forget thee?"

On the same river whose surroundings were thus described, was also born and still dwelt, Nathaniel G. Taylor—a near kinsman of the post-prandial orator. He it was who in debate at

Knoxville during the Presidential canvass of 1860, spoke with almost prophetic tongue of the civil war and its train of dreadful ills, which he alleged, the malcontent politicians of a great party were preparing to bring upon the country if Mr. Lincoln were elected. So vivid was the picture which he then drew of those evils, that, as before related, some of his hearers wept. But the tears they shed, compared with the many that fell from the eyes of women and children during the war, were as the few scattering drops that clouds in summer send down to tell of the torrents of rain, with which the land is soon to be drenched. The eloquent speaker on that occasion, had been, in 1863, grieved for more than two years by seeing and hearing of the unjust violences to which the Union people of East Tennessee were subjected. It is impossible now to determine with strict accuracy the details of wrongs they suffered from their enemies. To use his words, those wrongs included:

"The confiscation of property, merciless conscription, arrest, imprisonment, the execution of the death sentence by drum-head court-martial, running the gauntlet of rebel bullets and bayonets for great distances by 30,000 men to reach the United States flag and join its army; the martyrdom of from 2,000 to 3,000 non-combatant, unarmed Union people in thirty-one counties, by shooting, hanging or slaughtering in cold blood;* the despoilment of personal property, and conse-

* See Appendix: Note X.

quent upon all these, a widespread destitution of the very necessaries of life."

Mr. Taylor was known to be a Union man, and therefore could not be permitted to dwell peacefully at home with his wife and children. He was arrested and tried by a drum-head court-martial as an accomplice in the bridge burnings of 1862, but was acquitted. Afterwards, being threatened with arrest and imprisonment upon the charge of High Treason against the Confederacy—to end, perhaps, in his death—he sought refuge in secluded and very inaccessible gorges of the mountains. His concealment there was attended with privations, but it disconcerted enemies in their pursuit. Upon learning of Burnside's advent into East Tennessee, he became perplexed in mind as to his personal duty. He could not remain in his hiding place without danger of being discovered and hunted from it, if not seized. The Confederate troops were between him and Burnside at Knoxville, and he could reach there only with difficulty and risk. If he attempted to do so and succeeded, in what way under the protection of friendly power, could he best serve his country? He almost determined to seek for a suitable position in the United States army, but postponing a conclusion, he submitted the subject to God in prayer. Upon doing this, he was persuaded that his petition for guidance and direction was answered by the strong impression of a new idea upon his mind.

For some time he had been deeply moved at heart, in his daily and nightly reflections, by a vision which the unhappy condition of East Tennessee suggested; a vision of famine and death swiftly coming upon its people. Prayer in faith had been the means of opening his eyes as to what he should do in relation to those impending evils. He thought that the Spirit of the Lord spoke to his own spirit: "Your duty is to go and tell the people of the North, of this great, threatening destitution, that they may interpose with their beneficence between it and the suffering people of East Tennessee." He accepted the conclusion as from Him who inspires those who trust in Him to all good and praiseworthy undertakings. Escaping at once through the Confederate lines to Knoxville, he proceeded from thence to Cincinnati upon his humane and patriotic mission. There he met with sympathizing friends of his enterprise, to promote which several hundred dollars were contributed by citizens, after a public meeting had been held and an address heard from him. The amount would have been larger, had there not been already a stream of needy refugees from the seceded States to Cincinnati and other points on the Ohio River, which two months later grew into "great numbers." To provide for that out-flow of "thousands of women, children and aged men—all meanly clad, well-nigh starved, and many well-nigh heart-broken," the Refugee Relief Commission was established at Cincinnati.

Andrew Johnson, then Military Governor of Tennessee, gave Mr. Taylor a letter of endorsement and commendation, to which President Lincoln added a similar one, and on arriving at Philadelphia he was received most kindly. Nearly two months before, the extreme necessity which induced his visit, had been brought incidentally to the attention of a few patriotic and benevolent ladies of that city. Mrs. Joseph Canby and Mrs. Caleb W. Hallowell heard some soldiers of Kearney's regiment, early in December, 1863, speak of the famine in East Tennessee, and of how they themselves had sometimes lived on a cracker a day in order to give to the children who flocked to the camp, begging for the remnants of their rations. Touched with compassion, the two ladies quietly proceeded to sew and collect articles, and being joined by friends and neighbors, including some from Norristown and Lancaster County, a fair was held. Its cash proceeds and several boxes of clothing were forwarded to Knoxville and distributed to the needy.

In January, 1864, the Governor of Pennsylvania recommended to the State Legislature the subject of Mr. Taylor's mission, and the latter delivered an address in the Philadelphia Academy of Music. A Relief Association for East Tennessee was at once organized with Ex-Gov. Jas. Pollock, President, Joseph T. Thomas, Secretary, Caleb Cope, Treasurer, J. B. Lippincott, Chairman Committee on Collections, and Lloyd P. Smith, Chairman Executive Committee. The people of the city cheerfully responded to the call upon them for material aid and contributed over twenty-six thousand dollars. From that date, the Pennsylvania Association was of great benefit to the whole undertaking, (especially through the Chairman of its Executive Committee) in various ways—by wise counsels and active co-operation, as well as by warm sympathy, encouragement and gifts.

From Philadelphia, Mr. Taylor upon advice went to Boston. On the 10th of February, a crowded assembly in Faneuil Hall, including many ladies, gave him an enthusiastic greeting. Upon nomination by Hon. J. Wiley Edmunds, Officers of the meeting were elected: Hon. Edward Everett, President; Gov. Andrew, Mayor Lincoln, Hons. J. E. Field, A. H. Bullock (Speaker), Robert C. Winthrop and Chas. B. Loring; also Wm. Clafflin, Patrick Donahoe, Wm. B. Rogers, Chas. B. Goodrich, Jas. Lawrence, Rich'd Frothingham, Julius Rockwell, Chas. L. Woodbury and John M. Forbes, Esqs., Vice Presidents; and Col. F. L. Lee and Sam'l Frothingham, Jr., Secretaries.

Hon. Edward Everett stepped forward upon the platform and spoke. He requested the respectful attention of the assembly to Mr. Taylor on his own account, and also that they should "hear him for his cause"—the cause, not simply of the Union, but of faithful Union men who from the beginning of hostilities "had stood at the post of danger; on whom the storm of war first broke, and on whom from that day to this, it has beat with its wildest fury." "At this distance from the scene of war," he said, "we hear only the far-off roar of the tempest; but all its waves and billows have gone over the devoted region for which our honored guest comes to plead."

Mr. Everett then gave the true and beautiful description of East Tennessee, which has been repeated in the Introduction to these chapters. He said of that region:

"Overrun it may be by the armed forces of the rebellion, but all its sympathies and attachments are with the loyal States. While the aristocracy of the southeastern counties of Maryland, were shouting 'My Maryland,' the farmers in the western counties in Cumberland Valley shouted back, 'No, it's our Maryland.' Western Virginia, a portion of the same grand chain of mountain and valley, is as loyal as Massachusetts. Then comes Western North Carolina, and still more, Eastern Tennessee, the home of our honored guest, and of as true hearted, loyal, Union loving a population as there is on the continent. As far down as Northern Alabama, the mountain district is filled with Union sentiment. It was with the greatest difficulty it was engineered into secession."

In continuation the eloquent orator spoke of the large majority at the polls in East Tennessee, February, 1861, against a convention for the purpose of seceding and of the subsequent "outrages and cruelties, of which the Union-loving inhabitants were made the victims." He told how, that "thrown upon their own resources, they naturally sought to save themselves from being overrun by destroying the bridges on the chief lines of communication," and that in consequence, the great

REV. N. G. TAYLOR.

majority of the people of the region were subjected by the Richmond Government to great severities. In that connection he read and sharply censured the letter of Mr. Benjamin, Secretary (C. S.) of War, heretofore repeated.

In concluding, he said to his fellow-citizens that their brethren of East Tennessee, fighting battles and suffering persecution, represented a common cause, and he feared the promptest relief extended would be too late to save some from starvation. "This," he added, "must not be. If the Union means anything, it means not merely political connection and commercial intercourse, but to bear each other's burdens and to share each other's sacrifices; it means active sympathy and efficient aid."

Mr. Taylor followed with a fervent and impressive address, in which he briefly related the historical events in East Tennessee from the beginning of 1861, told of the wrongs inflicted upon its people, of the voluntary exile of its men and their enlistment in the United States army, of the desolation their homes and fields had suffered from the war, of the deep, wide and threatening destitution existing among them, and he appealed on their behalf to the prosperous people among whom he stood, to send them help. He spoke plainly, with strong and earnest convictions of the truth, and with the burning passion which a sense of the injustices he narrated had enkindled in his soul. Inspired with a profound and lofty patriotism, by the presence of distinguished persons and a thronged audience on a spot of lively associations with liberty and the Republic, and by the importance of his theme, his speech was with unwonted power. His hearers were carried away by his eloquence as on a mighty wave of enthusiasm, and all criticism of his style, wherein it was not in harmony with the demands of a higher culture, was forgotten in their glowing sympathy with his subject and the ardent love of country to which his words quickened them.

When he had finished, resolutions expressive of hearty fellowship with the Unionists of East Tennessee in their fidelity and sufferings, and of a ready mind to minister to their needs, were presented by Geo. B. Upton and unanimously adopted. Hon. Rob't C. Winthrop said a few words, and Judge Thomas Russell spoke ardently, more at length. He referred to the statements of Mr. Taylor concerning destitution among the people whose cause he pleaded, and said:

"Let me add that this testimony is confirmed by one of the Generals who marched to relieve Burnside. General Blair has just told me a touching story of the devotion of the women who crowded to the line of his forced march, to welcome the sight of our armies; to wave the flags which in evil days they had hidden in the secret recesses of their homes, even as they kept the love of the Union in their hearts; to bring the last piece of bacon, the last handful of meal, to feed the advancing soldiers of the Union cause. Often he forbade his men to take the scanty gifts of the poor. As often, he heard the reply, 'Take it; I have a husband, a son, at Knoxville; take it all for the Union.' These are the people for whom our aid is sought."

A letter was also read from Gen. Frank Blair, reciting the same facts, and expressing his hope that liberality would "be stimulated by remembrance of the kindness and devotion of the loyal women of Tennessee who succored our toil-worn soldiers on their march to the relief of their beleaguered brothers, many of whom were sons of Massachusetts."

CHAPTER XIX.

FUND FOR RELIEF OF EAST TENNESSEE AT BOSTON, PORTLAND AND NEW YORK—MR. TAYLOR AND FAMILY IN GREAT TROUBLE—THEIR TIMELY RELIEF—KNOXVILLE EAST TENNESSEE RELIEF SOCIETY—PENNSYLVANIA COMMITTEE—EFFECTIVE WORK IN RELIEVING DESTITUTION—SUMMARY OF RESULTS.

> The quality of mercy is not strained;
> It droppeth as the gentle rain from heaven
> Upon the place beneath; it is twice blessed;
> It blesseth him that gives and him that takes.
> MERCHANT OF VENICE.

The only measure of relief for East Tennessee contemplated by the resolutions adopted at Faneuil Hall, was an appropriation by the State Legislature, and no arrangement was made for obtaining individual subscriptions. Col. Taylor had, however, touched a chord which drew a sympathetic response from the community. On the day after the public meeting, a contribution of three dollars was received by the President of the Association from a "Teacher in a Public School," which within a week was followed by other gifts amounting to more than a thousand dollars. Means were then organized to receive and announce donations. Legislative aid was prevented by constitutional difficulties, and the executive committee of the relief society published an address to the people of Massachusetts, in order to enlarge the field of contributions. From that time the fund increased with remarkable rapidity. Soon it amounted to more than $90,000. Public opinion had assigned $100,000 as the sum to be raised by private subscription, and it was completed June, 4 by a gift of $1,000 from a children's fair.

Boston and its suburbs were chief sources of these donations, but many of them were made from other places and States. The enthusiasm to help in the work was ardent and prevailed among all the people. Mr. Everett kept the public constantly informed of the contributions as they were received and his patriotic presence inspired others to assist.*

In the spring Mr. Taylor visited Maine, and eleven thousand dollars were given through Gov. Cony, and a relief association organized at Portland. He also visited New York city upon invitation, but the holding of a metropolitan fair at the place and time, prevented any important results from his labors. His address there was well received and a society formed which adopted means to promote the object of his mission. A letter from Gen. S. P. Carter was read on the occasion, dated at Knoxville a few weeks previous, in which he said: "From 40,000 to 50,000 troops have been in East Tennessee for more than four months; of that number, 10,000 to 15,000 were cavalry. In a

* See Appendix: Note Y.

great measure both armies lived off the country. The rebels drew all their supplies from it. Of course nearly the whole of the forage subsistence of East Tennessee has been consumed. Many families have been left without a bushel of corn or a pound of meat. And it is certainly to the credit of the people, that although they have been stripped of their substance by their own friends—by our troops—there is no abatement of their love for the old Government. Many rations have been issued daily from the Government stores; but for this, more than a few would be without bread. Even those who have supplies have only enough to last for a short time, and then, unless assistance comes from abroad, many, I fear, will suffer terribly for bread." * * * * " From the destruction of fences, impressment of horses, and absence of forage as well as laborers, I fear that only a small part of our farms will be cultivated during the present year. Numbers of the people are driven to seek homes north of the Ohio; many others must follow, not willingly, but because there is no help for it."

An address to the people of the State of New York, drafted by William Cullen Bryant, Esq., was published by a large and influential committee; but the aggregate of contributions to the New York city relief fund was less than $20,000, of which one-fourth was from Buffalo.

Mr. Taylor's wife and children had of necessity left home, and with them he dwelt at Haddonfield, N. J. As strangers, with narrow means of support, their faith and patience were tried, and at one time severely. They were delivered when in great need, by an interposition that appeared to come from a Divine Providence.

The family of exiles, numbering thirteen, although not free from painful recollections of recent life in Tennessee, were no longer disturbed by alarms of war or shocked by atrocities of a hostile soldiery, and were contented and happy in their new home. In the afternoon of the day when Mr. Taylor returned from an absence of six weeks in New England, his wife said to him:

"We are nearly out of provisions. You must go to market in the morning. Besides, the rent is due next Monday and it must be met promptly."

"Well, of course I'll go to market, and I'll settle the house-rent; but I suppose (drawing an almost empty purse from his pocket) you will furnish the money, as I believe I am about broke."

"Why, dear me," she exclaimed, with lengthened face and fading color, "is it possible you have come back home without money? You are surely jesting."

"Indeed, my dear wife, I am in dead earnest. All I have in the world is this five dollar bill."

For the first time in all their troubles, she lost faith and hope, and was helpless. Overcome by emotion and unable to speak, she dropped into a chair, sobbing. When the power of speech returned, she bewailed their condition:

"Oh! oh! just think to what we have come. Here we are a thousand miles from home. · If we were there, enemies are ready to kill us. Here we are among strangers, in a rented house—rent due—provisions all gone—thirteen in family—and only that five dollar bill between us and starvation."

Confessedly, the case had a dark out-look, and to any person of desponding mind it would appear desperate. Her paroxysms of grief brought all the household together; they stood around in deep, silent sympathy; but the head of the family soon rallied courage to speak in a tone of cheerfulness, not very well sustained:

"My dear wife, I am astonished at your want of faith and extravagant apprehensions. We are indeed among strangers, but they are our friends. Would the Lord lead us through all the dangers we have survived, only to let us starve here in a peaceful, prosperous land? And that, when we are in His service—working for the poor and destitute in unhappy East Tennessee? Away with your fears, and be assured that the same God who has led us safely so far, will lead us safely to the end."

Her mind was calmed by these words, but they failed to remove all its doubts and forebodings. Next morning, the husband went to Philadelphia, armed with a bushel market basket, and after payment for a round ticket by railroad, with his five-dollar bill distressingly reduced in size. Prices of provisions were high. He had to buy inferior qualities to supply the needful quantity, and to use thought and skill lest his little means prove unequal to the occasion. At length he started homeward, with the basket cheaply but plentifully filled, and in passing through Haddonfield was hailed by the postmaster and given a letter for his wife. It was postmarked at Boston. Who could have sent it? "Perhaps some of our rebel kin," he thought, "have been captured and taken to that city, and have written to her."

All day he had been praying inaudibly to the Lord for help, and he believed it would come, but all his forecastings as to the whence, how and when of its coming, had only been perplexing. He did not dream it would be from strangers and a distance; yet his curiosity was so keen to know who had written the letter that, contrary to his habit, he broke the seal and read.

It informed Mrs. Taylor that its writers highly valued the important services her husband was rendering to the cause of humanity and of our country; that they were aware of his inability, because cut off from all home resources, to maintain his family while he successfully prosecuted his good work; and therefore they begged her to accept the within check as a testimonial of their appreciation of his labors and their kindly regard for his wife and children. The names of six persons were subscribed to the letter, and it enclosed a check on Philadelphia for one thousand dollars. A mountainous weight rolled from the heart of its surprised reader. Midnight had changed to day. His whole soul bowed itself in thankfulness to the God of Elijah, for he looked on the thousand dollars as sent directly from the Lord. Quickening his steps, home was soon reached. At its entrance stood the tearful wife, as he drew near whistling a joyful hymn-tune. Alarmed at his lightness of spirits, she cried out:

"What in the world is the matter, Mr. Taylor? You are surely deranged. How else could you come home whistling, with only the contents of that basket between your poor family and starvation? I know you must be crazy!"

"Never was of sounder mind in all my life. It is you that are deranged, my dear! Did not I tell you, 'The Lord will provide?' There, read that (handing her the letter). See how thankless it is to doubt His promises; and learn to trust the Lord."

She wiped away her tears and began to read. Gradually the signs of distress and depression disappeared from her face and it beamed with hope, gratitude and joy. Meanwhile *his* thoughts were busy concerning the Hebrew prophet and God's commissary-ravens—the replenished oil-cruse and meal-tub—the weary disciples tugging at the net, over-full of fish—and concerning Him who still and ever reiterates in men's dull ears, "Ask and ye shall receive." When she had finished reading, she wept tears of joy, and with uplifted hands exclaimed, "Never again will I distrust my Lord as long as I live."

In July, '64, Mr. Taylor, by request, undertook a tour through the State of New York, accompanied as he had been before to New England, by J. E. Peyton. The heat of August and the political excitement in the canvass for the Presidency soon brought these labors to an end.

Because of the scarcity of food in East Tennessee, the Sanitary Commission sent some supplies from Cincinnati to relieve it, but the evil was too great to be overcome without extraordinary means. Not long after Mr. Taylor's visit to Philadelphia, it was advised by his Eastern friends that an association should be organized in the destitute region, to receive gifts and administer help to the needy; and also that a competent committee, representing the distant contributors should visit the afflicted people, to observe their condition, confer with the society located among them and to report. Accordingly on February 8, 1864, at a public meeting in Knoxville, a relief association was formed and officers elected: Rev. Thomas W. Humes, President; Executive Committee, William Heiskell, Samuel R. Rodgers, John Baxter, O. P. Temple, William G. Brownlow, R. D. Jourolmon, George M. White and David Richardson; John M. Fleming, Secretary; M. M. Miller, Treasurer. Mr. Fleming was soon succeeded by George M. White as Secretary; and after one year David A. Deaderick became Treasurer of the Society. Needful agents were appointed for purchase and transportation of supplies.

About the same time, two Commissioners of the Pennsylvania Relief Society, Lloyd P. Smith and Frederick Collins, expended at Cincinnati, on their way to East Tennessee, over $8,000, in buying and shipping to that region, articles of food, chiefly flour, bacon, salt, sugar and coffee. These were transported to Nashville, free of charge, by means of a credential letter from Chas. H. Dana, Assistant Secretary of War, to Gen. Grant. Soon afterwards, $28,000 were used for like purchases at the former city by Mr. Hazen, agent of the Knoxville Society, which were forwarded by means of $2,000, kindly loaned by Hon. Joseph E. Fowler, of Nashville.

The Pennsylvania Commissioners were well qualified for the duties assigned to them, and which required they should make a tedious and uncomfortable journey of 2,500 miles and of nearly three weeks' time. They were heartily welcomed at Knoxville, and gave to its Association a memorandum of their own Society's judgment concerning the distribution of supplies. They advised first, that the provisions should be given away to those who were unable to buy, and secondly, that to all other applicants they should be sold; the preference to be given, among both classes, first to Union families who had suffered on account of their loyalty; second, to families, who, without having specially suffered, had adhered throughout to the Federal Government; thirdly, to people who, whatever their past conduct, had given their adhesion to the United States. Lastly, they recommended that the old men, women and children of families which then had representatives in the Confederate army should be permitted to share in the bounty, no part of which, they thought, was intended for secessionists of the fighting age. The plan thus proposed was adopted by the Knoxville Association, and practically observed.

The Pennsylvania Commissioners informed themselves as far as possible concerning the destitution said to prevail throughout the region. Before they reached Knoxville, refugees had been arriving there daily in growing numbers and some of them slept of necessity in the open air. Gen. Carter, U. S. Provost Marshal, and Wm. G. Brownlow, U. S. Treasury Agent, provided shelter for the needy. Rations were also issued to them for a time and until the necessities of the army prevented.* The destitution was found to be all that it had been represented to persons at a distance.

Thrifty and well-to-do people were not exempt from it. One instance came directly to the knowledge of the Commissioners. A member of the Society of Friends from Blount County, sought for help from the the U. S. Quartermaster at Knoxville, saying that he and all his people had nothing to eat. Before the peace of the country had been broken, they lived in plenty. At various places the visitors met with refugees on their way to the North in search of bread, not only from East Tennessee, but from Western North Carolina, Northern Georgia and Northern Alabama. Their losses

---

* After the siege of Knoxville, soldiers of Burnside's army had only half rations of bread. Sergeant White, in his Diary, Walcott's History 21st Massachusetts Regiment, says: "I have to-day seen soldiers scrambling after corn in the ear, as though it was the greatest of luxuries. We parch it. Officers eat it, as well as privates. Well, its all for the Union and we are driving the rebels to the wall, thank God!" A committee of citizens requested Gen. Foster to send the people out of the country, rather than the U. S. army should evacuate it.

had been entire, and having no means to buy food and shelter by the way, they kept on fleeing, for behind was threatening starvation. In their poorly clad and dispirited condition, sickness among them, especially of women and children, was inevitable. Pitiful cases of afflicted families came to the knowledge of the Commissioners, such as that of a mother and four children, all prostrated at the same time by disease. These unhappy emigrants were to be counted by thousands, not always impelled only by hunger and losses of property. Fear of being coerced to do military service for the Confederacy was in some instances an additional motive. At one town, a Western North Carolinian, nearly three-score years old, lay dangerously ill. His distressed wife, standing at his bed-side, said: "We came away because the 'Rebs' took away every thing from us and were about to force my husband and my son, 17 years old, into their army."

At a point between Bridgeport and Chattanooga, the Commissioners, detained by a railroad accident, approached a group of passengers, decently but poorly dressed, huddling around a fire. They were three families, thirteen persons in all, on their way to Vincennes, Indiana, where they had friends. One old man, dressed in home-spun and wearing a straw hat, said simply, "All gone!".* He lived eleven miles east of Knoxville, and when Burnside arrived, he volunteered and was in camp five

---

* NOTE.—" To which," say the Commissioners, "he might have added, and with more truth than Francis the First at the battle of Pavia, 'save honor.'"

weeks, but he was then refused on account of his age—being over sixty-six years old.

The evidences of a superior loyalty to the United States among East Tennesseeans (and Western North Carolinians) were as conclusive to the visitors from Philadelphia, as were those of great destitution. A farmer who had emigrated and was returning home, told them that if secession had succeeded, he would have left all and remained at the North. He said, "I would rather protect the Government than protect my property. If I had one bushel of corn, I would be glad to give one-half of it to the Union men. We could do a heap of good, if we could only stay there and raise truck for the army." The mind he expressed was that of the people generally, and justified the opinion that "with the men of East Tennessee, devotion to the Union was not a mere sentiment, but a passion."

In March, 1864, Mr. Thomas G. Odiorne of Cincinnati, was appointed purchasing and forwarding agent of the Society. He consented to serve, reluctantly and only upon condition that no remuneration be paid him. Too much can scarcely be said of the wisdom and fidelity with which he fulfilled his office.

As the summer advanced the beneficence administered by the Society told perceptibly upon the destitution. Clothing as well as food was distributed. Two thousand dollars were invested in goods which were made into garments by the Ladies' Sewing Circle of Boston, and numerous boxes of clothing were contributed from various sources, all of which—timely and useful—were issued with discretion to the needy by Mrs. Maynard and Mrs. Humes at Knoxville, and by chosen agents at other places. Shoes amounting in value to $7,000 were bought by Mr. Everett at Boston, and $4,000 worth of woolen goods by Mr. Lloyd P. Smith at Philadelphia, and shipped on a U. S. Government steamer; but they were burned at Johnsonville, on the Tennessee River, by order of the Commandant of the Post, along with a quantity of Government stores on board, to prevent their capture by the army of Gen. Hood. No compensation was made.

The friends of the work of relief were not unmindful of the needs of refugees at Nashville, through which city more than 9,000 of them passed in the first two months of 1864, from different parts of the South, being chiefly old men, women and children. The Pennsylvania Association, by its Commissioners contributed $1,500 of its funds to the Nashville Aid Refugee Society, in March, to which the Knoxville Association added a donation of $1,000 the following October.

In August, 1864, Mr. A. G. Jackson resigned the office of resident General Agent, and was succeeded by Rev. E. E. Gillenwaters, who continued to serve to the end of the work. Both were competent and faithful in the conduct of affairs.

The Hon. Edward Everett, to whom the people of East Tennessee are so largely indebted for the means of deliverance in their time of trouble, departed this life, January 15, 1865, and a meeting of the citizens of Knoxville—Hon. Seth J. W. Lucky, President and D. A. Deaderick, Secretary—was soon after convened to honor his memory. Sincere sorrow for his death and strong esteem for his character and life were expressed in resolutions by the assembly and appropriate addresses were made. The speakers' hearts were in profound sympathy with their subject and their minds found ready utterance in apt and glowing words. Gratitude to the deceased statesman and patriot, was conspicuous in all that was said. The common sentiment was well expressed by one of those who spoke:

"It is not saying too much to affirm that the history of our people during the last four years, is one of the most remarkable chapters in the history of the race. Enough is already known of it to excite the admiration of all friends of the country. In Mr. Everett's case, it took a practical form—resulting in a fund of upwards of one hundred thousand dollars in cash, expended with a sagacity and fidelity that, aided by the benevolent of both sexes among our own citizens, will make thousands of humble sufferers bless the memory of their distant and unknown friend."

The orator concluded with the words:

"As we follow his retreating form and begin to take the account of our loss, I cannot help feeling that from the aggregate of learning, the sum total of human knowledge, all that makes up the complex idea of civilization and lends grace to the affairs of men, he, in departing, has taken away a larger measure, than will in like manner be withdrawn by any one he has left behind." *

Twelve months after the work of relief began, the destitution was largely diminished but still serious, especially in the most eastern counties of the State, which military conditions had prevented from being reached with supplies. When hostilities ceased, the people of those counties being the most needy, received chief attention and help from the Association, which distributed among them in 1865, fifty thousand dollars in goods and provisions. Its ability to do this, and at the same time assist the needy in other counties was due to the faithful observance of the plan recommended by the Pennsylvania Commissioners —by which, the supplies, excepting issues without charge to the penniless, and sales at cost to soldiers' wives and widows who had means, were sold to citizens, able to pay, at an advance. The results obtained, were as follows:

First, the aggregate receipts of the Association by gifts from a distance, of one hundred and sixty-seven thousand dollars, were increased to two hundred and fifty-two thousand dollars.

Second, the amount of cash paid for food and clothing, alone, was more than that originally contributed. From the proceeds of sales were also paid the cost of freight and insurance, the salaries, wages and expenses of all officers, agents and employes; all other necessary expenses; twelve

* Hon. Horace Maynard.

thousand dollars for shoes and woolen goods destroyed at Johnsonville; three thousand dollars for aid to refugees at Nashville, and five hundred dollars sent to Portland, Maine, which had given thousands to East Tennessee, and later had suffered by a great fire.

Third, as the benefit of the poor and needy was the controlling purpose of the Association in all its deliberations and transactions, that supreme end was practically reached in the use of the fund originally contributed. The articles of food purchased and distributed were judiciously chosen, and the wearing apparel, in buying which fifty thousand dollars were expended, was suited to the wants of the people.*

Altogether, there was much cause for congratulation among the friends of the undertaking both at home and abroad, that at a period of time when because of civil war, vast sums of money were lavishly expended and temptations to mis-use of them were strong, more than one hundred and sixty thousand dollars should have been managed with such prudence and efficiency and with such strict integrity, for the relief of the suffering people of East Tennessee. The generous givers and the thankful beneficiaries were far away from each other in space. A deep gulf of deadly strife intervened between them; but across that gulf, their hearts went forth and were clasped together—the prosperous and the comfortless,—in love for the American

* See Appendix: Note Z.

Union, and in brotherly love as fellow-countrymen.

> "Those friends thou hast and their adoption tried,
> Grapple them to thy soul with hooks of steel."

Sincere human friendships by no means perish with the loss of their mortal surroundings. To a pure mind, inspired by the truth, they are spiritually related to the invisible and permanent. Else, hopelessly we should often have to cry—

> "For the touch of a vanished hand,
> And the sound of a voice that's still."

Just so with human citizenship, wisely conceived and cherished. It is more than a mere symbol of one higher and nobler. As one has well said:

"There is a mystery in all affections which rises above vulgar instincts; it is thus with the love of country. The patriot sees in her more than can be seen by those who are without; and yet he remembers that there remains in her much that cannot meet his eye; for it is part of the greatness of a nation, that though her fields and cities are visible things, her highest greatness and most sacred claims belong in part, like whatever includes a spiritual element, to the sphere of 'things unseen.'" *

The archetype of *our country* is the "better country, that is, an heavenly," for which prophetic souls—children of faith and promise—have yearned

* Aubrey de Vere.

throughout all the centuries. A man dwelling here, may have there his citizenship, and in its fulfillment is required and insured the performance of all other civic duty.

APPENDICES.

CONTENTS.

Note A: Love of Religious Excitement.
" B: Contrary Statements; Sevier and Tipton.
" C: A Southerner's Letter, in 1861.
" D: Rev. Herman Bokum.
" E: A New-Yorker's Letter, in 1861.
" F: Col. David Cummings.
" G: Delegates to Union Convention.
" H: "   "   "   "
" I: Employment of Bloodhounds.
" J: Verse on the Execution of Haun and the Harmons.
" K: Edward J. Sanford's Narrative.
" L: Heroism of East Tennessee Women.
" M: Gen. Samuel P. Carter's Raid.
" N: Lieut. S. T. Harris, at Columbia, S. C., &c.
" O: Report of Col. Wm. P. Sanders' raid.
" P: Report of Col. R. C. Trigg, (C. S. A.)
" R: Letter from Gen. Longstreet.
" S: Concerning Knoxville refugees.
" T: Capt. Poe's Topography of Knoxville.
" U: Gen. Sherman's dinner with Gen. Burnside.
" V: Col. E. P. Alexander, (C. S. A.) concerning the siege.
" W: List of superior U. S. A. officers from East Tennessee.
" X: Martyrdoms of non-combattant Unionists.
" Y: Concerning gifts at Boston to East Tennessee relief.
" Z: Receipts and expenditures for East Tennessee relief.

APPENDICES.

Appendix: Note A: Page 27.

The love of religious excitement, attributed by the ex-United States Consul at Singapore, to the mountaineers of East Tennessee, is apt to exist among a civilized, yet, uneducated people, who lead a simple, natural life. Its indulgence was formerly much greater in the Western States.

A religious excitement sprung up in East Tennessee in 1802, which was attended with remarkable bodily manifestations, familiarly called "the jerks." The affection included among its subjects equally the young and old, the strong and weak, the good and bad in previous moral character, those who desired and those who hated it. Involuntary, it had no premonitory symptoms, and left the patient as he was before. The very atmosphere seemed to be laden with an influence that brought the mind and body into relation and sympathy that were abnormally close. If the preacher, after a smooth and gentle course of expression suddenly changed his voice and language to the awful and alarming, instantly some dozen or twenty persons or more would simultaneously be jerked forward where they were sitting, with a suppressed noise, once or twice, like the barking of a dog. And so it would continue or abate, according to the tenor or strain of the discourse.

This extraordinary nervous agitation commenced in East Tennessee at a "sacramental meeting," and on that day several hundreds of persons were seized with it. At first uniformly confined to the arms, the quick, convulsive motion went downwards from the elbow, and these jerks succeeded each other after short intervals. For some time no religious meeting was held in which this novel, involuntary exercise was not exhibited by more or less of the audience in that part of the country where it originated. Generally, all who had once been its subjects, continued to be frequently affected, and not only at meeting but at home, and sometimes when entirely alone. After the commencement of the "jerks" they spread rapidly in all directions. Persons drawn by curiosity to visit the congregations where they existed, were often seized, and when they returned home they would communicate them to the people there. In some instances they occurred in remote valleys of the mountains, where the people had no opportunity of communication with the infected. In East Tennessee and the southwestern part of Virginia, their prevalence was the greatest. Soon the "exercise" began to assume a variety of appearances. While the jerks in the arms continued to be the most common form, in many cases the joint of the neck was the seat of the convulsive motion, and was thrown back and forward to an extent and with a celerity which no one could imitate, and which to the spectator was most alarming. A common exercise was dancing, performed by a gentle and not ungraceful motion, but with little variety in the steps. One young woman had what was termed, "the jumping exercise." It was truly wonderful to observe the violence of the impetus with which she was borne upwards from the ground: it required the united strength of three or four of her companions to confine her down. None of these varieties however, were half so terrible to the spectator, as that which affected the joint of the neck, in which it appeared as if the neck must be broken. Besides these exercises, there were some of the most curious and ludicrous kind. In one, the affected barked like a dog, in another, boxed with fists clenched, striking at any body or thing near, in another, ran with amazing swiftness,--imitated playing on a violin, or sewing with a needle, &c.

The affection was "imported into Kentucky" as well as Virginia. Not only was it contagious, but particular kinds of exercise were caught from a stranger visiting a congregation that had known it in other forms of bodily movement.

These nervous agitations were at first received as supernatural agencies, intended to arrest the attention of the careless multitude, and were therefore encouraged and sustained by many of the pious, but after a while they became troublesome. The noise made by the convulsive motions in the pews was such, that the preacher could not be composedly heard; and in several of the exercises the affected person needed the attention of more than one assistant. Besides, subjects of the jerks became weary of them, and avoided serious and exciting thoughts, lest they should produce this effect. However, they all united to testify, that in the most violent and convulsive agitations, when the head would rapidly strike the breast and back alternately, no pain was experienced; and some asserted, that when one arm only was affected with the jerks, it felt more comfortable than the other through the whole day. In some places the persons affected were not permitted to come to the church on account of the noise and disturbance produced. The subjects were generally pious or seriously affected with religion, but not universally. There were cases in which the careless, and those who continued to be so were seized. The dread of the jerks was great in many persons, both religious and careless, and the affection did not contribute to the advancement of religion. There were persons however, who after much experience still approved them.

APPENDIX: NOTE B: Page 75.

According to Haywood and Ramsey, the ex-Governor of Frankland, when attempting to escape in the mountains on the way to Morganton, was pursued, became entangled in the woods, was fired upon by one of the guard, was recaptured unhurt and delivered to the High-Sheriff of Burke County, N. C. Gen. McDowell, Sevier's compatriot at King's Mountain and another friend, procured him a brief liberty, which the Sheriff renewed. The Court was then in session and the prisoner was arraigned before it as a traitor to North Carolina. Six of his friends had separately come from west of the mountains to Morganton:—Dr. James Cozby, his former Army Surgeon; Maj. Evans, his tried fellow-soldier; his two sons James and John, and two others, Greene and Gibson.

Dr. Ramsey's history repeats the narrative in MS. of one who lived at that time. He tells that four of the six men above named concealed themselves outside the town, while Cozby and Evans went into it and entered the crowd attracted to the scene by the prisoner's fame. Evans, apparently an unconcerned visitor, led Sevier's horse, (celebrated for swiftness,) in front of the Court house, and threw the bridle carelessly over its neck. Cozby went into the house, and his eyes met those of the prisoner. Sevier at once knew that rescue was at hand, but a sign from Cozby restrained him. There was a pause in the trial. Cozby stepped forward in front of the Judge and asked him with quickness and energy: "Are you done with that man?" His hearers were startled and wondering, and while their attention was turned aside, Sevier sprang to the door, then to the saddle on the waiting horse and speedily was gone. He was followed by his rescuers and welcomed by the two friends who were without the town. Then, away the whole party went homeward, leaving their pursuers hopelessly behind.

There have been recent publications concerning Sevier, in which his antagonist, Tipton, has been spoken of unfavorably. J. C. Tipton, an aged grandson of Col. John Tipton, has been moved to publish, that there are two errors in current history of that early period One of these is in the statement that Tipton would have hung Sevier's sons, his prisoners, but was persuaded by friends to spare their lives. The second error, relates to Sevier's deliverance from captivity. Mr. Tipton affirms that "Col. Tipton started Gov. Sevier to North Carolina for trial under a guard of two men, that Sevier escaped in the mountains on the way, and was not taken to Morganton." He represents that these facts were received by him from his father, Jonathan Tipton, to whom they were communicated by Col. John Tipton. He admits that the errors of which he writes, should have met long since with correction, but the general character of both Tipton and Sevier having been that of "honorable, brave and magnanimous men," the necessity for it sooner has not seemed urgent. The historical revival of the subject now invites this act of justice to the memory of his ancestor.

APPENDIX: NOTE C: Page 88.

The following letter to the author of these Reminiscences, is from his friend,—a gentleman of superior social and professional standing, and a citizen of Richmond, Virginia. It expresses his mind, and probably that of many other intelligent and reflecting persons in Virginia at the time it was written, concerning the civil and political situation.

RICHMOND, Dec. 26, 1860.

"There are times when friends are indeed blessings. I prize a sympathizing friend more and more every day: and I almost think that the time has come when union with Christ is the only bond that can certainly survive the shock and the disintegration that threaten our social structure.

After a conversation held last evening with a circle of intelligent friends, I retired to my room convinced that we are, as a nation, all adrift,—under cross tides,—under high and variable winds, without chart, compass or generalship,—except the secret purposes of the Eternal Mind.

Paul's experience on the Adriatic,—without sun, moon or stars for many days, comes up to my mind. This only I know, that God is serene; in knowledge and power,—the sure trust of His Church and people.

The work of disintegration goes on,—without any combination, as yet, of the forces. The inauguration of Mr. Lincoln, (if he is inaugurated,) will give proportions and type to the entire Southern elements, which will present a distinct and palpable issue to the North and South.

I incline to think that the South will become substantially a unit upon the main points at issue, whilst the North is likely to be divided both on the moral and political questions pressing upon them. Then a line will have to be conceded or fought for, or a reconstruction of the Federal Government will take place. The West and North West are inoculated already with the doctrine of free trade; and if Baltimore, Norfolk, Charleston, Savannah, Mobile and New Orleans are declared free ports of entry, the laws of trade will prove invincible powers, aided by foreign diplomacy and interests, before which manufacturing New-England will have an unequal struggle.

The trouble is with Pennsylvania and her iron interests; but New

York will force Philadelphia into Southern sympathies, and Commerce will butter the bread of politicians. Such are my poor thoughts.

I go with a United South on such grounds as Kentucky, Tennessee, Georgia, North Carolina and Virginia may consent to. The Cotton States cannot, as I think, make themselves respected as an independent power, at home or abroad. They will feel this before their Conventions dissolve.

Our pride needs to be humbled! our national and public sins to be felt and deplored. I trust the fourth of January will bring the people of God before Him in such an attitude, that He, as He alone can, will deign to hear and save us yet.

* * * * * * * * If this Union is to be dissolved, and especially if extreme Cotton ideas are to prevail, I would willingly accept a home in England or Scotland. The thought of exile from America! Strange!!! But I am now humiliated and grieved, so that I know not what more I could feel except at the horrors of *blood* shed by brothers."

APPENDIX: NOTE D: Page 88.

This Bible Colporteur was Rev. Herman Bokum, a Minister of the German Reformed Church and a Pennsylvanian, who had resided for five years on a farm near Knoxville. His education was superior in kind, and he had the Germanic conscientiousness with which Martin Luther was so magnificently gifted. Under his eccentric, decidedly brusque manners, there lay hidden a tender heart and a deep vein of piety. Whatever disturbances his mind had once suffered from outward troubles, it certainly had emerged from them (as is sometimes the outcome in such cases,) with a sharpness of discernment, of which minds are blameless that have never been moved from their even tenor and plodding ways. His mental astuteness was of little or no use to him in the conduct of his own affairs,—his poverty always keeping in front along with his sincerity. But he early saw the fatal drift of the Secession movement and the magnitude of the proportions to which it would grow. Dr. Hill, then President of Harvard University, told a Tennesseean after the war had closed, that his eyes had been first opened by Mr.

Bokum, to the reality of the Rebellion, early in its progress, as *a great and portentous fact*. Being an ardent Union man and of a fearless nature, he soon became obnoxious to the Confederate authorities. Eventually they detailed a file of soldiers to arrest him at his home. But he heard of their coming and made his escape over the mountains through Kentucky to Philadelphia. There he was appointed a Hospital Chaplain and in 1863 published in pamphlet, "A Refugee's Testimony,"—being a narrative of his personal experiences in Tennessee.

APPENDIX: NOTE E: Page 95.

The young New-Yorker soon went on his way homewards. At Washington City he was forced to tarry, and from there he wrote to his friend at Knoxville as follows:

April 23, P. M., 1861.

"I have succeeded in effecting a junction with my other forces—my brother and brother-in-law—but we are all now prisoners of war! Not that I would give you to understand that we are in the power of either of the belligerents, but because of the war we are most decidedly prisoners in this place.

I found the whole line of the road in a blaze of enthusiasm and excitement from Knoxville to Lynchburg, which place I reached the next morning. Having occasion for a business purpose to introduce myself to ———, Warden of the Church there, (the Clergyman being absent), he very kindly asked me to stay at his house, which I did until Monday morning, when I came on here without interference.

The people of Virginia display a noble spirit of patriotism if it were only in a right cause, which I cannot feel to be the case. The very soil seems to teem with armed men. Even the boys and the old men are enlisting, and the cry is 'To Washington!' Senator Mason addressed them on the route and said, 'War has begun,' and Jeff. Davis with two thousand Carolinians is already at Richmond. I regret the policy of the Government and think it is a grand mistake; but it is the most absurd dream in the world that Lincoln wishes to lead an army against the South. The truth is, Virginia's sympathies are so much more with the South than with the Government, that although denouncing utterly both South Carolina and Secession, she preferred uniting her fortunes with them, to sustaining a policy which involved force against them to any degree at all·

I am struck with the fact that at the South the loyal feeling goes to the State, while at the North it goes to the General Government. The radical difference of belief concerning the relations of the separate States to the Nation, is a principal cause in the whole trouble. The very same act which crazes Virginia, crazes the whole North in an opposite direction, and brings Pierce, Buchanan and Fillmore out in support of the Government.

My friends (at Lynchburg) did not dare invite me to take part in the services, and the most atrocious sentiments were uttered in my hearing against Lincoln and the Yankees. Here all seems quiet—no cannon in the streets and few soldiers to be seen. Martial law is not proclaimed and there is a wonderful contrast to the feverish atmosphere of Virginia. Still I believe the Government is wide awake and more ready than people dream of. Communications have been open to Baltimore but broken up beyond. To-day Rev. Mr. P—— and I concluded to go there and try to make our way around through Harper's Ferry and Hagerstown, but we found that since morning the Government had seized the depot and would allow no train to leave. So here we are.

I despond very much about peace. Perhaps I am superstitious, but the two singular portents (which have so many parallels in history) of the first lesson last Sunday from Joel, and the co-incidence of the Baltimore fight with the anniversary of the battle of Lexington, dishearten me.

The Potomac is now fortified and the Government must march its troops through Maryland or give up its Capital. Unless this should be seized soon, it will not be done; and if Maryland refuses passage through her borders to men and provisions, Maryland must be put down, if it burns her every town and makes the State a desert. Self preservation will extort that.

But in these exciting times we must do what we can to check the madness of the people. Do not let yourself suppose, as so many seem to do, that all this excitement at the North is hatred of the South. No such thing. The very same feeling of patriotism which in Lynchburg called six hundred men to arms and equipped them with eighteen thousand dollars, is at the North rallying all to the support of the old and loved Government—no conglomeration of States but the Federal Union. That hates will arise on both sides now, we must expect. War lets loose fearful passions, and I know human nature is alike every where; and judging from what I saw in Virginia, I can readily believe the North will be about as bad."

Appendix: Note F: Page 101.

Colonel David Cummings, of Anderson county, an officer of the Tennessee (Confederate) troops, was conspicuous in preserving peace at the time of the imminent deadly collision between Union men and Secessionists on the principal street of Knoxville. It was he, who with two Union citizens,—Abner Jackson and John Williams—afterwards succeeded by persuasion in halting hundreds of State soldiers on their way from camp to the town with a destructive purpose against Charles Douglass, and so, in preventing a bloody encounter between the soldiers, and Douglass with his friends. It was also Col. Cummings, who on a subsequent day, as the body of the murdered Douglass was borne along the street to its grave, relieved the occasion of its reproach in the eyes of unfriendly observers, by magnanimously joining on horseback the officiating minister in leading the sad procession.

Appendix: Notes G and H: Pages 107 and 115.

Delegates to the Union Convention at Knoxville and Greeneville, Tenn., May 30 and June 17, 1861.

Names unmarked are of members present only at Knoxville.
Names marked * are of those present only at Greeneville.
Names marked † are of those present on both occasions.

ANDERSON COUNTY.

T. Adkins,	Lindsey D. Hill,	James Ross,
J. Ayres,	L. Hockworth,	Philip Sieber,
H. H. Baker,	Oliver Hoskins,	William Smith,

ANDERSON COUNTY—CONTINUED.

John Black,
J. C. Chiles,
J. H. Cox,
William Cross,
J. A. Doughty,
Edward Freels,
John Freels,
W. S. Freels,

†L. C. Houk,
J. B. Lamar,
G. W. Leath,
Samuel Moore,
L. A. Powell,
Grandison Queener,
Wm. Reynolds,

J. Thompson,
P. C. Wallace,
John Weaver,
W. W. Weaver,
A. T. Williams.
D. K. Young,
S. C. Young.

BLEDSOE COUNTY.

S. P. Doss,
J. W. McReynolds,

Wm. S. Findlay, M.D.,

†J. G. Spears.

BLOUNT COUNTY.

S. F. Bell,
Henry Brakebill,
Rev. J. S. Craig,
*F. M. Cruze,
W. H. Cunningham,
†Rev. W. T. Dowell,
W. L. Dearing,
Rev. W. T. Dowell,
Robert Eagleton,
†Solomon Farmer,
S. C. Flannigan,
H. Foster,
David Goddard,
William Goddard,

John Godfrey,
*J. R. Frow,
Henry Hammell,
J. M. Heiskell,
*H. J. Henry,
James Henry,
Spencer Henry,
Isaac Hinds,
W. A. Hunter,
G. W. Hutsell,
John Jackson,
Alex. Kennedy,
Edward Kidd,
Jefferson Kidd,

James Henry,
†A. Kirkpatrick,
Sanders Leeper,
Stephen Matthews,
Fleming Mays.
Andrew McBath,
M. McTeer,
Robert Pickens,
Thomas Pickens,
James H. Rowan,
John Trew,
Jas. H. Walker,
†Lavater Wear.

BRADLEY COUNTY.

S Beard,
J. S. Bradford,
*J. G. Brown,
J. M. Campbell, M. D.,
T. L. Cate,

C. D. Champion,
A. A. Clingan,
J. N. Dunn,
†R. M. Edwards,

S. P. Gaut,
C. T. Hardwick,
J. L. Kirby,
John McPherson,

APPENDICES.

CAMPBELL COUNTY.

George Bowling,
William Carey,
†Joseph A. Cooper,
David Hart.

Joseph Hatmaker,
John Jones,
J. L. Keeny,

John Meader,
Wm. Robbins,
R. D. Wheeler.

CARTER COUNTY.

*B. P. Angel,
*J. L. Bradley,
John W. Cameron,
J. T. P. Carter,
*L. Carter,
*W. B. Carter.
*W. J. Crutcher,
*J. Emmet,
*J. Hendrickson.

*T. M. Hilton,
*J. G. Lewis,
*Wm. Marsh,
*B. M. G. O'Brien,
*J. Perry,
*V. Singletary,
*H. Slagle,
*L. Slagle,

*H. C. Smith,
*John M. Smith,
Daniel L. Store,
*D. Stover,
†Abram Tipton,
†C. P. Toncray,
*Robert Williams,
*C. Wilcox.

CLAIBORNE COUNTY.

*J. J. Bunch,
†E. E. Jones,

*F. Jones,
*V. Myers,

*H. Sewell,
*J J. Sewell.

COCKE COUNTY.

*J. Bible,
*W. A. Campbell,
†J. W. Clarke,
†P. H. Easterly,

*W. Graham,
*W. Hornett,
*S. H. Inman,

*W. Nicely,
*G. L. Porter,
*William Wood.

CUMBERLAND COUNTY.

F. Kindred,

A. C. Yates,

*R. K. Byrd; Proxy.

FENTRESS COUNTY.

*E. B. Langley; Proxy.

GRAINGER COUNTY.

†John Brooks,
†Harmon G. Lea,

†James James,
*Edward L. Tate.

†D. C. Senter.

GREENE COUNTY.

*Thos. D. Arnold,
†Samuel H. Baxter,
*Jacob Bible,
*H. B. Boker,
*J. Brannon,
†James Britton,
†James Britton, Jr.,
T. G. Brown,
*W. R. Brown,
†Wm. Cavender, M.D.,
†G. Click,
†R. A. Crawford,
*William H. Crawford,
*W. D Culver,
*E. Davis,
*Thomas Davis,
*J. B. Dobson,
*B. Earnest,
*N. Earnest,
A. G. Easterly,
†Jonathan Easterly,
Reuben Easterly,
R. M. Easterly,
Adam Farnsworth,
*James A. Galbreath,
†Charles Gass,
*George F. Gillespie,
†Solomon Goode,
†Abram Hammond,
*C. Harden,
*Peter Harmon,
*J. W. Harold,
*J. P. Holtsinger,
*A. W. Howard,
†Chas. Johnson, M.D.,
†Robert Johnson,
*James Jones,
†John Jones, Jr.,
†William Jones,
*J. Kerbaugh,
*George Kinney,
†Alexander A. Lane,
*John Love,
†John Maloney,
W. A. Maloney,
†W. D. McClelland,
*B. McDannel,
†Jas. P. McDowell,
*Samuel McGaughey,
*Anthony Moore,
*J. Myers,
*Hon. D. L. Patterson,
*J. G. Reeves,
*David Rush,
†B. B. Sherfie,
†D. G. Vance,
*C. M. Vestal,
†A. W. Walker,
†Wm. West, M. D.,
*Israel Woolsey.

HAMILTON COUNTY.

John Anderson,
J. D. Blackford,
F. G. Blacknall,
A. M. Cate,
G. O. Cate,
E. M. Cleaveland,
†William Clift,
Wm. Crutchfield,
William Denny.
J. F. Early,
R. Hall,
Wilson Hixson,
J. D. Kenner,
Monroe Masterson,
J. A. Matthews,
P. L. Matthews,
*S. McCaleb,
A. W. McDaniel,
R. C. McRee,
Peter Mounger,
A. A. Pearson,
I C. Rogers,
A. Selser,
J. G. Thomas,
†D. C. Trewhitt,

HANCOCK COUNTY.

*Charles L. Barton, Wm. G. Brownlow and Wm. C. Kyle: Proxies.

APPENDICES.

HAWKINS COUNTY.

*Thomas Benny,
†John Blevins,
†A. P. Caldwell,
*C. W. Hall,
*A. B. Keel.

†Wm. C. Kyle,
*A. A. Kyle,
*C. J. McKinney,
*H. Mitchell,

*John Netherland,
Robert G. Netherland,
John Vaughn,
*James White,

JEFFERSON COUNTY.

*John Alderson,
†Sam'l Anderson, M.D.
J. M. Bewley,
*Rev. J. R. Birchfield,
†A.A. Caldwell, M. D.,
†——— Cawood, M. D.,
*J. L. Coile,
†William Dick,
†Wiley Foust,
*Wm. Harris.

W. A. Haun,
Joel Johnson,
†William Jones,
*W. Kirkpatrick,
†L. F. Leeper,
*L. McDaniel,
Wm. McFarland,
†J. Monroe Meek,
*N. Newman,

*R. D. Rankin,
*E. A. Sawyers,
*C. K. Scruggs,
†J. P. Swann,
*N. B. Swann,
†John Tate,
*M. Thornburg,
*John Thornhill,
*Edward West,

JOHNSON COUNTY.

*Alexander Baker,
†R. R. Butler,
†J. W. M. Grayson,
*Samuel Howard,
M T. Locke, M. D.,
Rev. L. Madron,
*H. P. Murphy.

*Kemp Murphy,
†John Murphy,
J. Norris,
*J. H. Norris,
*J. F. Norris,
*H. C. Northington,
†S. E. Northington,

*A. G. Shown,
G. H. Shown,
F. Slimp,
†A. D. Smith,
D. Smithpetre, M. D.,
†J. H. Vaught,
†Rev. L. Venable,

KNOX COUNTY.

F. A. Armstrong,
John Armstrong,
Caleb H. Baker,
J. P. Barger,
†John Baxter,
William Beard,
James D. Bell,

R. B. Gibbs,
A. Gideon,
Wilson Groner,
James Hall,
R. M. Hall,
Robert Harper,
R. A. Harrison,

John H. Mynatt,
R. G. Mynatt,
David Nelson,
Jacob L. Nelson,
J. M. Nelson,
Nicholas Nelson,
H. Osborne,

THE LOYAL MOUNTAINEERS.

KNOX COUNTY—CONTINUED.

J. S. Bell,
R. M. Bell,
R. M. Bennett,
F. H. Bounds,
H. R. Brown,
John Brown,
John M. Brown,
T. W. Brown,
†Wm. G. Brownlow,
†J. F. Bunker,
Absalom Burnett,
David Burnett,
John A. Callaway,
*A. C. Callen,
P. H. Cardwell,
C. W. Carnes,
T. W. Carnes,
W. B. Carnes,
M. Childress,
Henry Chiles,
†H. R. Clapp,
William Clapp,
William Coker,
John M. Conner,
W. A. A. Conner,
George Cooper,
F. Coram,
John J. Craig,
Robert Craighead,
O. H. Crippen,
John Currier,
†A. Davis,
D. F. DeArmond,
P. Derieux,
†John Devers,

James Hartley,
W. E. Hedgcock,
F. S. Heiskell,
John Henson,
A. D. C. Hinds,
William Hines,
Daniel Hommell,
Joseph Hubbs,
*Abner G. Jackson,
L. D. Johnson,
William D. Johnson,
W. Kennedy,
Daniel King,
John Kirk,
†Andrew Knott,
Joseph Larew,
W. R. Lawrence,
M. D. Lea,
Seth Lea,
John Lester,
John Letsinger,
*Lewis Letsinger,
Thomas Long,
John Looney,
Jas. C. Luttrell,
John Luttrell,
J. Luttrell,
J. M. Marcum,
†James Maxwell,
W. N. Maxwell,
John J. May,
*Horace Maynard,
†Samuel McCammon,
Wm. McClelland,
Levi McCloud,

†D. W. Parker,
James Raison,
†A. P. Rambo,
Lewis Reed,
Jacob Reid,
B. Roberts,
*Henry Roberts,
Milton Roberts,
Samuel R. Rodgers,
Thomas Rodgers,
†Wm. Rodgers, M. D.,
*P. A. Ruble,
Frederick Rule,
P. Rutherford,
William Sharp,
Joseph Shell,
Matthew Simpson,
P. H. Skaggs,
James Smith,
†John Smith,
†T. A. Smith,
†Robert Sneed, M. D..
Jesse Stubbs,
W. H. Swan,
James Tarwater,
†O. P. Temple,
†Andrew Thompson,
G. W. Tindell,
†C. F. Trigg,
A. R. Trotter,
John Tunnell,
H. Turner,
John Vance,
P. Walker, M. D.,
Thos. J. White,

APPENDICES. 353

KNOX COUNTY—CONTINUED.

J. R. Draper,	J. C. S. McDaniel,	†John Williams,
†John M. Fleming,	J. A. McMillan,	Calvin Wood,
Joseph W. Fowler,	A. A. Meek,	John Wood,
B. Frazier,	J. H. Morris,	R. H. Wood,
*J. D. French,	A. K. Mynatt,	F. M. Yarnall,
Joseph Garner,	Col. Mynatt,	Martin Yarnall,
J. O. Gentry,	Hugh Mynatt,	R. A. York,
P. George,	H. D. C. Mynatt.	

MARION COUNTY.

†William G. Brownlow: Proxy.

M'MINN COUNTY.

W. W. Alexander,	O. Dodson,	T. B. McElwee,
†M. D. Anderson,	Wm. L. Dodson,	†John McGaughey,
†George W. Bridges,	C. Foster,	N. J. Peters,
David Brient,	J. H. Hornsby,	Wm. Porter,
Rev. H. Buttram,	A. Hutsell,	E. T. Renfro,
Charles Cate,	Nathan Kelly,	B. Wells,
Robert Cochran,	Wm. L. Lester,	Rev. John Wilkins,
*A. C Derrick,	M. R. May, M. D.,	D. P. York,
J. J. Dixon.		

MEIGS COUNTY.

Andrew Campbell,	†T. J. Matthews,	Thomas Sessell,
Thomas Miller.		

MONROE COUNTY.

I. C. Brown,	W. H Dawson,	Samuel M. Johnson,
A. W. Cozart,	†B. Franklin, M. D.,	J. R. Robinson,
*T. H. Davis,	†William Heiskell,	Wm. M. Smith.

MORGAN COUNTY.

*T. H. Davis,	†E. Langley.	M. Stephens,
†S. C. Honeycutt,	†J. M. Melton,	†Jesse Stonecipher,
*Rev. W. R. Jackson,	B. T. Staples,	

v

POLK COUNTY.

*W. M. Biggs,
*W. J. Copeland,
J. M. McCleary,

ROANE COUNTY.

*J. Adkisson,
†W. M. Alexander,
†Joseph Anderson,
J. W. Atkisson,
F. Bales,
†J. W. Bowman,
R. W. Boyd,
E. W. Brazeale,
†R. K. Byrd,
T. F. Carter,
Samuel L. Childress,
Isaac A. Clark,
William Clark,
E. S. Clarke,
T. T. Coffin,
J. I. Dale,
Reuben Davis,
John DeArmond,
P. I. Doremus,
G. W. Easter,
W. L. Goldston,
A. L. Greene,
*J. S. Hagler,
Wesley Harwell,
†D. F. Harrison,
John Hays,
J. O. Hays,
*W. J. Hornsby,
E. D. Hoss,
†James H. Johnston,
†George Littleton,
William Lowry,
Joseph B. Martin,
†Thomas J. Mason,
W. S. Patton,
Wm. E. Pope,
†M. Rose,
W. P. Rose,
T. Russell,
†J. T. Shelley,
Wm. H. Selvidge,
J. Y. Smith,
*W. B. Staley,
†T. J. Tipton,
†J. J. West,
C. C. Wester,
J. W. Wester,
†L. M. Wester,
Samuel Williams,
John Womble,
*J. Wyatt,
†F. M. Wylie,
*L. M. Wylie,
†F. Young.

SCOTT COUNTY.

*S. C. Honeycutt: Proxy.

SEVIER COUNTY.

*L. D. Alexander,
†J. H. Caldwell,
*J. Caldwell,
*J. Cate,
William Catlett,
Harvey Cowan,
R. M. Creswell,
†Rev. Jas. Cummings,
*John Douglass,
Lemuel Duggan,
†Wilson Duggan,
*F. L. Emmert,
†J. K. Franklin,
†J. T. Havis,
†R. H. Hodsden, M.D.,
†Edmund Hodges,
*C. Inman,
David Keener,
Alexander McBath,
†D. McCroskey,
*H. Mount,
†J. C. Murphy,
William Petty,
†Samuel Pickens,
†D. M. Ray,
Isaac Russell,
E. H. Williams.

APPENDICES.

SULLIVAN COUNTY.

P. N. Easley,
*J. Hughes,
†James Lynn,

William Mullenix,
†G. R. Netherland,

†Jacob Shewalter,
†R. L. Stanford, M. D.

UNION COUNTY.

†Isaac Bayless,
John Cox,
F. P. Hansard,
L. Huddleston,

*M. V. Nash,
A. McPheters,
J. G. Palmer,

J. M. Sawyers,
S. H. Smith,
†J. W. Thornburg.

WASHINGTON COUNTY.

D. B. Barkley,
*J. Biddle,
*C. Bashor,
†A. J. Brown,
*M. H. Clark,
*Jas. W. Deaderick,
*C. A. Eames,
*J. W. Ellis,
*J. A. Estes,
*R. L. Gillespie,
*T. S. Gillespie,
*W. Glaze,
J. F. Grisham,
*P. H. Grisham,
*J. W. Hartman, M. D,

*E. S. Harvey,
†A. Hoss,
*E. Keezell,
*A. Kibbler,
†S. T. Logan,
†J. F. Mahoney,
*E. S. Matthews,
*Wm. H. Maxwell,
*R. B. McCall, M. D.,
*D. M. McFall,
*R. M. McKee,
*G. W. Nelson,
†Thos. A. R. Nelson,
*D. Onk,

*E. W. Oughbrough,
†R. H. Palmer, M. D.,
†S. K. N. Patton,
*John Pennybaker,
*H. Presnell,
*W. M. Reese,
*J. Slack,
*W. Slemmons,
*W. Smith, M. D.,
*A. B. Tadlock,
*E. H. West,
†S. West,
*G. W. Wilson,
*J. Yerger.

APPENDIX: NOTE I: Page 139.

A comparison of the date of Gen. Zolicoffer's letter from Campbell County to Col. Wood, announcing his purpose immediately to disarm the Union population, with the date of the following advertisement in the *Memphis Appeal* by two Confederate officers, written from the same county, seriously weakens the plea given in the advertisement for the barbarous use of so many dogs against that population. For disarmed Union men could scarcely carry on an irreg ular warfare that would require or justify the employment to their damage of sanguinary beasts.

"BLOODHOUNDS WANTED."

"We, the undersigned, will pay five dollars per pair for fifty pairs of well-bred hounds, and fifty dollars for one pair of thorough-bred bloodhounds that will take the track of a man. The purpose for which these dogs are wanted is to chase the infernal, cowardly Lincoln bushwhackers of East Tennessee and Kentucky, (who have taken advantage of the bush to kill and cripple many good soldiers,) to their haunts and capture them. The said hounds must be delivered at Captain Hammer's livery stable by the 10th of December next, where a mustering officer will be present to muster and inspect them."

(Signed)   F. N. McNAIRY,
                   H. H. HARRIS,
Camp Crinforth, Campbell Co., Tenn., November 16.

APPENDIX: NOTE J: Page 151.

In proof that the hanging of young Harmon before his father's eyes, while the latter awaited death by the same method, was not, as a grave judicial procedure, without censorious comment at the time, are these satirical lines by one who was more of a wag than a poet. Necessarily, they had a very limited circulation in *M. S.* among friends.

To General ———

Plentiful heroes from this War will spring,
With praise of whom shall Fame's proud arches ring,
And unborn generations with pains be taught,
At mother's knee and school, what deeds they wrought.
But thou, as Jupiter excels in light
Planets and stars which deck the robe of night,
Shalt for thy courage and milit'ry skill
Above compeers, historic pages fill.

APPENDIX.

They have won battles,—strong batteries storm'd,
And such small deeds, common in War, perform'd:
But thou, with soaring aim, hast hung three men,
Sentenced by Martial Court and thy brave pen.
These loved their country; one, in prime of life
Bequeathed it all he had, children and wife;
The second, gray with age, the third, his son,
Whom thou didst order,—by no pity won,
Should to life's closing scene together go,
And while one died, the other see his woe!
Brave General! goodness ever is allied
With greatness. Be thou, thy country's pride!

APPENDIX: NOTE K: Page 167.

NARRATIVE BY EDWARD J. SANFORD OF KNOXVILLE, TENN.

In February, 1862, the Rebel Conscript Law was enacted in Tennessee declaring every man between the ages of eighteen and forty-five a soldier of the Southern Confederacy, and the then Governor, I. G. Harris, made a call for the entire militia force of the State. Consequently the prospect of being speedily compelled to do battle against their sense of right and justice, added to the already precarious condition of those citizens who were known to entertain Union sentiments, and many companies of Union men were formed in East Tennessee for the purpose of running through the rebel lines and joining the Federal army in Kentucky.

For several days previous to April 18, 1862, such a company was forming in Knox and Blount counties. Guides were procured who knew the mountain-paths and who were constantly passing to and from the Federal camp in Kentucky. For the ostensible purpose of buying beef in the mountain region for the Confederate army, passes were procured by men who employed their time in preparing a boat on the Clinch river, about twenty miles north of Knoxville and secreting it from the watchful eyes of rebel pickets, so that the company could be set over without delay.

The place of *rendezvous* was on Bullrun creek, fifteen miles north, and its time midnight, April 18. The party was to number three hundred and seventy-five men; but the authorities at Knoxville having got wind of the matter, placed a strong guard around the town which prevented seventy-five of this number from their purpose. I was fortunately one of the few citizens who intended to join the party and were outside of the town before nightfall when the guard was stationed. A carriage ride with my wife early in the evening, as though only for recreation, gave me the opportunity without suspicion, to pass into the country; and leaving her at the house of a friend five miles from town to return home the next day, I went on foot to the house of the well-known Unionist, Andrew Knott, Esq., and remained there until nearly dark. By that time six others had come to bear me company. Two of these were the son and son-in-law of Squire Knott, who united with his family to bestow their best wishes on the little band at its departure. Accessions to it were almost constantly received, as we cautiously proceeded on our way to the *rendezvous*. We avoided the intervening houses of rebels by going through the fields. But happily this precaution was seldom necessary, for from almost every house we passed, one at least was added to our number, and many were the words of encouragement given and bitter tears shed by mothers, sisters and wives, as those they held dear stepped noiselessly forth from their homes and joined the marching column. Before reaching the appointed place of meeting, our number had increased to seventy-five, and there we found seventy-five men awaiting us. Every one had a haversack of provisions; all were without blankets and extra clothing and only one-third of the company had succeeded in arming themselves for defence with guns or pistols. One half of the whole party did not arrive at the time agreed upon.

We had no shelter, our clothes were completely wet by the rain which had fallen during the entire night and we dared not make a fire, as it would have exposed us to the enemy who, we had reason to know had discovered our movements. For a small scouting party of theirs had captured a few miles back two of our party who had fallen behind the main body. After a short consultation we pushed on as fast as possible and found our boat unmolested where it had been hidden. One-half of our company at one time were set over the river and it so happened that I went with the first boat load. We found relief from fatigue in putting off our haversacks and, (although the rain was pouring down,) in sitting upon the ground on the north side of the stream, while the boat returned for the rest of our party. But scarcely were we seated when a startling cry arose that the rebel cavalry were upon us We knew at once that if such were the case, our only safety was in fighting, for the river behind us barred our escape in that direction. In a moment a line was formed;—those fortunate enough to have either gun or pistol stood in front and the unarmed behind;—and the expected attack was awaited.

Two horsemen could be seen approaching through the woods, but in the darkness it could not be told whether they were in advance of a column of troops or not. In either case we concluded they were enemies and with weapons levelled, we listened for the word of command to fire upon them. Much to our joy however, they gave us the friendly countersign, and we found that they were an Official of Anderson county and others, who had come to show us on our way. It was then about two o'clock in the morning and without waiting for the second half of our party to cross the river, we went forward under the guidance of our recently supposed enemies at a "double quick" pace. Not a word was spoken as we pressed on without halting,—sometimes through woods and sometimes through fields. As day began to break, from a very secluded spot in a piece of thick woods through which we were going, out stepped a small man with dark eyes and determined look, who without a word motioned us to follow him and then went rapidly ahead. The Anderson County Official who had guided us, immediately turned back homeward, bidding us adieu with a wave of his hand. Our new guide started off at such a quick gait that it was difficult for our leg-weary party to keep up with him. Some of them finding it impossible to do so, were obliged to fall behind and risk the chance of capture. We had walked almost forty miles during the night, through a hard and constant rain and over muddy, slippery ground. Our guide, (Wash Vann by name,) seeing that all were much fatigued, led the way to a secluded place near Nelson's Ridge and there halted the company for needed rest. Haversacks were then opened, a breakfast made from their contents and nearly all stretched themselves upon the wet ground for repose. A few men were put upon the watch and soon the others were fast asleep. All was quiet for about two hours, when (at 9 A. M. of the 19th) we, who served as sentinels, discovered a man walking very fast and coming upon the trail we had made. He seemed to be scrutinizing our tracks and was evidently following us, but for what purpose of course we could not tell. He approached within thirty yards of us before he raised his eyes or perceived that we were near. At the first glance, he turned and began to run; but hearing the word, Halt! he looked over his shoulder and seeing that several rifles were drawn upon him, he thought it wise to obey the summons. When he came up, we catechized him very closely,—asking him where he was from? how far he had followed us? Where going? &c. To none of these questions could he give a satisfactory answer; but crossed himself frequently and seemed much confused. He said he was a rebel, but could tell nothing about the rebel troops. We concluded that he had been sent to pursue and discover us for the information of our armed enemies, and that our longer delay at the spot would be dangerous. Our short rest and breakfast, with the excitement consequent upon taking a supposed spy, made us all ready to start at once. Our prisoner was ordered to fall in and told that if he attempted to escape, he would be shot.

We soon ascended Nelson's Ridge and from its summit we could see the rebel cavalry scouts hunting for us in the valley road below, and trying to cut us off, as they were not able on horses to follow us over the Ridge. By going very cautiously through the thickets we managed to escape discovery, safely crossed the valley road north of Walson's Ridge and soon began the ascent of the Cumberland Mountains, where for the time we felt secure from pursuit by cavalry.

In order to understand our real condition at that time and what had saved us from capture, it will be necessary to revert to the place where we had crossed Clinch river, and notice what was transpiring there. As before stated, one-half of our company crossed Clinch river before two o'clock in the morning. But the remainder, numbering about one hundred and fifty, did not do so until near daylight. In consequence they were discovered by a rebel, named

Jones, who lived in the vicinity. He gladly hurried off to a rebel camp a few miles below and gave information. The rebels were on the alert, for they had previous notice that a party of Union men were in the neighborhood, and they gave quick pursuit. But fortunately, a Union man hearing that our friends would probably be overtaken by their enemies, hurried along a near way and told them of their danger. Upon receiving this warning, they had but time to hide in a thicket close at hand, when the pursuing cavalry went rushing by at the top of their speed upon the trail the first half of our company had made hours before, without discovering that any of the fugitives were being left behind them. As the cavalry moved with the utmost possible speed, they reached the spot where we had rested, only an hour after we had left it, and where, but for our capture of the spy, they would no doubt have found us. The hour we had, in advance of the troopers, had been well improved and enabled us to find safety from them in the Cumberland Mountains.

It was then dark. We had walked rapidly for twenty-four consecutive hours, excepting the two hours of halt. The rain, which had fallen during the whole period, came down in torrents at its close. Every one suffered with fatigue, but some were so overcome by it they could not proceed at all. Soon the darkness became intense; we had almost to grope our way; no one could pick his footsteps, and there were many bruises and scratches of the flesh. But over the rocks and through the brush we had to go in the gloom of that dreadful night. At length the joyful sound of "halt!" was heard. Our guide said that we were five miles from any shelter or habitation. It must have been a dismal spot at all times. On every side arose high hills which would almost shut out the light of the mid-day sun. But in the then impenetrable darkness and pouring rain, the thick forest seemed a fit abode for evil spirits. Yet it afforded security from enemies, and we were glad to rest even there. No one of the company would be apt ever to forget the wretched night we spent at that place. After supper from our water-soaked haversacks, we lay down to rest as best we could, without blankets or other means of protection from the wet ground and drenching rain, having agreed without a dissenting voice that the place ought to be known for all time as Camp Misery!

As soon as it was light enough the next morning, we again moved forward and soon began to ascend the highest point of the Cumberland Mountains, known in that vicinity as "The Smoky Range." On its top, alternate snow and rain were substituted for the continuous, soaking rains of the previous thirty-six hours, and added much to our discomfort. On the top of that and adjacent peaks we travelled nearly the whole day,—keeping upon the roughest and highest surfaces to prevent successful pursuit on horses. Our experience during the remainder of the journey was like that already related. The enemy tried to intercept us, when in passing from one hill to another we crossed over the valley roads, as we were obliged to do. On such occasions one or two of our number would first advance cautiously and reconnoitre. If no danger appeared, the whole company would then pass over the road swiftly, making as little trail as possible, and sometimes by walking backwards, leaving deceptive impressions on the soil.

One incident of the trip will show after what manner the people of Scott county were organized to resist their enemies. They were most thoroughly loyal to the United States and both determined and active. Through one of the narrow and deep vallies among the hills over which we traveled, runs New River. Usually it is little more than a creek, but at that Spring-time because of the heavy and steady rains, it was a formidable stream. When arrived on its southern bank we could find but one small canoe; and knowing it would be imprudent to wait until the whole company could be carried in it over the river, the guns and provisions were placed in the boat, and all who could swim jumped in and breasted the waters. Upon the hillside about the fourth of a mile in front of us, could be seen a small cabin, and as our guide said that the occupant was a Union man, we did not hesitate to approach it. We saw no one about the house until one of our guns, in being placed in the canoe, was accidentally discharged. Immediately a man ran from the house to the stable, mounted a horse and rode rapidly up the hillside. We thought this a suspicious circumstance, and on reaching the house and making known who we were, it came to light that the horseman, in the belief that our company was one of rebels, had sped over the hills to inform the "Home Guards" of which he was a member, and that they would probably fire upon us from every convenient spot, or as it was commonly termed "bush-whack" us. But upon this a woman of the family went ahead of our party, and let the "Guards" know their mistake; and the wounds or death they would have inflicted upon us were averted. Knowing us to be friends of the Union, we were in their eyes as brothers, and instead of resistance and blows, they would have given us help and comfort to the utmost limit of their power.

At the end of the sixth night of this kind of travel we arrived at the Federal Army Camp at Boston, Kentucky. The second half of our original company, whom we had left behind at Clinch river, joined us the day before that termination. This accession made us three hundred strong. The sight of that camp gave us relief, joy and thankfulness, which they only can understand who have had complete deliverance from protracted sufferings and trouble. Beneath the flag of our choice we found nourishment, rest, protection and a hearty welcome from friends who had gone before us and were anxious to hear from dear ones at home. In six hours, three companies of as good soldiers as were ever dressed in blue were added to the Sixth East Tennessee Regiment and went forth to do battle for their homes and country. But they all united afterwards in saying that no week of their lives as soldiers, would begin to compare in hardships with the one they spent in this trip over the mountains.

Before closing this narrative, I should state that the supposed spy whom we captured at our first halting-place and whose capture saved us from being overtaken by the pursuing cavalry, proved to be one of a party of Union men who had several days previously been attacked on their way to Kentucky and all either scattered or captured. Being lost in the woods, he accidentally came upon us while resting, and under the supposition that we were Rebel soldiers, he gave us confused statements. In a short time he learned the true character of his captors; but fortunately for us, we did not find out that he was on our side, until we had reached for the night a secure position. He afterwards carried a musket in the Sixth East Tennessee Regiment and was called one of its best soldiers.

APPENDIX: NOTE L: Page 185.

Mrs. Edwards, wife of Mr. Edw. C. Edwards, of Campbell county, carried information, at the cost of exposure to inclement weather and risk of arrest and punishment, to the Union troops in several[1] instances. Once she traveled from her home in a buggy to Lenoir's Station on the East Tennessee and Georgia Railway, and thence by Rail to Athens, 55 miles southwest of Knoxville, and quickly returned. She was accompanied by a neighbor's adult daughter, Miss Bettie Carey, to whom she did not divulge her purpose. They traveled with passports from the Confederate authorities, and accomplished the journey of more than 150 miles with remarkable celerity. Upon arriving again at home, Mrs. Edwards mounted her horse, and with the valuable knowledge concerning intended movements of the Confederate troops which she had obtained on her recent visit among them, she went alone through the rain over Pine Mountain to the encampment of Gen. J. G. Spears, near the Kentucky border. He was of Bledsoe county, East Tennessee, and in May and June, 1861, a member of the Union Convention at Knoxville and Greeneville. The information given him by Mrs. Edwards, was the means of saving from capture, him and his soldiers, and also, several hundreds of East Tennessee refugees who were on their way to the interior of Kentucky. General Spears thought that she deserved for her daring, patriotic exploit, so useful in its results to his army, more than wordy gratitude; and that she should be paid two thousand dollars by the Federal Government; but the papers he gave her to prove that reward was justly due her failed of their purpose. The United States has never paid it in whole or in part; but her work was not done for the sake of money.

On another occasion, when Winter was about passing into the Spring of 1863, she went on a patriotic errand to Williamsburg, Kentucky, accompanied by Miss Bettie Carey,—both on horseback, their cavalier being a son of Mrs. Edwards, ten years old, mounted on a mule, but as on the previous trip, she kept her special purpose from her companion. Their ostensible object was to purchase supplies needed by their households. As the first night closed in upon the travelers, they lost their way on Pine Mountain. Mrs. Edwards preserved her cheerfulness and hopefully said, that by and by they would find a house. This they did after tedious wandering in the cold and darkness. Observing a light, they found the hospitality they sought in a log cabin which had but one apartment. Their supper, consisting of coffee corn bread and bacon, was kindly provided by the family, and one of the beds in the room was assigned to their use. The two women, with the lad nestling at their feet, slept as comfortably as the cold wind which found entrance through the crevices of the house would permit.

The journey had several difficulties, not the least of which was in fording rivers that were in such a swollen condition, that the horses had almost to swim and their riders were compelled to mount high in their saddles to escape the waters. Mrs. Edwards alone knew what communications she had with others at Williamsburg in relation to the War. In returning home, they were hospitably fed and lodged at the house of a worthy Union man, of whom, as illustrating the wanton cruelties inflicted here and there upon country people by the Confederate soldiery, it has to be said, that not long afterwards, he was arrested by them at his home, and deliberately shot to death, and two of his neighbors of like mind, at the same time shared his fate.

"Were the three men charged with any offence?" was the question asked of the lady who told of the occurrence in connection with the above narrative. "O, no!" was her reply; "they were only Union men."

There was an instance of dangerous adventure in behalf of the United States, which a young lady and a boy who had just entered his teens undertook during the siege of Knoxville. According to a report made to the House of Representatives, (50th Congress, 1st Session,) by its Committee on War Claims, Gen. Grant sent an important dispatch to Gen. Burnside. So overrun was the territory between Chattanooga and Knoxville by Confederate troops, that it could only be delivered, if at all, with great difficulty and hazard. At length, Miss Mary Love, of Kingston, Tennessee, agreed to take the message through the Confederate lines. She went, attended by a guide, Thomas F. Carter, as far as Louisville, Tennessee. Being there compelled to abandon personally the attempt, she could find but one person who was willing to prosecute it: and to him, a boy, John T. Brown, only 13 years of age. she entrusted the dispatch. He carried it safely to its destination, but has never received from the Government, any acknowledgment of his brave and patriotic service.

APPENDIX: NOTE M: Page 194.

[From the Official Report of General Carter.]

A movement of troops into East Tennessee was proposed as early as November 25, 1862, but was not ordered until December 19, when arrangements for it had been completed. It was hoped that the force to be sent on this hazardous but important expedition, would have been much larger than that which the Commander of the Department felt could be detached for that service when the time to enter upon it arrived.

The original design was to divide the force into two columns, and strike the East Tennessee and Virginia Railroad at two points at the same time, distant 100 miles apart, and by moving towards the centre, destroy the road for that distance.

A junction of the forces (consisting of two battalions 2nd Michigan Cavalry, Lieut. Col. Campbell; the 9th Pennsylvania Cavalry, Major Russell; and one battalion 7th Ohio Cavalry, Major Raimey) was made near the mouth of Goose Creek, Clay County, Kentucky. As ordered by Gen. Burnside, Col. Charles J. Walker of the 10th Kentucky Cavalry was placed in command of the cavalry brigade.

The troops were ordered to move without baggage, with ten days rations, and 100 rounds of ammunition; but as it was feared some difficulty would be met with in obtaining forage, a supply train was ordered to proceed some 60 miles on the route and then transfer forage and rations to a train of pack mules. On the 22nd December Gen. Carter, who left Lexington on the 20th, came up with the two battalions of the 2nd Michigan and the 9th Pennsylvania at McKee, Jackson county, Kentucky, and after one day's necessary detention, they effected a junction on the 26th with the remainder of the troops, (1st Battalion of 7th Ohio Cavalry) at Heard's on Goose Creek. The whole force amounted only to about 1,980 men,

APPENDICES. 367

and of that number a considerable portion were in the field for the first time.

The marches owing to the roughness and narrowness of the roads, (being merely bridle paths along the banks of creeks and over steep and rugged mountains) were of necessity slow and tedious, and their length had to be governed by the distance to the several points at which forage could be obtained. It was not until about meridian of the 28th, that they reached the foot of the Cumberland mountain (on the north side,) opposite "Crank's Gap," 12 miles to the southward and eastward of Harlan Court House. The pack train was sent back in charge of a detachment of the Kentucky State Guard.

A little before sunset they reached the summit of the Cumberland mountain, and had the field of their operations, with its mountains and vallies spread out before them. Gen. Carter then consulted with the officers of his command, and it was the unanimous opinion that the force was entirely too small to venture on a division according to the original plan. This decision seemed to be the more necessary from the news they had received through East Tennessee refugees at the foot of the mountain, relative to the disposition of the rebel forces along the line of the railroad.

Soon after dark, the advance commenced the descent of the mountain, hoping to make a long march before sunrise, but owing to the steepness, narrowness and roughness of the way, the rear of the column did not reach the foot of the mountain, until 10 p. m., having consumed four hours on the way. Gen. Carter was told there were 400 rebel cavalry in the vicinity of Jonesville one mile distant. As it was important to move through Lee County, Virginia, without exciting suspicion, he moved down Cane Creek, and passing through a Gap in Poor Valley ridge, crossed Powell's Valley about five miles east of Jonesville. On leaving the valley road, his guides were at fault and valuable time was lost in finding the way. The march was continued through the night and at daylight the troops reached the top of Wallen's Ridge, 22 miles distant from the foot of Cumberland Mountain, and halted. Thus far they had advanced without giving any alarm, or even exciting any suspicion as to their character. The village of Shelbyville lay immediately below, and but for the imprudence of an officer in allowing the men to visit the village, they could have passed on as rebel cavalry. A number of rebel soldiers belonging to Trigg's battalion were within Carter's lines, supposing they were among friends and were captured.

In a short time the U. S. troops were again in the saddle,— passed through Stickleyville, across Powell's Mountain, and through Pattonsville. Before sunset, they crossed Clinch River 12 miles from Estillville, Scott County, Virginia, and halted for a couple of hours. News of their approach had gone before them, but few of the rebels were disposed to credit it, believing it impossible that a Government force would venture so far within their territory. Upon arriving at Estillville at 10 P. M., they were told that a considerable rebel force was in possession of "Moccasin Gap," prepared to resist their passage. Gen. Carter could not afford to lose time. The Michigan Battalions were dismounted, and under Lieut. Colonel Campbell, a portion was deployed and moved through the Gap. Being unacquainted with the ground, and having to guard against an ambuscade in this strong pass,—which could have been held by a strong force against greatly superior numbers— they advanced with great caution. It was midnight before the rear of the column had passed through. The enemy, deterred by this resolute advance, fled towards Kingsport, East Tennessee, without firing a gun. A rebel Lieutenant and several soldiers with their arms, were captured on the south side of the Gap, on the Blountville road. During the remainder of the night the men moved forward as rapidly as was practicable over unknown roads,—picking up rebel soldiers by the way. Owing to the darkness of the night, a portion of the command lost their way and became separated from the main body. A small force of the enemy's cavalry, hovering about the rear, killed a Sergeant of the 2nd Michigan, and captured two others who had wandered from the road. At daylight on the morning of 30th December, the troops reached the town of Blountville, Sullivan County, East Tennessee, surprised and took possession of the place, captured some 30 soldiers belonging to the 4th Kentucky Rebel Cavalry and paroled them. They were there informed that at Bristol, some eight miles distant, there was a large amount of stores, besides the meat of a considerable number of hogs, belonging to the Rebel authorities, but as the place was guarded, according to the best information obtained, by a regiment of Infantry under Colonel Slimp, (said to be 900 strong,) a Cavalry force under Colonel Gettner and a battery, they were reluctantly compelled to leave it on their left, and move towards the railroad bridge at Union, six miles from Blountville. The General sent forward Lieut. Colonel Campbell, with a portion of the 2nd Michigan under the direction of Col. Jas. P. T. Carter of 2nd East Tennessee Infantry, towards Union, with orders to take the place and destroy the railroad bridge across the Holston river. As soon as the remainder of the troops which had been separated during the night, came up, he moved them rapidly forward in the same direction. When he reached Union, he found the town in the possession of his men, and the railroad bridge, a pine structure some 600 feet in length, slowly burning. The rebel force, about 150 strong, consisting of two companies of the 62nd North Carolina troops under command of Major McDowell, had surrendered without resistance; the Major himself having been first captured by the advance of the U. S. troops while endeavoring to learn if there was any truth in the report of their approach. The prisoners were paroled, and a large number of them were that afternoon on their way to the mountains of North Carolina, swearing they would never be exchanged. Their joy at being captured seemed to be unbounded.

The stores, barracks, tents, a large number of arms and equipments, a considerable amount of nitre, a railroad car, the depot, &c., &c., were destroyed; also a wagon bridge across the river, a few hundred yards below the railroad bridge. As soon as the work of destruction was fairly under way, Gen. Carter dispatched Colonel Walker with detachments from the 2nd Michigan, 9th Pennsylvania and 7th Ohio Cavalry,—in all 180 men, the whole under the guidance of Col. Carter,—towards the Watauga bridge at Carter Depot, 10 miles west of Union. On their way they captured a locomotive and tender, with Col. Love of the 62nd North Carolina troops, who having heard of the approach of the "Yankees," had started on the locomotive to Union, to ascertain the truth of the rumor. On the detachments reaching the Station about sunset, they found the enemy, consisting of two companies of North Carolina troops, esti-

w

mated by Colonel Walker at nearly 200 men, falling into line. Col. Walker gallantly attacked them and after a brief but warm resistance, they broke and fled to the woods. The gallant Major Roper of the 6th Kentucky Cavalry, with two Companies of the 9th Pennsylvania Cavalry under Capt. Jones of that Regiment, made a dashing charge and captured and destroyed many of their number. Maj. Roper's loss was 1 killed, 1 mortally, 1 severely and 2 slightly wounded. The entire loss of the enemy, owing to the darkness of the night, could not be learned with certainty, but it was in killed, 12 to 16. The railroad bridge across the Watauga River, some 300 feet in length, was soon in flames and entirely destroyed; also a large number of arms and valuable stores. The captured locomotive was run into the river and completely demolished, destroying in its passage one of the piers of the bridge

The men and horses, especially the latter, were much worn and jaded from constant travel and want of rest. The alarm had been given. The rebels had the road open to Knoxville and could move up a strong force. The General also learned that some 500 cavalry and 4 guns, under Col. Folks, were within three miles; that an Infantry force would be concentrated at Johnson's depot, six miles west of Carter's station by daylight; and further, that Humphrey Marshall, who was at Abingdon, Virginia, was moving his troops to occupy the mountains and thus cut off his egress. It was deemed prudent therefore to return. The command left Watauga, and after a hard march, reached Kingsport at the mouth of the North Fork of the Holston River at sunset on the 31st of December. After feeding and resting a short time and issuing meat to the men, they were again in the saddle, passed eight miles north of Rogersville, and reached Looney's Gap on Clinch Mountain late in the afternoon, passed through without opposition, and about 11 P. M., January 1st, reached a place on the edge of Hancock County, Tennessee, where forage could be procured, and bivouaced for the night. This was the first night's rest the men had been able to take since the night of the 27th ult. They had been annoyed during the day and night by bushwhackers, but Providentially escaped with only two men slightly wounded.

Soon after daylight on the morning of the 2d inst., the command proceeded towards Jonesville, Lee County, Virginia, with the intention of reaching the foot of Cumberland Mountain on the Kentucky side before halting. Its march was much impeded during the day by bushwhackers, who constantly annoyed the front and rear. Just before reaching Jonesville, they endeavored to check Gen. Carter by occupying the hills in his front with two companies, (supposed to be Larimore's and Staley's); but they were soon driven from their strong position by the skirmishers of the 2d Michigan. The command reached Jonesville late in the afternoon; but before its rear guard had passed, it was attacked by about 200 rebels. Col. Walker took charge of the rear guard, reinforced by two light companies and drove the assailants back to the woods. Several of their number were killed,—one in the village of Jonesville and some twenty were captured during the day, without suffering any loss. From prisoners the General learned that the passes in Powell's and Clinch mountains, through which he marched in going to Union, had been blockaded and were occupied by three or four companies of infantry. He reached the foot of Cumberland Mountain, passing through "Crank's Gap," at 11 P. M., and bivouaced;—men and horses completely jaded and worn, having been in the last five days and seventeen hours, but thirty hours out of the saddle.

On the 5th inst., the command reached Manchester, Clay County, Kentucky, and rested on the following day.

Gen. Carter says in conclusion, that "notwithstanding the inclemency of the weather, the severity of the march and the scanty supply of rations, for no inconsiderable portion of the time; both officers and men bore their hardships without a single murmur or word of complaint. They returned after a journey of 470 miles, 170 of which were in the enemy's country, in high spirits and in good condition, proud to think they had accomplished a feat which for hazard and hardship has no parallel in the history of the war."

Appendix: Note N: Page 196.

When the United States Army under Burnside approached Knoxville, September, 1863, Captain S. T. Harris was taken with other prisoners to Columbia, S. C. He was there put in chains that weighed from 12 to 15 pounds, and cruelly imprisoned. His father applied to President Davis, and in consequence, he was transferred from the filthy and almost airless cell where he lay, to a better one.

In the same prison were confined a scaling party of the United States Naval Officers, who had been captured in a night attack on Fort Sumter, September, 1863. One of them was Ensign Porter, of whom the Rev. H. Clay Trumbull says in the Church Magazine, August, 1886; "A part of the time he was in irons as one of the hostages for two Confederate privateersmen who were held by our (the United States) Government as pirates. He was the life of the party. He was always taking a cheery view of the situation. * * * * In a room of the jail, adjoining that of the naval officers, there was confined in irons a Captain Harris of Tennessee, held as a hostage for some Confederate prisoner under special charges. It was a delight of Ben. Porter to put his mouth to the key-hole of the intervening door and whistle a lively tune, while the Captain danced to it with the accompanying clanking of his chains. After Porter had been himself in irons, he taught Captain Harris how to remove and replace his handcuffs and fetters, without the knowledge of the prison officials. It was through this instruction, that Captain Harris's life was saved when the Columbia jail was burned, early in 1865."

Captain Harris relates that he was hurried off with other prisoners under guard from Columbia, that they might not be delivered by Gen. Sherman's army, and that, having learned while in prison at Knoxville the trick of slipping off his chains at pleasure, he released himself of those with which he had been bound in Columbia and left them in a swamp. He was paroled at Charlotte, N. C., and in exchange for Captain Ellison of the C. S. Army, a prisoner at Nashville held as hostage for him by order of President Lincoln, he was finally transferred from Wilmington, to the United States authorities. On his return to Knoxville, where he had forgiven all his enemies when expecting soon to be executed, he did not fully illustrate the saying of the poet, that young men "soon forget affronts;" but meeting with one who had sought his life when a helpless prisoner, he remembered the wrong, and in a brief interview redressed it to his enemy's discontent.

APPENDICES. 373

Appendix: Note O: Page 207.

[From official reports concerning the Sanders raid in East Tennessee, June 14—24, 1863.]

Colonel William P. Sanders, in obedience to special instructions from the General Commanding the Department, left Mount Vernon, Kentucky, June 14, 1863, with a force of 1,500 mounted men, composed of detachments of different regiments, as follows: Seven hundred of the 1st East Tennessee mounted Infantry, under Colonel R. K. Byrd; 200 of the 44th Ohio mounted infantry, under Major Moore; 200 of the 112th Illinois mounted infantry, under Major Dow; 150 of the 7th Ohio Cavalry Volunteers, under Captain Rankin; 150 of the Second Ohio Cavalry volunteers, under Captain Welch; 100 of the First Kentucky cavalry Volunteers, under Captain (G. W.) Drye, and a section of Captain Konkle's battery, First Regiment Ohio Artillery Volunters, under Lieutenant Lloyd,—for the East Tennessee and Virginia Railroad. From Mount Vernon to Williamsburg, on the Cumberland river, a distance of sixty miles, a train of wagons containing forage and subsistence stores, accompanied the expedition. From this point, he followed a route known as the Marsh Creek road to near Huntsville, Tennessee, leaving that place a few miles to his left. He reached the vicinity of Montgomery, Tennessee, on the evening of the 17th of June, and learning that a small party of rebels were stationed at Wartburg, one mile from Montgomery, he sent 400 men from the 1st East Tennessee to surprise and capture them, following one hour afterward himself with the remainder of the command. The surprise was complete. They captured 102 enlisted men and two officers (one of them an aide to General Pegram,) together with a large number of horses, sixty boxes artillery ammunition, several thousand pounds of bacon, salt, flour, and meal, some corn, 500 spades, 100 picks, besides a large quantity of other public stores, and six wagons with mule teams. The prisoners were paroled, and the property destroyed.

A small portion of this command, who were out some distance from the camp, with their horses, escaped and gave the first notice of Sanders's approach, at Knoxville, Kingston, Loudon and other places. From that point he marched toward Kingston. When within eight miles of it, he learned positively that Scott's brigade and one battery were at that place, guarding the ford of Clinch River. For this reason, leaving Kingston to his right, he crossed the river eight miles above, at Waller's Ford on the direct road to Loudon. At daylight, on the 19th (June), he was within three miles of Loudon, and about the same distance from Lenoir's. He there learned that a force of three regiments was at the Loudon bridge, with eight pieces of artillery, and that they had been for two weeks strengthening the works at that place, digging rifle pits, ditches, &c. A courier was captured from the commanding officer at Loudon, with dispatches ordering the forces from Kingston to follow in Sanders's rear, and stating that the troops from Lenoir's had been ordered to join them. Sanders determined to avoid Loudon and started immediately for Lenoir's station, which place he reached about 8 A. M., arriving there about thirty minutes after the departure of the rebel troops. At that station he captured a detachment of artillerymen, with three 6 pounder iron guns, eight officers and fifty-seven enlisted men, burned the depot, a large brick building, containing five pieces of artillery, with harness and saddles, two thousand five hundred stand of small arms, a very large amount of artillery and musket ammunition, and artillery and cavalry equipments. The depot was entirely occupied with military stores, and one car filled with saddles and artillery harness. He also captured some seventy-five Confederate States mules and horses. There was a large cotton factory with a large amount of cotton at the place, and he ordered that it should not be burned, as it furnished the Union citizens of the country with their only material for making cloth, but it was burned by mistake or accidentally. He had the telegraph wire and railroad destroyed from there on to Knoxville, at points about one mile apart. He met the enemy's pickets at Knoxville about 7 P. M. on the 19th (June,) and drove them to within a mile of the city. Leaving a portion of the 1st Kentucky Cavalry on the southwest side of the town, he moved the rest of his command as soon as it was dark by another road entirely around to the other side, driving in the pickets at several places, and cut the railroad, so that no troops could be sent to the bridges above. At daylight he moved up to the city on the Tazewell road and found the enemy well posted on the heights and in the adjacent buildings, with eight or nine pieces of artillery. The streets were barricaded with cotton bales, and the batteries protected by the same material. Their force was estimated at 3,000, including citizens who were impressed into service. After about one hour's skirmishing Sanders withdrew, capturing near the city two pieces of artillery, 6 pounders, the tents, and all the camp equipage of a regiment of conscripts, about eighty Confederate States horses, and thirty-one prisoners.

He then started for Strawberry Plains, following the railroad, and destroyed all the small bridges and depots to within four miles of the latter place at Flat Creek, where he burned a finely built, covered bridge and also a county bridge. The guard had retreated. He left the railroad three miles below the town, and crossed the Holston River, so as to attack the bridge on the same side the enemy were. As soon as he came in sight they opened on the advance with four pieces of artillery. He dismounted the infantry and sent the 44th Ohio, under Major Moore, up the river, and the rest under Colonel Byrd and Major Dow, to get in their rear. After about an hour's skirmishing, the enemy was driven off, and leaving a train and locomotive with steam up in waiting, a portion of them escaped. All their guns (five in number), 137 enlisted men and two officers, a vast amount of stores, ammunition, and provisions, (including 600 sacks of salt) about seventy tents and a great quantity of camp equipage were left in his hands. He remained at the place all night and destroyed the splendid bridge over the Holston River, over 1,600 feet long, built on eleven piers, the trestle included.

At daylight on the 21st (June) he started up the railroad for the Mossy Creek bridge, destroying the road at all convenient points. At Mossy Creek, New Market and vicinity, he captured 120 prisoners and destroyed several cars, a large quantity of stores, several hundred barrels of saltpetre, 200 barrels of sugar, and a large amount of other stores. The bridge burned at Mossy Creek was a fine one, over 300 feet in length. Near this place he also destroyed the machinery of a gun factory and a saltpetre factory.

He determined to leave the railroad here and endeavor to cross the mountains at Rogers' Gap, as he knew every exertion was being made on the part of the enemy to capture his command. Fording the Holston, at Hayworth's Bend, he started for the Powder Spring Gap of Clinch Mountain. There a large force was found directly in his front, and another strong force overtook and commenced skirmishing with his rear guard. By taking country roads he got into the Gap without trouble or loss, and had all this force in his rear. On arriving within a mile and a-half of Rogers' Gap, he found that it was blockaded by fallen timber, and strongly guarded by artillery and infantry, and that all the gaps practicable were obstructed and guarded in a similar manner. He then determined to abandon his artillery and move by a wood path to Smith's Gap, three miles from Rogers' Gap. The guns, carriages, harness and ammunition were completely destroyed, and left. He had now a large force, both in front and rear, and could only avoid capture by getting into the mountains, and thus place all his foes in the rear, which he succeeded in doing, after driving a regiment of cavalry from Smith's Gap. The road through this pass was only a bridle path, and very rough. He did not get up the mountain until after night. About 170 of his men and officers got on the wrong road, and did not rejoin the command until it reached Kentucky.

Owing to the continual march, many horses gave out and were left, and although several hundred were captured on the march, they were not enough to supply the men. He reached Boston, Ky., on the 24th, with a loss of two killed, four wounded and thirteen missing. The number of prisoners paroled by him was 461.

After acknowledging his indebtedness for the success of the expedition to several officers of his command, Col. Sanders did so chiefly to Sergeant Reynolds, First East Tennessee volunteers, and his guides. He said: "Reynolds' knowledge of the country was thorough, reliable and invaluable." "All the officers and men deserved great credit and praise for the cheerfulness with which they submitted to great hardships and fatigue, and their energy and readiness at all times either to fight or march."

APPENDIX. NOTE P. Page 207.

[Confederate account of the fight at Knoxville, in the Sanders Raid, condensed from the Report of Lieut. Col. Milton A. Haynes, C. S. Artillery, to Maj. Von Sheliha, Chief of Gen. Buckner's staff.]

APPENDICES.

DEPARTMENT OF EAST TENNESSEE,

KNOXVILLE, JUNE 21, 1863.

Major General Buckner had marched toward Big Creek Gap with all the artillery aud all the other disposable force at this post, except Colonel Trigg's 51st (54th) Virginia Regiment, and Colonel J. J. Finley's 7th (6th) Florida Regiment; effective force about 1,000 men; leaving Colonel Trigg temporarily in command at Knoxville. On the morning of the 19th, Maj. Von Sheliha, Acting Chief of Staff, was informed that the enemy in large force had passed by Loudon, and were at Lenoir's Station, twenty-four miles from Knoxville, and he requested Lieut. Col. Haynes to take charge of the artillery defence of the city, and to organize his force from the convalescents in the hospitals and from citizens, to man his guns then in the city. At the same time he ordered Maj. S. H. Reynolds, Chief of Ordnance, to issue to Lieut. Col. Haynes as many field pieces as could possibly be put in condition within a few hours, and to furnish him with all necessary equipments and one hundred rounds of ammunition. This order was fulfilled as far as was practicable

In the mean time the citizens of Knoxville had been ordered to report to Col. Haynes or to Col. (E. D) Blake for duty for the defence of the city.

At 3 o'clock in the afternoon of that day it was known that the enemy was within five miles of the city, and their advance were skirmishing with thirty-seven of our cavalrymen, being all that were then in Knoxville. The eight pieces of artillery at the ordnance department were immediaiely posted in sections. First, at College Hill, under Maj. Baker (the exposed point); second, on McGhee's Hill, under Capt. Hugh L. McClung, and third, under Lieut. Patterson and Lieut. J. J. Burroughs, at Summit Hill. This last battery had been fortified during the afternoon, under the superintendence of Capt. (W. F) Foster, of the engineers, with a cotton bale revetment. During that evening, the enemy failing to advance, Colonel Trigg removed Major Baker's battery from College Hill to a point near the Asylum Hospital. In the evening about 200 persons, citizens and convalescent soldiers from hospitals, had reported for duty, and each of the batteries was fully manned, although in the morning of the same day there was no artillery force whatever in the city.

During the night the pickets of the enemy advanced upon the city, but the Confederate pickets, thrown out by Col. Trigg, after an hour's skirmish, drove them back at about 2 o'clock in the morning.

At 7 o'clock on the 20th, four pieces of artillery, detached by Gen. Buckner from his command, reached the ordnance depot, and were immediately taken to the rear as a reserve. Soon after, the enemy advanced at double quick time from beyond the workshops in North Knoxville, where the Confederates had neither battery nor soldiers to oppose them. Colonel Haynes took "a section of Wyly's battery, and moved them at a gallop to a point immediately in front of the advancing column, and opened fire upon them with spherical case. The enemy took shelter behind houses and fences, and threw forward sharpshooters within 200 yards of the Confederate Battery which was entirely unsupported by infantry, and 400 yards from any support. At the same time a battery of three-inch rifled guns belonging to the enemy opened upon the Confederates at 800 yards, and during the first two or three shots killed and wounded some of their men and several horses. The battery was then advanced and ordered not to fire at the artillery, but at the infantry. The enemy at this moment forming a column, advanced rapidly, but after receiving two rounds of canister, they retreated."

"During the same time the battery under Lieut. J. J. Burroughs and Lieut. Patterson on Summit Hill, were also engaged and kept up a continual fire, during which Capt. McClung and Lieut. Fellows were killed. The section under Lieut. Whelon, before ordered by Col. Trigg to Temperance Hill, opened fire from there upon the retreating enemy, which, with the fire from Wyly's battery, Burrough's battery and Maj. Baker's, completed the victory. * * * * *

"The enemy had one battery of artillery and about 2,600 men, opposed by about 1,000 men, part of whom were citizens and convalescent soldiers."

Col. Haynes says in his report: "Among many citizens who reported to me that day for duty, I must not forget to mention Hon. Landon C. Haynes, Hon. Wm. H. Sneed, Hon. John H. Crozier, Rev. Joseph H. Martin and Rev. Mr. Woolfolk, and many others who do not desire me to mention their names. With such compatriots and such fellow-soldiers a man might willingly at any time meet the foe.

"Our loss was two officers and two enlisted men killed and four enlisted men wounded. Loss of enemy, forty-five."

APPENDIX: NOTE R: Page 227..

[Gen. Longstreet, concerning the military situation in East Tennessee, Nov., 1863.]

Whether or not the movement of Longstreet against Burnside originated with Mr. Jefferson Davis, as Gen. Grant was informed, it appears from the following letter published in 1871,* that Gen. Longstreet was dissatisfied with the way in which Gen. Bragg had ordered things and was conducting operations in front of Chattanooga; that he attributed the idea of his own expedition to Bragg's mind; that he thought it was the least favorable of opportunities for relief to the situation, but that having heard of it, he had proposed, without avail, a plan to make the movement greatly advantageous. Gen. Grant in his Memoirs, puts the force with which Longstreet left Chattanooga "to go against Burnside" at about 15,000 troops besides Wheeler's Cavalry, 5,000 more.

Extract from a letter written by Gen. Longstreet, dated July 12th, 1871:

"I have just concluded to send you a copy of a letter written by me just on the point of mounting my horse to start upon the East Tennessee campaign. It was written after my tent was struck, sitting in the rain, (a light drizzle) from the head of an empty flour barrel; but I think that, concise and hurriedly as it was written, it plainly indicated that I understood what Grant's campaign would be; that is, I understood the conditions and situations of the two armies well enough to know what Grant *should* do, and it is always safe to assume, with such a man, that he will do what he should do. Seeing the letter that I send a copy of, amongst my papers that I was overlooking, I determined to send it, in order that you might be assured of our force and of my appreciation of the campaign when it was projected by General Bragg:"

* In a pamphlet, entitled "Recollections of the East Tennessee Campaign," by Will H. Brearley, Company E, 17th Michigan Volunteers." Detroit.

HEADQUARTERS, CHATTANOOGA, Nov. 5, 1863.

"S. B. BUCKNER, MAJOR GENERAL.

MY DEAR GENERAL—I start to-day for Tyner's Station, and expect to get transportation to-morrow for Sweetwater. The weather is so bad, and I find myself so occupied that I shall not be able to see you to say good bye.

When I heard the report around camp, that I was to go into East Tennessee, I set to work at once to try and plan the means of making the move with security, and the hope of great results.

As every other move had been proposed to the General and rejected, or put off till time made them more inconvenient, I came to the conclusion as soon as the report reached me, that this was to be the fate of our army; to await till all good opportunities had passed, and then, in desperation, to seize upon the least favorable one.

As no one had proposed this East Tennessee campaign to the General, I thought it possible that we might accomplish something by encouraging his own move, and (I) proposed the following plan, viz: To withdraw from our present lines, and the forces now in East Tennessee: the latter to be done in order to give the impression to the enemy that we were retiring from East Tennessee, and concentrating here for battle or for some other movement, and place our army in a strong (concentrated) position. The moment the army was together, make a detachment of 20,000 to move rapidly against Burnside and destroy him; and by continued rapid movements, to threaten the enemy's rear and his communications to the extent that might be necessary to draw him out from his present position. This, at least, is a tedious process, but I thought it gave promise of some results, and was therefore better than lying here destroying ourselves.

The move, as I proposed it, would have left this army (Bragg's) in a strong position and safe, and would have made sure the capture of Burnside. That is, the army here could spare 20,000 if it were in the position that I proposed, better than it can spare 12,000, occupying the lines that it now does. Twenty thousand men well handled could surely have captured Burnside and forces. Under present arrangements, however, the lines are to be held as they now are, and the detachment is to be of say, 12,000. We thus expose both to failure, and really take no chance to ourselves of great results. The only notice my plan received was a remark that General Hardee was pleased to make: ' I don't think that that is a bad idea of Longstreet's.' I undertook to explain the danger of having such a long line under the fire of the enemy's batteries, and he concentrated, as it were, right in our midst, and within twenty minutes march of any portion of our line. But I was assured that he would not disturb us. I repeated my ideas, but they did not even receive notice. 'Twas not till I had repeated my plan, however, that Gen. Hardee even noticed me.

Have you any maps that you can give or lend me? I shall need every thing of the kind. Do you know any reliable people living near and east of Knoxville, from whom I might get information of the condition, strength, &c., of the enemy. I have written in such hurry and confusion of packing and striking camp, that I doubt if I have made myself understood.

I remain very sincerely your friend,
(Signed)   J. LONGSTREET,
Lieutenant General.

APPENDIX: NOTE S: Page 246.

[The night ride of Refugees to Kentucky.]

One of the party of refugees from Knoxville, as Longstreet approached it, relates: "The attention of wayside inhabitants, on the occasion of this escapade was the sharper, because the news of Longstreet's advance had already spread through the country; and many were the questions with which the excited and curious population plied the fleeing party; such as "What is the matter," etc., etc. The discomfort of the travellers was especially relieved by the tongue of an elderly woman whom they encountered. In order to relish the amusement her sallies afforded them it should be remembered that "Parson Brownlow" as he was often called, not only had great popular notoriety, but was as highly esteemed by one party to the strife as he was intensely hated by the other. By the rebels he was thought to be,

"The very head and front of their offending."

By the Union people he was everywhere known as their fearless and indomitable champion; and the idea of his giving way before the coming of their foes, could find place in their minds only along side of a desperate emergency.

"As we plunged along with the north star for our main guide, we were continually hailed to know what was the trouble, and what was the state of things at Knoxville? It is specially remembered that just after entering Anderson County, we were saluted by one of the numerous families peculiar to that region, headed by the matron, torch in hand:

"What in the name of goodness does all this mean? and where are you men going? Is Burnside retreating? or who are you any how?"

It was mildly answered to her by one of the more polite-mannered gentlemen of the party, that Gen Burnside, so far from being able to retreat, was in all probability a prisoner with his whole army.

'And are you running,' exclaimed she, 'without firing a gun?' 'Oh no!' said an elderly gentleman; 'we are simply retiring in good order, to save the country.'

'Yes!' said she, as she flamed her torch with a sort of patriotic fierceness; 'I expect the next thing I'll hear will be that Old Bill Brownlow is running too!'

At this juncture, the reverend gentleman so irreverently referred to, in a subdued tone of voice, remarked:

'Gentlemen, this is no place to make a stand; I think I'd rather encounter Longstreet's army, or Vaughn's cavalry, than that woman.' "*

Capt. A. J. Ricks, the military escort of the party says: "One man of the group, from the beginning of the hazardous ride, impressed me with the coolness, judgment and courage, with which he confronted dangers, and advised as to the best means of avoiding them; and it was soon apparent that the distinguished band looked to him as leader and adviser. And when, at an hour that all agreed my orders required me to leave them to their own chances and I parted from them with many misgivings as

---

* "The Nashville (Tenn.) Union."

to their safety, I noticed that they all instinctively turned to John Baxter, as pilot and commander."

They did so with good reason, for he had quick and accurate judgment and a powerful will. Mr. Ricks, now of Massilon, Ohio, in his address at a meeting of the bar of northern Ohio, held at Cleveland, Ohio, April 6, 1886, concerning the recent death of the Hon. John Baxter, of the U. S. Circuit Court, related some interesting incidents in the Judge's personal history during the civil war.

"No one of all the famous Union men of that conspicuously loyal section, (East Tennessee,) was more fearless, consistent or aggressive in the struggle against secession than our departed friend. He was a leader in the historic Union Convention of 1861, which held its session, planning open opposition to the Confederacy, while rebel regiments by the train load, destined for Virginia, were passing by within hailing distance. Johnson, Maynard, Brownlow, Nelson and Baxter were the leading spirits in its deliberations."

"Although the disposition of many members of that convention to make organized armed resistance at once, and to put Baxter in command of the forces was not approved by his knowledge of the environment, he was recommended from Greeneville to President Lincoln for a Brigadier General's commission in the army. This honor was tendered, but for satisfactory reasons was declined.

"In 1862, while on professional business at Memphis, he was arrested by the Confederate military authorities and confined to prison sixteen days, refusing to take the oath of allegiance to the Southern Confederacy, but finally, he was unconditionally released."

"In 1861, he defended three Union men* before a Confederate Military Commission. They were charged with having burned railroad bridges in aid of the Union cause. He argued against the jurisdiction of the tribunal, contending that so long as the civil courts were open and the due course of legal proceedings was uninterrupted, the citizens arraigned were entitled to a trial by jury, after indictment by a grand jury, a doctrine long afterwards affirmed by the Supreme Court, in the Milligan case."

"In 1862, a gallant band of Ohio soldiers, known as the Mitchell

*Haun, and the two Harmons, father and son, executed at Knoxville.

raiders, who, in a lawful military expedition, had seized some engines and cars and run them towards the Federal lines, were captured and tried before a court martial as spies. Baxter volunteered to defend them and made a fearless argument for them before the court martial at Knoxville, urging that they were not spies engaged in a sneaking expedition, but that taking the risks of war, they had made an open venture as soldiers under legitimate military orders, and were entitled to be treated as prisoners of war, subject to exchange, &c. But the spirit of animosity was then so great, that the argument of the Union lawyer was of no avail, and seven of the brave men were shot as spies, while five others escaped during the excitement of a retreat. One of them is now a prominent Methodist clergyman of this State.

"One other incident of this stormy and eventful part of his life, forcibly illustrates his fearless character. In 1861, happening one day to step into the Court-house, he found a meeting of citizens called to devise means for raising troops for the rebel army. A person in the audience, unfriendly to him, and desiring to provoke him to talk in the presence of soldiers, suggested that perhaps Colonel Baxter would make them a speech. He did so, and made quite a different speech from what they wanted to hear. He compared the resources of the North and South—told them that superior numbers and wealth and advantages in arming and equipping forces were sure to give the North success; and that the war, if prosecuted long, would end in the liberation of their slaves, loss of life and treasure and final defeat. He also argued against the policy of conscripting Union men for the Confederate army, and advised the soldiers present, that such men would be of no service or aid to them. A garbled report of the speech was published in a Confederate paper, making it even more obnoxious than it was as delivered. A Georgia regiment stopped a few days afterwards, on the way to Virginia, and a few personal enemies of Baxter supplied them with drink and copies of the paper containing the garbled speech and suggested that he ought to be hanged. They proceeded to the Court-house where, it was reported, that Colonel Baxter was engaged in the trial of a case. His friends, learning of the danger that threatened him, reached the Court-house in advance of the soldiers and advised him to flee for his life. Instead of doing so, he walked out of the Court-house in the midst of ˙the soldiers and inquired if they were looking for him. One of the leaders thrust a copy of the rebel paper into his hands and asked him if he was the man who made that speech? He told them in a cool, deliberate, fearless manner of the circumstances under which he had made a speech and of the character of the one actually delivered—of the spirit that actuated the men in calling on him for the speech, and of the motive that prompted the publication of it in a garbled form; and then portrayed the cowardice of those who had incited them through drink to come by hundreds to take the life of an unarmed and unprotected man. He asked them if they proposed to be the tools of such men, who dared not confront him personally? His manner, his tact, his manly courage, first startled them, then arrested their attention to his defence and finally won their admiration. Instead of hanging him, they applauded his pluck and approved his denunciation of his enemies. And it is believed that he could easily have turned their fury against his assailants, if he had made the attempt."

APPENDIX: NOTE T. Page 251.

[The Topography of Knoxville and Its Vicinity.]

"On the north bank of the river, a narrow ridge is formed, extending from a point about two and a-half miles east of Knoxville, to Lenoir's. It has an average base of about one and a-half miles in width. At Knoxville, the width is about one mile. This ridge is cut through at short intervals by small streams, two of which, First and Second creeks, run through the town of Knoxville at a distance from each other of about three-fourths of a mile. The main part of the town is built upon that portion of the ridge bounded on the northwest by the valley, on the southwest by Second Creek, on the southeast by the Holston River and on the northeast by First Creek. It has the appearance of a table, elevated about 150 feet above the river, and about 100 feet above the valley. Again, Third Creek is found about seven-eighths of a mile below Second Creek, forming a second similar table. A depression in the ridge about the same distance east of First Creek, forms still another table upon which is built East Knoxville. This elevated ground is called Temperance Hill. From this eastward, the ridge is more broken until it disappears and other ridges spring up. This last division is known as Mabry's Hill, and is the highest ground by some twenty feet to be found on the north side of the river within cannon range of Knoxville."

CAPTAIN O. M. POE,
Chief Engineer, Dept. of the Ohio.

APPENDIX. NOTE U. Page 282.

Gen. Sherman found on Gen. Burnside's table such a good dinner, that he exclaimed at its contradiction of statements he had heard, that the besieged army was starving. Gen. Burnside explained that he had access to supplies from farmers on the south side of the river. No doubt the dinner was exceptional in the family and had been provided at extra pains, in honor of the guest. Had he shared the rations of the soldiers during the siege, he could have verified the reported scarcity.

The Comte de Paris seems to have read between the lines of Gen. Sherman's Memoirs, for he represents that "Gen. Sherman relates his astonishment when entering a place (Knoxville) which he believed to be reduced to the last extremities, he beheld a park of the finest cattle, and when afterwards, Burnside bade him sit down to a table abundantly served, he understands that the peril has been exaggerated." (History of the Civil War in America: By the Comte de Paris, Vol. IV., page 329.)

The Count is here distressingly inaccurate. Gen. Sherman does not say that at Knoxville he beheld a park filled with the finest cattle. He could not have done so, for they were not there to be seen. The "park and the finest cattle" are figments of the imagination.

APPENDIX. NOTE V. Page 285.

Will H. Brearley of Michigan quotes from a letter written by Col. E. P. Alexander, Chief Engineer of Gen. Longstreet, dated October 18, 1870, as follows:

"I believe I know as much or more of the assault on Fort Sanders than any one living, as I first proposed and planned it—not, however, as it was carried out, for several days' delay was caused by the arrival upon the ground of Bragg's engineer, Gen. Leadbetter, who insisted on an attempt *above* the town, which, however, he gave up in a *reconnoisance*; and by an additional delay of one day of bad weather, during which Gen. Leadbetter suddenly decided to give up the plan we had agreed upon and try a surprise!!! I was then too young and modest to say a word of objection, and the attempted surprise ended as you well know—though doubtless was and will always remain a surprise to you, in one sense at least." (See "Recollections of the East Tennessee Campaign.")

Mr. Brearley also states in his sketches, that during the truce ordered at the conclusion of the Fort Sanders fight, Capt. Poe and Col. Alexander, who had been acquaintances at West Point, had an interview. "Col. Poe very naturally felt like bantering Col. Alexander about the morning's work, and asked him if they 'intended to try it again?' which was answered in the negative. Col. Alexander then said, 'We did not know there was a ditch in front of the Fort;' which was responded to by an invitation from Col. Poe to 'go up and see it,' but was politely declined with, 'I am fully satisfied on that point.'"

Appendix. Note W. Page 298.

Commissioned Officers of the United States Army from Tennessee, in 1861-'65, above the grade of Lieutenant:

Major Generals by Brevet—Samuel P. Carter, Joseph A. Cooper, Alvin C. Gillem.

Brigadier Generals—William B. Campbell, Andrew Johnson, James G. Spears.

Brigadier Generals by Brevet—James P. Brownlow, George Spaulding, William J. Smith.

Colonels—Spencer B. Boyd, R. K. Byrd, J P. Carter, Wm. Cross, L. C. Houk, Fielding Hurst, Robert Johnson, George McPherson, James M. Melton, John K. Miller, George W. Moore, John Murphy, Samuel K. N. Patton, Joseph H. Parsons, William C. Pickens,

William F. Prosser, Daniel M. Ray, Felix A. Reeve, James W. Scully, James T. Shelley, William B. Stokes, Daniel Stover, Isham Young.

Lieutenant Colonels—James T. Abernathy, Joseph H. Blackburn, Albert F. Beach, Stephen Beard, W. K. M. Breckenridge, George W. Bridges, J. W. Bowman, Andrew J. Brown, Roderick R. Butler, John C. Chiles, William J. Cleveland, William J. Clift, William R. Cook, R. Clay Crawford, James J. Dail, R. A. Davis, Calvin M. Dyer, John Ellis, John Feudge, Frank F. Fisher, Frank T. Foster, Robert Galbraith, Abraham E. Garrett, J. W. M. Grayson, George A. Gowin, Charles C. Halfling, Owen Haney, Isaac R. Hawkins, Charles C. Holding, William H. Ingerton, John S. Kirwan, George D. La Vergne, Edward Maynard, John B. Minnis, Charles C. McCaleb, Michael L. Patterson, Milton L. Phillips, Thomas H. Reeves, Pleasant C. Rutherford, William M. Sawyers, Orlando H. Shearer, James W. Spaulding, Brazilian P. Stacy, William P. Story, Duff C. Thornburgh, Jacob M. Thornburgh, D. C. Trewhitt, Fremontin Young.

Majors—John F. Armstrong, William S. Barnett, Benjamin J. Bingham, Edward Black, Luther M. Blackman, James S. Bradford, Jason A. Bradshaw, William H. Bean, Sater Boland, James O. Berry, Thomas H. Boswell, David G. Bowers, Morgan F. Buckhart, D. A. Carpenter, Favor Cason, Albert C. Catlett, M. Cleaveland, Henry Crumbliss, Ben. Cunningham, William B. Davis, James E. Deakins, William J. S. Denton, James M. Dickerson, Oliver M. Dodson, David C. Donett, Robert H. M. Donnelly, George W. Doughty, R. H. Dunn, Patrick F. Dyer, John Elliott, John Ellis, Daniel D. Emerson, Henry G. Flagg, A. Marion Gamble, Joseph Grigsby, Sterling Hambright, Abram Hammon, John S. Herman, James H. Hornsby, George W. Hutsell, Charles Inman, James H. Johnson, Christopher C. Kenner, Gaines Lawson, Mack J. Liaming, William R. McBath, Francis M. McKey, Louis Mandazy, Middleton L. Moore, John Parr, Samuel W. Pickens, John M. Sawyers, Charles C.* Shoyer, Eldridge S. Sidwell, Burton Smith, Meshac Stevens, Benjamin F. Taylor, Robert M. Thompson, Russell Thornburgh, Alexander Thurneck, William R. Tracy, Eli N. Underwood, Joseph H. Wagner, S. L. Warren, Shelah Waters, Thos. Waters, H. W. Wells, C. C. Wilcox, Wilson W. Willis, John Wortham, John C. Wright.

APPENDICES. 389

Captains—James W. Adkisson, William C. Allen, Allen G. Anderson, Francis M. Anderson, Max H. Andrea, William Ausmus, Alfred C. Aytse, Julius Aytse, Daniel W. Baker, Frederick W. Baker, R. M. Baldwin, A. B. Barner, William S. Barnett, Charles L. Barton, Thomas J. Barry, Ezekiel W. Bass, Albert F. Beach, William H. Bean, William O. Beebe, James W. Bell, Rufus M. Bennett, Charles S. Berry, James W. Berry, William S. Bewley, John C. Bible, Thomas Bible, James M. Bishop, Edward R. Bladen, Joseph H. Blackburn, Leonidas Blizard, Ainsworth E. Blount, James L. W. Boatman, James S. Bonham, Francis H. Bounds, James J. R. Boyd, John C. Boyer, John S. Bowers, James W. Branson, Jacob P. Brient, Davis Brooks, David W. Brown, John D. A. Bryan, S. S. Buck, Charles H. Burdick, William C. Burnett, John H. Byrd, Robert E. Cair, David M. Caldwell, William A. Campbell, Thomas J. Capps, Andrew C. Card, James L. Carter, Landon Carter, Robert C. Carter, Alfred M. Cate, William L. Cate, Charles D. Champion, Elisha Chastain, Joseph W. Chockley, William J. Cleveland, James Clift, Judge R. Clingan, Robert H. Clinton, Samuel S. Cobb, William A. Cochran, Charles W. Coker, Lafayette Coil, Gillon O. Collins, Joseph A. Collins, Louis Collins, James E. Colville, George B. Colver, Albert Cook, Bennett J. Cooper, Alfred Couch, Reuben C. Couch, Adam T. Cottrell, William J. C. Crandall, Jordan W. Creary, Robert C. Crawford, Jacob P. Crooker, Charles W. Cross, John H. Cross, Thomas J. Cypreh, John A Davis, Ross R. Davis, Thomas Davis, James A. Davison, John F. DeArmond, Jas. E. Deakins, Spencer Deaton, Risden D. Deford, John G. Dervan, David J. Dickinson, Dennis Donahue, Alf. T. Donnelly, Robert H. M. Donnelly, James A. Doughty, John C. Dougherty, Thomas J. Dougherty, Rufus Dowdy, Thomas P. Duggan, John C. Duff, James L. Dungan, Pat. F. Dyer, Thomas H. Easley, Thomas D. Eddington, John H. Edwards, James H. Elkins, Daniel Ellis, John W. Ellis, Richard Ellis, Peter Engels, Samuel E. Erwin, Samuel P. Evans, James T. Exenn, William Farmer, Eli G. Fleming, David Floerke, Munro M. Floyd, Michael Fogarty, Asbury Fowler, Richard B. Freeman, Jacob Fritts, Fred. F. Fulkerson, James H. Galbraith, Theodore W. Gambee, A. Marion Gamble, Robert L. Gamble, William A. Garner, Andrew J. Garrison, Joseph W. Gibson, Homer Gillmore,

Ellas Goddard, James A. Goddard, Pastede L. Good, George W. Gorman, Thomas J. Gorman, William M. Gourley, John T. Graham, George W. Gray, Benjamin F. Green, James C. Green, Joseph Grigsby, Gid. R. Griffith, George E. Grisham, Martin V. Guest, Robert A. Guthrie, Newton Hacker, John N. Haggard, Jacob S. Hagler, Jonathan H. Hall, Henry D. Hamm, Abram Hammond, Drury P. Harnell, John W. Harrington, Shadrick Harris, William Harrison, John Harrold, William L. Hatherway, William C. Hayworth, George W. Heard, John Heavy, Willis E. Hedgecock, Jacob M. Hendrickson, James M. Henry, Chester J. Hoag, Elijah J. Hodges, Harry Hodges, Henry G. Hodges, George W. Holtsinger, Samuel C. Honeycutt, Robert N. Hood, James Howe, George E. Huckaba, William Hughes, Levi Hurst, John W. Isbell, Solomon Irick, Otta Jacobi, Wilson C. Jackson, Alexander J. P. Jarcroy, S. M. Jarvis, David B. Jenkins, William D. Jenkins, Lafayette Jones, Thomas A. Jones, Wade Jones, Armine T. Julian, John O'Keefe, Henry C. Kelly, Nathan D. Kemp, James P. Kendrick, Henry C. Kerner, William A. Kidwell, Jno. F. Kincheloe, James H. Knight, Alfred Lane, Morgan Lane, Richard S. Lane, Ephraim Langsley, William L. Lea, James L. Ledgerwood, Wash. L. Ledgerwood, Henry N. Lee, Samuel Leinart, George Littleton, Jesse M. Littleton, Henry C. Lloyd, Jacob K. Lones, William S. Long, Richard H. Luttrell, Alexander Lynch, Vanatta MacAdoo, James R. McBath, J. T. C. McCaleb, Samuel McCaleb, Oliver P. McCammon, Moses McConnell, Thos. McDermott, Francis M. McFall, James McGill, John McKay, Francis M. McKey, Nelson McLaughlin, Thomas McNish, George McPherson, Rufus McSpadden, Fielding L. McVay, Daniel McWilliam, John W. Magill, Daniel D. Markwood, James M. Martin, John Martin, John H. Martin, Samuel H. Martin, George W. Massey, Monroe Matterson, Goldman G. Meador, Daniel Meador, Bayless A. Miller, John A. Miller, Mitchell R. Millsaps, James A. Montgomery, William F. Morgan, William W. Mosier, William W. Mount, W. M. Murray, Archibald Myers, James C. Myers, Vincent Myers, David M. Nelson, Jacob H. Norris, Samuel E. Northington, Polasky W. Norwood, George Oatley, David Odell, Will Odle, William J. Patterson, Robert J. Patty, James P. Patey, William B. Pearson, E. L. Pennington, John C.

APPENDICES. 391

Penoyar, Daniel T. Peterman, George W. Peters, William C. Peterson, W. W. Phillips, Chas. A. Pickens, Samuel W. Pickens, Levi Pickering, John D. Poston, Pleasant M. Pryor, William Pryor, James H. Queen, Norton E. Quinn, Robert W. Ragon, Thomas Rains, David Ressh, Alexander D. Rhea, Elias H. Rhea, William O. Rickman, Barney J. Riggs, Andrew J. Roberts, James G. Roberts, John C. Rodgers, John T. Robeson, Harbert S. Rogers, Robert A. Rogers, Thomas J. Rodgers, Samuel P. Rowan, Samuel W. Scott, Andrew P. Senter, James B. Sharp, David Sharp, John Sharp, William C. Shelton, Chas. W. Shipmate, H. N. Y. Shipp, John Simpson, Alex. P. Slatery, John C. Slover, Francis A. Smith, John W. Smith, Louis Smith, Samuel H. Smith, Brazilia P. Stacy, Thomas Stephens, Alex. D. Stone, Van Stuart, Fred Slimp, John B Tape, Isaac A. Taylor, John W. Taylor, Spencer J. Tedder, James B. Terry, William P. Testerman, Samuel Tewls, James R. Thompson, Robert M. Thompson, Samuel W. Tindell, Thomas D. Tipton, John H. Trent, Jacob F. Tregler, William A. Tuiggs, Joseph D. Turner, Joseph D. Underdown, John A. Wagner, James H. Walker, John P. Walker, Theophilus F. Wallace, Henry E. Warren, Shelah Waters, Thomas Waters, John W. Watkins, William C. Webb, William D. Webster, Robert Weitmuller, Louis M. Wester, Samuel West, William O. White, Galyon Wiley, Moses Wiley, Pleasant Williams, Eli P. Willis, Joseph N. Witt, William R. Willoughby, A. H. Wilson, John Wilson, Jonathan E. Wood, Martin V. Wood, Robert A. Woolen, Gideon Wolf, Cushbert B. Word, James Wortham, Edwin F. Wiley, James B. Wyett, David K. Young.

Adjutants—Noah Acuff, Samuel P. Angel, John K. Beckner, Charles H. Bently, Moses C. Brown, Nathaniel B. Brown, Frank Cameron, James B. Carpenter, Henry A. Cobin, Lawrence Forkner, Joseph P. Galbraith, James R. Gettys, Charles C. Haefling, William S. Hall, John M. Harris, W. R. Harris, John W. Hines, Jacob Leab, William A. McTeer, George B. Morehead, Spencer Munson, John Murphy, Henry W. Parker, Jesse S. Reeves, William H. Roberts, William Rule, Eli T. Sawyers, William J. Scott, Ashley L. Spears, William J. Stokes, Gustavus E. Teubner, Horace H. Thomas, John Thomas, John H. Thorington, William B. Tickering, William Van Dorn.

APPENDIX. NOTE X. Page 307.

MARTYRDOM OF UNION PEOPLE.

Mr. N. G. Taylor undertook after the war ended, to collect materials for its "Unwritten History" in East Tennessee, and they not only confirmed but enlarged the knowledge he acquired in 1861-'2 and '3 concerning the cruel treatment of Union people during those years. His estimate of those unarmed, who were put to death in various ways throughout that region, is founded upon diligent inquiries. In writing to a friend, February 22, 1886, he says, "I was at some pains to gather up from the different counties the facts on this point, and the result showed an aggregate of 2,500 to 3,000 non-combatants massacred for their Union sentiments. I had at that time a list of those thus slaughtered in this (Carter) county, which aggregated 70 or 75; in Greene County over 200; in Washington County over 100, &c., &c."

Hon. C. W. Hall, of Rogersville, Tenn., in 1861-2, in "Threescore Years and Ten, by a Lawyer" (Cincinnati, 1884), tells of such atrocities. He says: "Guerilla bands claiming to belong to the Rebel army, were engaged generally in the plunder of Union families. One of these bands was commanded by one William Owens. His company was a band of cut-throats, marauding around, seeking to shed blood. They found a lad of some sixteen years, whose name was Lizemore. His father was a Union man and quite aged. This gang of desperadoes arrested the old man, took the boy into the woods and deliberately murdered him. Whether the Confederate Commander in East Tennessee commissioned Owens to plunder and kill in order to subdue the loyal sentiment of that section, as Reynolds and others were trying to do in other counties is not stated. One fact is known, viz.: that Owens was recognized by the Rebel military as a Captain." After detailing the cruel treatment to which Union people were subjected, Judge Hall adds: "These outrages were not confined to the more populous portions of the counties, but were often perpetrated in the hills and hollows, and usually upon men reputable at home, but bold enough to confess their loyalty. Indeed it was a rare thing to find a man who had a bad character before the war, advocating the Union cause."

APPENDIX: NOTE Y. Page 317.

The list of contributors to the Boston Fund for the relief of East Tennessee, is interesting. Some sent their proper names with their gifts. Mr. George F. Bartlett, of New Bedford, wrote to Mr. Everett: "In response to Col. Taylor's touching appeal in behalf of our suffering loyal brethren in East Tennessee, I cheerfully part with the only thing saved from the whaleship 'Lafayette,' burned by the pirate 'Alabama,' April 15, 1863, off Fernando de Noronha, and enclose the same to you herewith, viz: (6) six English sovereigns, worth about forty-three dollars. Captain Lewis was fortunately on shore with this gold to purchase stores, when Capt. Semmes steamed around the island and burned his ship. I will regard it as a *forced* contribution from Capt. Semmes, in the name of the immortal Lafayette, who loved our country and its Father, and I am most happy in being able to make so worthy a bestowal of it."

Hon. J. L. Motley, Jr., U. S. Minister at Vienna, wrote: "I enclose a check for $200, and I wish it was in my power to send a much larger sum. When, in after days, the history of this unexampled insurrection against Liberty comes to be written, there will be few episodes more moving or more instructive than the record of those Tennesseeans who have so long sustained the Republic and its principles, amid such trial and at such sacrifices. Certainly it is no *charity* on our part to assist them, but a sacred duty, which I am sure that all will fulfill in proportion to their means."

Master John W. Pierce, Jr., twelve years old, wrote from S. W. Harbor, Tremont, Maine: "Dear Sir: Enclosed please find twenty-five dollars, which I have collected for the suffering East Tennesseeans. I had read and heard so much of these loyal people that I wished very much to do something for them. I said to my mother, I will give them my dollar, *all my money*. She said that will do very little good alone, but I might go round and ask my young friends to give for this noble cause. I was pleased to do so, and have collected this sum. I found both old and young ready to give me something; very few refused. In one family I got almost five dollars. I know this is a small sum compared with the thousands you are receiving, but if some little boy in each town in this State would go round among his friends, the sums thus collected would make thousands of dollars, and oh! how much suffering would be relieved."

Some, in transmitting their gifts, substituted for their proper names, such inscriptions, as "A little boy, six years old, his own money,"—"A poor ex-teacher,"—"A school girl's monthly allowance,"—"A law student at Cambridge, being one-half of all he has,"—"C. and J., two poor young men,"—"Three little sisters," —"A Vermont soldier on the Potomac,"—"One day's pay of a navy yard employe,"—"A lady, aged 83,"—"Acts, 11th ch., 26 and 27th verses,"—"The earnings of a little boy,"—"A poor old duster." The citizens of historic Lexington sent $280, and eight little girls, $80, the proceeds of a fair they held at Plymouth. The Pastor of the Second Church in Dorchester, in remitting its contribution "for the patriots of East Tennessee," said: "We observe a fourth Sabbath evening of each month as a time for prayer for our country, and last evening thought it fitting to *act* as well as *pray*." The Pastor of the Congregational Church at Taunton, delivered a special sermon in the same behalf, and the responsive offerings of his people amounted to $870. From the Unitarian Society at Watertown, founded in 1630, its Pastor sent a handsome contribution "for brothers who suffer for their dear country's cause and glory." The 44th Regiment of Massachusetts volunteers had been given $5,000 by fellow-citizens. One-fifth of the sum was transferred through the Colonel to the fund "for the relief of the suffering loyalists of East Tennessee." "Anonymous" enclosed $500 in a note, saying. "I have stood in the fight many a day by the side of those East Tennesseeans, but I see that there are yet other ways of doing one's duty towards them, so I add my contribution to their aid." Another "Anonymous" wrote: "Fifty dollars from one, who in days of yore was a short sojourner about Knoxville, and whose then estimate of East Tennesseeans has been borne out and tested." "A Young Ensign" left his gift, as he "went forth to serve his country."

The tone of the communications received, showed the ardent patriotism and abounding liberality of the people. Mr. Everett styled it "a noble letter," in which the Selectmen of Dorchester sent about $3,000—the gifts of its citizens and Churches. Three school-girls at Chelsea devoted their afternoons to visiting "from house to house in the little town, which is far from rich, with a subscription paper, asking from each person the small sum of ten or fifteen cents." They wrote to Mr. Everett: "It might be a comforting thought to the suffering Tennesseans, if they could know how generous and interested even the poorest people have been in their cause. One poor old woman gave all the money she had (seven cents), with the earnest wish that it was a great deal more, and that it might also do a little good." Their collections amounted to $45. The boys of Mr. Allen's School at New Bedford made their gifts under the caption:

"The loyal boys of Massachusetts, to the loyal boys of Tennessee, send greeting. Having heard through Col. Taylor of the hardships and privations that you have endured while your fathers and our fathers have been struggling side by side for the support of the Union cause and the defence of Liberty, and feeling that, although remotely situated, we are brothers and have a united interest in the prosperity of our glorious country, we wish to manifest to you our sympathy."

Appendix. Note Z. Page 331.

CASH BALANCE SHEET OF THE EAST TENNESSEE RELIEF ASSOCIATION.
RECEIPTS.

From the E. T. R. A. at Boston, by Mr. Edward Everett,	$100,000 00
From the New England Loyal Relief Society, by M. Brimmer, Esq................	10,000 00
From the E. T. R. A. of Pennsylvania, at Philadelphia	26,184 55
" " " at New York City........	15,675 18
" " " at Portland, Me., $7,641 16; also, through Governor Cony, $3,518 90......	11,160 06
From Stamford, Connecticut..................	1,200 00
" Wilkesbarre, Pennsylvania................	1,000 00
" Brooklyn, N. Y.; Packer Institute, $236 36; Boys' C. and P. Institute, $271 17................	507 53
From Utica, New York....................	500 00
" Cincinnati, Ohio.......................	402 00
" Knoxville, Tennessee...................	211 25
" Providence, Rhode Island................	200 00
" Springfield, Mass.....................	156 75
" Springfield, Ohio.....................	134 00
" Quincy, Illinois, (Ladies' Needle Picket)......	100 00
	$167,431 32
From sales at Knoxville, from 1864 to 1868, $46,413 82	
" " by County Agents " " " 37,557 92	
" Loans to poor, 185 00; interest in Cincinnati, &c., 172 08................ 357 08	
From various sources, 191 55; cash in excess, 253 82.................... 445 37—	84,774 19
	$252,205 51

Boxes and barrels of clothing, &c., were received: From Massachusetts towns and Boston, 34 packages; N. E. Refugee Aid Society, 15; American Union Commission, 13; Unknown, 15; Philadelphia Ladies' Relief Association, 9; Ladies' Aid Society, Wilmington, Delaware, Refugee Commission, Cincinnati, and Sag Harbor, New York, 2 each; Dunkirk, Binghampton, and Saugerties, N. Y., 1 each.

APPENDICES.

EXPENDITURES OF THE EAST TENNESSEE RELIEF ASSOCIATION.

1864.

Feb.—For supplies of food at Cincinnati, by Philadelphia Committee; freight, insurance, &c.	$8,106 66
Mar.—For supplies of food at Cincinnati, by General Agent; freight, insurance, &c.	32,759 49
1864 & '5—For supplies of food from Cincinnati, by Thos. G. Odiorne; freight, insurance, &c.	90,892 10
Goods made into clothing by Ladies' Sewing Circle, Boston.	2,000 00
Dry Goods bought by General Agent at Philadelphia and New York	11,000 00
Dry goods and groceries bought at Cincinnati by General Agent	45,963 70
Wheat bought at Cincinnati by General Agent	4,133 51
Freight, insurance, &c., on above purchases	4,075 08
Shoes at Boston and woolen goods at Philadelphia (Mr. Everett and L. P. Smith)	12,041 10
Stipends and expenses of Agents (including Nashville), buying and forwarding	3,596 56
Supplies bought at Knoxville in successive years to 1868.	2,409 37
	$216,977 57
1864-'5—Salaries and expenses attending contribution of fund.	11,187 57
For 4 Years—Home Agency, officers of the Association, employes, &c.	10,442 73
Cash for support of refugees and poor at Knoxville, Nashville and Cincinnati.	6,961 15
House rent, labor, drayage, printing, &c.	3,911 31
Gift towards Everett Hospital, Knoxville.	2,000 00
Gift for relief of sufferers by fire, Portland, Me.	500 00
	$251,980 33
Balance cash on hand, July, 1868.	225 18
	$252,205 51

INDEX.

Arnold, Thomas D.. 109
Baxter, John 106, 108, 119, 156, 246, 323
Bell, John 83, 102
Benjamin, Lieut............ ....241, 251, 274, 275, 277, 279
Benjamin, J. P....................................140, 155, 157, 313
Blue Springs, fight at................................ 223
Bragg, Gen. Braxton................ ....171, 227, 234, 237, 280
Bridges, Hon George W.... 128
Bridges on railways In East Tennessee burned 133
Brownlow, Wm. G...........83, 106, 147, 153–158, 166, 246, 323, 325
Buckner, Gen. Simon 201, 208–9
Burnside, Gen. A. E., 201, 210, 211, 212, 214, 215, 217, 219–224, 227,
    230–232, 236–238, 241, 250–54, 256, 258, 265, 272–3, 279, 280, 283
Byrd, Col. R. K...........................201, 215, 220, 222, 294
Campbell, Col. Wm.............. ... .43, 46, 52-5
Campbell's Station, battle of............................241-2-3
Carroll, Gen 147, 155, 163
Carter, Gen. Samuel P..........194, 222, 230, 245, 247, 248, 317, 325
Carter, Col, J. P. T................................ ... 167, 214, 220
Church Ministers..................... 180-1-2
Churchwell, Col. Wm. M. 173, 174, 187
Cooper, Col. (Gen.) Joseph A........................116, 119, 294
Cox, Gen. J. D 214, 293, 296
Crittenden, Gen. (C. S. A.) 155, 156, 163-4
Cumberland Gap 128, 131, 161, 186, 187, 207, 216, 223, 226
Dana, Charles A 226, 236, 324
East Tennessee Relief Society 310, 311, 317, 323
Everett, Edward........... .... 12, 22, 311, 317, 328, 329

INDEX. 399

Executions 147, 150, 151
Ferrero, Gen..................................223, 241, 252, 276
Foster, Maj. Gen..............................286, 289, 291
Foster, Col ....215, 221, 223–'4, 226
Grant, U. S. .... 225, 226, 227, 234–'5–'6, 237, 267, 281, 288
Halleck, Gen................................... 220, 221, 222
Hartraupt, Gen................................240, 241, 252, 264
Heiskell, William 108, 323
Humphreys, Judge W. H. 124, 141, 143
Imprisonments 145, 146
Johnson, Hon. Andrew..........100, 102, 114, 129, 158, 309
Kirby Smith, Gen. E..................170, 171–'3, 186, 187, 301
Knoxville...................................... 34, 35
Lenoir's 201, 225, 238, 239
Lincoln, President A..................92, 94, 235, 286, 309
Longstreet, Gen... 226, 227, 234, 238, 241, 261, 265–'6–'7, 271, 275–'6, 279, 281, 291
Loudon..........................134–'5, 201, 222, 225, 236–'7, 239
May, M. R., M. D................................ 108
Maynard, Horace................102, 127, 158, 174, 236 329
Military League 100, 104, 113
Murphy, J. C................................... 108
Nelson, Thomas A. R 100, 102, 108, 128, 323
Pennsylvania Commissioners.................323, 324, 326, 330
Poe, Capt. Orlando M..................250, 253, 256, 263, 284, 285
Potter, Brig. Gen. 223, 225, 236, 241, 271
Reynolds, Robert B..............................145, 157
Rosecrans, Gen..................................219, 221–2
Sanders, Col. (Gen.) Wm. P......199, 201–'2, 207, 213, 238, 253, 254, 255, 256
Schofield, Gen..................................293, 294, 295–'6
Sevier, Col. John............42, 43–'4, 46, 53, 59–60, 63, 67–'71- 76
Shackelford, Gen...............................223, 226, 244
Shelby, Col. Isaac ....42, 43–'4, 46, 50, 52–'3
Sherman, Gen. W. T.......234, 237, 281, 282, 287, 288, 293, 296, 297
Slavery in East Tennessee.........................30–34, 78
Smith, Lloyd P..................................34, 310, 323, 328

Spears, J. G...108, 119
Stanford, Dr. R. L...159–163
Taylor, Nathaniel G....80, 306, 307, 308, 309, 310, 311, 313, 316, 317, 322, 323
Temple, O. P..82–'3, 106, 246, 323
Thomas, Gen..163, 227, 235, 294
Trigg, Connelly F......................101, 106, 109, 153, 158
Union Convention at Knoxville and Greeneville............105–119
University, East Tennessee............................179–180, 298
Wheeler, Gen..234, 238 244, 293
Wheeler, R. D..108
White, Gen..214, 222, 236, 241
Wilcox, Gen..214, 223, 224, 226, 267
Williams, John..106, 108
Wood, Col. W. B..131, 132, 136, 139
Woolford, Col..214, 222, 225, 244
Yancey, Wm, L..81–85
Zolicoffer, Gen. Felix 122–126, 131, 139, 153, 163

BELMONT COLLEGE LIBRARY

E   73091
531   HUMES
H92
1974